MCSE
TestPrep

Networking
Essentials

que®

MCSE TestPrep: Networking Essentials

By Michael W. Barry, Joe Casad, Robert J. Cooper III, Mark D. Hall, Howard Hilliker, Ron Milione, and David Yarashus

Published by:
New Riders Publishing
201 West 103rd Street
Indianapolis, IN 46290 USA

Printed in the United States of America 1 2 3 4 5 6 7 8 9 0

Library of Congress Cataloging-in-Publication Data

CIP data available upon request

ISBN: 1-56205-826-6

Warning and Disclaimer

Publisher *David Dwyer*
Executive Editor *Mary Foote*
Managing Editor *Sarah Kearns*

Acquisitions/Development Editor
Danielle Bird

Project Editors
Amy Bezek, Christopher Morris

Copy Editors
Amy Bezek, Audra McFarland

Technical Editor
Bob Reinsch

Team Coordinators
Stacey Beheler, Amy Lewis

Manufacturing Coordinator
Brook Farling

Book Designer
Glenn Larsen

Cover Designer
Dan Armstrong

Cover Production
Casey Price

Director of Production
Larry Klein

Production Manager
Laurie Casey

Production Team Supervisor
Victor Peterson

Graphics Image Specialists
Kevin Cliburn, Wil Cruz, Oliver Jackson

Production Analysts
Dan Harris, Erich J. Richter

Production Team
Lori Cliburn, Kim Cofer

Indexer
Tim Wright

About the Authors

Michael W. Barry has 16 years of programming experience. Upon receiving a BSEE from the University of Texas at Austin, Mike went to work for Datapoint Corporation where he was involved in networking and desktop video conferencing. Mike holds numerous patents ranging from video teleconferencing to color-image processing to cluster printing. He has been involved in NT Kernel and User mode programming since the Windows NT 3.1 beta and is considered an expert on the Windows NT operating system. Currently, Mike is Vice President of Development at T/R Systems, Inc. (the inventors of cluster printing), where he and his group are pioneering cluster printing systems based on Windows NT.

Mike lives in Atlanta, Georgia, with his wife and two children. In his free time, he enjoys scuba diving, tennis, camping, water skiing, and knee boarding.

Joe Casad is a freelance writer and editor who specializes in programming and networking topics. He was the managing editor of the short-lived but well-received *Network Administrator Magazine*, a journal of practical solutions for network proessionals. Joe received a B.S. in engineering from the University of Kansas in 1980 and, before becoming a full-time writer and editor, spent ten years in the computer-intensive areas of the structural engineering profession. He now lives in Lawrence, Kansas, with wife Barb Dineen and a pair of pint-sized hackers named Xander and Mattie. Look for his recently published books, *MCSE Training Guide: Windows NT Server 4* and *MCSE Training Guide: Networking Essentials*, by New Riders Publishing.

Robert J. Cooper III has worked in information systems for the past ten years and is a contributing author *of Managing Windows NT Server*. Robert is employed as a senior consultant for Interim Technology in Minneapolis, Minnesota and is a Microsoft Certified Product Specialist. He lives in Minneapolis with his wife Gael Fashingbauer Cooper and their two cats.

Mark D. Hall is a Novell CNE and a computer consultant with a Masters degree in Computer Science Education. He has co-authored two previous titles, PC Magazine's *Webmasters Ultimate Resource Guide* and New Rider's *Inside Windows NT 4.0 Ras*. He has also performed technical edits on 52 other computer titles in the last 7 years.

Howard Hilliker built his first computer in the late 70s. His major source of influence came from his father, whose career in electrical engineering, communications, and Defense work challenged his engineering mind. He has been involved in the microcomputer industry since its infancy. He holds over 70 certifications with major vendors including Microsoft, IBM, Hewlett-Packard, Epson, Zenith, NEC, and Okidata, and has been involved as a Microsoft Certified Professional since the program's infancy (LAN Manager 2.0). He has nearly a decade of network and hardware field experience and holds key networking credentials, including Compaq ASE and Hewlett-Packard Network Professional. Howard has done technical editing and illustration work on several occasions in the past. He has taught classes on Microsoft Windows and Microsoft Networking products. His experience includes advanced topics such as SNA Server and SQL. Howards also enjoys the benefits associated with being an experienced Pascal, C++, and Foxpro developer. He has been involved with several key Microsoft BETA programs. Howard also holds an amateur radio license and is an active member of the Network Professional Association. He lives with his charming wife and two beautiful young daughters.

Ron Milione is Chief of Technology at Integrated Systems Group in Hauppauge, New York. He is a Microsoft Solution Provider Partner and earned his BS and MS in Electrical Engineering from City College of New York. He holds the following certifications: MCSE, MCT, Master CNE, CNE, CNP (Certified Network Professional), Compaq ASE in Windows NT and Novell NetWare, and a Commerical License (GROL) from the Federal Commications Commission.

David Yarashus is a Senior Network Engineer with TimeBridge Technologies in Landover, Maryland. He specializes in designing, managing, and troubleshooting large, multiprotocol internetworks. Mr. Yarashus has contributed to several books and magazine articles, has been a featured speaker at the Network Analysis Forum's annual meeting, and is a member of Novell's Master CNE Advisory Council. His major industry certifications include Cisco Certified Internetwork Expert (CCIE), Microsoft Certified Systems Engineer (MCSE), Novell Master CNE, and Certified Network Expert (CNX).

About the Technical Editor

Bob Reinsch is an independent contractor, providing services as a Microsoft Certified Systems Engineer and Microsoft Certified Trainer. He has been working on personal computers and networks for almost 20 years, dating back to Commodore Pets with 16 KB of RAM. In his career, he has served as a network administrator on Unix, Macintosh, Novell, and Windows NT networks. He has been working with Windows NT since 3.1 and has pursued certification since NT 3.5. He has been a trainer since 1994 and has worked with students from Boeing, Chase Manhattan Banks, John Hancock Companies, Cinergy, and the Department of Defense. He has taught classes from Portland, Oregon to Wiesbaden, Germany.

Bob is husband to Dr. Lisa Friis, PhD, and father to Bonnie Reinsch, a beautiful baby girl who learned to whistle when she was eight months old.

Trademark Acknowledgments

Contents at a Glance

Table of Contents

Introduction

The MCSE TestPrep series is written as a study aid for people preparing for Microsoft certification exams. The series is intended to help reinforce and clarify information with which the student is already familiar. This series is not intended to be a single source for student preparation; rather, it is a review of information and a set of practice tests to help increase the likelihood of success when taking the actual exam.

Who Should Read This Book

The Networking Essentials book in the MCSE TestPrep series is specifically intended to help students prepare for Microsoft's Networking Essentials Exam (#70-58). This is one of the core required tests in the MCSE program, although Microsoft waives the requirement for individuals who are already certified as Novell CNEs, Master CNEs, or CNIs, or as Banyan CBSs or CBEs. This is done in recognition that these people have already demonstrated a good knowledge of networking.

In addition to presenting a summary of information relevant to each exam objective, this book provides a wealth of review questions similar to those you encounter in the actual exam. This book is designed to help you make the most of your study time by presenting concise summaries of information that you need to understand to succeed on the exam. The practice problems at the end of each objective help to reinforce what you have learned. Each answer is explained in detail in the Answers and Explanations section following the practice problems. Also, key words are noted for that section. The practice exam at the end of each chapter helps you to determine if you have mastered the facts. In addition, the book contains two full-length practice exams.

When you feel prepared for the exam, use this book as a test of your knowledge. Use this book for a final quick review just before taking the test to make sure all the important concepts are set in your mind.

The Networking Essentials Exam (#70-58)

The Networking Essentials Exam focuses on determining your skill in four major categories of network-related skills. They are:

> Standards and Terminology
>
> Planning
>
> Implementation
>
> Troubleshooting

The specific objectives for these topics are described in the following sections.

Standards and Terminology

The Standards and Terminology part of the Networking Essentials Exam tests your familiarity with networking standards, such as Ethernet and Token Ring, as well as with common terms used to discuss networking technologies and topics.

The objectives for the Standards and Terminology section are:

- Define common networking terms for LANs and WANs.

- Compare a file-and-print server with an application server.

- Compare user-level security with access permissions assigned to a shared directory on a server.

- Compare a client/server network with a peer-to-peer network.

- Compare the implications of using connection-oriented communications with connectionless communications.

- Distinguish whether SLIP or PPP is used as the communications protocol for various situations.

- Define the communication devices that communicate at each level of the OSI model.

- Describe the characteristics and purpose of the media used in IEEE 802.3 and IEEE 802.5 standards.

- Explain the purpose of NDIS and Novell ODI network standards.

Planning

The Networking Essentials Planning section focuses on the concepts needed to plan a network. You must understand networks before you can be trusted to plan them. Before designing a network, you need to analyze your network needs, your budget, and the technologies available. This section of the test focuses on the physical, data link, and network layers of the OSI model. It specifically tests your knowledge of technologies that you need to understand before designing your network.

The objectives for the Planning section are:

- Select the appropriate media for various situations. Media choices include:

  Coaxial cable

  Twisted-pair cable

  Fiber-optic cable

  Wireless communications

- Select the appropriate topology for various Token Ring and Ethernet networks.

- Select the appropriate network and transport protocols for various Token Ring and Ethernet networks. Protocols include:

  DLC

  AppleTalk

  IPX

  TCP/IP

  NFS

  SMB

- Select the appropriate connectivity devices for various Token Ring and Ethernet networks. Connectivity devices include:

  Repeaters

  Bridges

  Switches

  Routers

  Brouters

  Gateways

- List the characteristics, requirements, and appropriate situations for WAN connection services. WAN connection services include:

  T1

  X.25

  ISDN

  Frame Relay

  ATM

Implementation

The Implementation section covers the daily tasks associated with networking. These are tasks that a typical network administrator may have to deal with on a regular basis.

Doing implementation work well helps make the next section (troubleshooting) easier and can prevent the need for troubleshooting in many cases.

The objectives for the Implementation section are:

- Choose an administrative plan to meet specified needs, including performance management, account management, and security.

- Choose a disaster recovery plan.

- Given the manufacturer's documentation for the network adapter, install, configure, and resolve hardware conflicts for multiple network adapters in a Token Ring or Ethernet network.

- Implement a NetBIOS naming scheme for all computers on a given network.

- Select the appropriate hardware and software tools to monitor trends in the network.

Troubleshooting

Troubleshooting is the process of identifying and fixing problems on your network. Skill in troubleshooting differentiates between an excellent network administrator and merely a good one. This section of the exam verifies that you can identify common networking problems and can provide good solutions to those problems.

The objectives for the Troubleshooting section are:

- Identify common errors associated with components required for communications.

- Diagnose and resolve common connectivity problems with cards, cables, and related hardware.

- Resolve broadcast storms.

- Identify and resolve network performance problems.

Hardware and Software Recommended for Preparation

MCSE TestPrep: Networking Essentials is meant to help you review concepts with which you already have training and hands-on experience. To make the most of the review, you need to have as much background and experience as possible. The best way to do this is to combine studying with working on real networks using the products on which you will be tested. This section gives you a description of the minimum computer requirements you need to build a solid practice environment.

Computers

The minimum computer requirement to ensure you can study everything on which you'll be tested is one or more workstations running Windows 95, Windows NT Workstation, and two or more servers running Windows NT Server, all connected by a network.

Workstations: Windows 95 and Windows NT

Computer on the Microsoft Hardware Compatibility List

486DX 33-Mhz (Pentium recommended)

16 MB of RAM (32 MB recommended)

200-MB (or larger) hard disk

3.5-inch 1.44-MB floppy drive

VGA (or Super VGA) video adapter

VGA (or Super VGA) monitor

Mouse or equivalent pointing device

Two-speed (or faster) CD-ROM drive

Network Interface Card (NIC)

Presence on an existing network, or use of a hub to create a test network

Microsoft Windows 95

Servers: Windows NT Server

Two computers on the Microsoft Hardware Compatibility List

486DX2 66-Mhz (or better)

32 MB of RAM (64 recommended)

340-MB (or larger) hard disk

3.5-inch 1.44-MB floppy drive

VGA (or Super VGA) video adapter

VGA (or Super VGA) monitor

Mouse or equivalent pointing device

Two-speed (or faster) CD-ROM drive

Network Interface Card (NIC)

Presence on an existing network, or use of a hub to create a test network

Microsoft Windows NT Server

Networking Equipment

The Microsoft Networking Essentials Exam is different from most of the other Microsoft exams because it concentrates less on servers and workstations than it does on the connections between them and the network standards they use. For this reason, you should try to learn as much as you can about the non-host components in networks. Although it is impossible for most people to get hands-on access to everything in the following list, you should become familiar with as many of them as your circumstances allow, concentrating especially on Ethernet, the world's most popular data link protocol.

Network Equipment

IEEE 802.3 Ethernet network interface cards with connectors for 10BASE-T, 10BASE2, and 10BASE5

IEEE 802.3 Ethernet 10BASE-T hub and UTP cable

IEEE 802.3 Ethernet 10BASE2 coax and terminators

IEEE 802.3 Ethernet 10BASE5 coax and transceivers

IEEE 802.5 Token Ring network interface card

IEEE 802.5 Token Ring MSAU and STP (IBM Type 1) cable

Multiprotocol router/brouter

FDDI network interface cards

62.5/125 micron multimode fiber cable

Modems

CHAPTER 1

Standards and Terminology

1.1 Define Common Networking Terms for LANs and WANs

A. Definition of a Network

A *network* is a group of interconnected computers that share information and resources. Connected computers sharing resources is referred to as *networking*. The physical pathway in which computers are connected is the *transmission medium*. When a computer is not connected to a network, it is referred to as a *stand-alone* system. The simplest network consists of two computers communicating over a single cable.

B. The Local Area Network

The most common form of networks is the *local area network* (LAN). The LAN is a group of computers interconnected within a building or campus setting. The most common network topology is Ethernet. Ethernet comes in many types.

C. Network Topologies

The physical layout of a network is the *network topology*. The three common topologies are:

Bus

Star

Ring

1. Bus Topology

The *bus topology* or *linear bus* is the simplest form of networking, making it the least expensive to implement. This topology consists of a single cable that connects all computers of the network in a single line, without any active electronics to amplify or modify the signal. This bus must be terminated at each end. Without *termination*, the signals on the bus reflect back upon reaching each end of the bus. This reflection causes serious network errors.

The most common form of the bus topology is *10Base2*. 10Base2 is also referred to as *Thinnet*. 10Base2 employs *RG58* type cable, which has a 50-ohm impedance. This bus must be terminated with a 50-ohm terminator on each end. The maximum segment distance on a 10Base2 network is 185 meters (607 feet).

Another bus topology is *10Base5* or *Thicknet*. 10Base5 networks use RG6 cable, which is much thicker and harder to work with than RG58.

The bus network is a *passive topology* because each computer only monitors the signals on the bus. The signals do not pass through the NIC board in the computer. As the distance between these signals increases, their level decreases. This is referred to as *attenuation*. One way to increase the distance for this bus is to add *repeaters*. Repeaters are active devices that regenerate incoming signals. Signals are boosted as they pass through the repeater.

2. Star Topology

In a star topology, all devices on the network are connected directly to a hub. This type of network is usually easy to troubleshoot because each device can be individually unplugged from the hub. The first star network was *ArcNet*, invented by Datapoint Corporation in 1977. This *token-passing* network used RG62 cable, which is about the same size as RG58 but with a higher impedance.

The most common star topology in use today is 10Base-T. 10Base-T is an Ethernet network running over *category 3 unshielded twisted pair* (UTP). On 10Base-T, the data rate is 10 Mbits per second. Logically, the star topology sends data like the bus topology.

A newcomer to the star topology is 100Base-T, which has a data rate of 100 Mbits per second. This network requires *category 5* UTP cable.

A variation of the star topology is the *star bus* topology. In the star bus topology, hubs are interconnected with linear bus trunks. This enables networks to grow beyond the number of ports on a single hub.

3. Ring Topology

In a ring network, all computers are connected by segments of cable in a ring fashion, with no ends to the network. The signal passes through each computer on the network and is reconditioned before being retransmitted. If any network adapter fails then the entire network goes down.

This network was invented by IBM and is referred to as *Token Ring*.

D.   Bus Arbitration

Network Interface Cards (NICs) must implement a standard signaling methodology to gain access to the network bus. There are three popular access methods in use today.

   CSMA/CD (Carrier Sense Multiple Access with Collision Detection)

   CSMA/CA (Carrier Sense Multiple Access with Collision Avoidance)

   Token passing

1. CSMA/CD

Ethernet employs CSMA/CD, which is the most popular access method today. When a computer wants to send data, the following sequence of events occurs:

1. The computer *senses* the cable to make sure there is no traffic on the cable. If this is the case, then the computer can access the cable. If not, the computer must wait until the cable is free of traffic.

2. When the cable is free, the computer can transmit a signal onto the cable.

3. If two or more computers transmit at the same time, they each detect that a collision has occurred. Each computer backs off for a random amount of time, then tries the entire sequence again until the message is transmitted.

In CSMA/CD networks, as the number of computers communicating on the network increases, so does the number of collisions. It is best to break up large networks into segments with switching hubs or bridges.

2. CSMA/CA

CSMA/CA is slower than token passing and CSMA/CD; thus, it is not as popular. In this access method, a computer wanting to transmit waits a random amount of time after the last transmission on the cable. When this timer has expired, the computer transmits data. The transmitting computer does not detect collisions; instead, it waits for a response from the destination computer. If a response is not received in a certain amount of time, the computer waits for the cable to be idle and tries again. *LocalTalk,* which is the transmission medium for AppleTalk, uses CSMA/CA.

3. Token Passing

Datapoint developed the first token-passing network in 1977. ArcNet computers do not transmit data onto the medium until they own a token. The token is passed sequentially to each computer on the network based upon the NIC ID. ArcNet networks require the system administrator to set the NIC ID between 1 and 255. Duplicate IDs can be a real problem in ArcNet networks. If a computer has no data to transmit, that computer simply passes the token along. ArcNet supports both active and passive hubs.

E.   The Wide Area Network

When computers must share information over long distances, the *wide area network* (WAN) is used. WANs are typically much slower than LANs but can span distances from a few miles to around the world. WANs are typically created using telephone lines, but they are also created with fiber links, microwave radio, leased lines, and satellite links.

Several telephone line technologies are in use today:

*   *PSTN* (Public Switched Telephone Network) is in use in most homes.

*   *ISDN* (Integrated Services Digital Network)is divided into three channels—two for data and one for control. These channels are referred to as 2B+D. Each of the B channels moves data at 64 Kbps while the D channel is 16 Kbps. If both B channels are utilized, 128-Kbps data transfers can be achieved.

*   *T1* lines are used by many businesses to achieve transfer rates of 1.544 Mbps.

F.   Protocols

For computers to successfully communicate, they must follow a common set of communication rules (*protocols*). Thousands of communication protocols are in use today, each with its own acronym.

1. Internet Protocols

One of the most popular protocols in use today is the Internet suite of protocols. The Department of Defense funded development of this suite of protocols along with the Internet in the 1970s. The original name for the Internet was *ARPAnet* (Advanced Research Projects Agency Network).

Included in the Internet suite are two of the best known protocols, *TCP* (Transmission Control Protocol) and *IP* (Internet Protocol). This suite is often referred to as *TCP/IP.* The Internet protocols are routable.

When a corporation uses the Internet suite of protocols on a local LAN, the term *intranet* is used. Some other Internet protocols are:

FTP (File Transfer Protocol)

SMTP (Simple Mail Transfer Protocol)

SNMP (Simple Network Management Protocol)

NFS (Network File System)

ARP (Address Resolution Protocol)

DNS (Domain Naming Service)

Telnet

UDP (User Datagram Protocol)

2. NetWare Networks

NetWare networks have their own suite of protocols, the most popular being *Internetwork Packet Exchange* (IPX) and *Sequenced Packed Exchange* (SPX). These protocols are referred to as *IPX/SPX.* These protocols are routable.

3. NetBEUI

NetBEUI (NetBIOS Extended User Interface) is an extension to NetBIOS (Network Basic Input/Output System). NetBEUI was developed by IBM and is targeted toward small workgroups; thus, it is not routable.

4. The World Wide Web

The protocol to transfer web pages to browsers is Hypertext Transport Protocol (HTTP), which has become very popular in the last few years.

1.1 Exercise

1. Your company wants to set up a temporary classroom that will be used once per month for Windows NT training classes. The room must be set up the night before each class begins, it is used for 3 days, then it is torn down. The class is designed for 15 workstations and must be configured as inexpensively as possible. Choose a network topology and explain the reasons for choosing this topology.

2. You work for a brokerage firm in which uptime is of utmost importance. Thus, the time required to isolate and fix network problems must be minimized. This firm employs over 300 brokers, each with their own computer. Choose a network topology and explain the reasons for choosing this topology.

1.1 Exercise Explanation

1. Because the network is contained in one room, distance between computers is not an issue with any available topology. The entire network contains only 15 workstations, which could be easily handled by all topologies.

   Ease of setup and cost are the driving factors for determining the best topology.

   > A ring network can be used, but the NICs for ring networks typically cost more than NICs for other topologies.

   > A 10Base-T–type network can be used. However, a 15-port hub significantly adds to the cost.

   > ArcNet is a low-cost alternative. However, 15 ports are too many for inexpensive ArcNet passive hubs.

   In this case, the bus topology 10Base2 is the best choice. Because no hubs are required, cost is reduced. Installation is simple because a T connector on the back of each computer is all that is required to wire the network.

2. Reliability is the issue here. This immediately disqualifies the ring topology because any individual computer can bring down the entire network.

   An ArcNet implementation would be complicated by the fact that there are more than 255 computers in the network. ArcNet IDs only allow for 255 computers.

   10Base2 or 10Base5 could be implemented, but the time required to diagnose a problem can be quite long. A bad connector can require testing at least half the segments in the network.

   10Base-T is probably the best choice because diagnosing problems does not require much time. One problem with 10Base-T is that, if the hub fails, all connected computers lose their networking capability. Purchasing backup hubs can solve this.

1.1 Practice Problems

1. CSMA of CSMA/CD stands for:

   A. Copper System Media Access

   B. Collision Sense Media Access

   C. Collision Sense Multiple Access

2. Which media access network tries to detect collisions instead of avoiding collisions?

   A. Token Ring

   B. CSMA/CD

   C. AppleTalk

   D. ArcNet

   E. CSMA/CA

3. Which is a media?

   A. Twisted-pair wire

   B. Television

   C. Radio waves

   D. Microwave signals

   E. Disk drive

   F. Tape backup

   G. All

   H. None

4. Which company invented ArcNet?

   A. DEC

   B. XEROX

   C. Datapoint

   D. Apple

   E. Standard Microsystems Corporation

5. Token Ring networks use CSMA/CA network arbitration.

   A. True

   B. False

6. 10Base5 is also called:

   A. Thinnet

   B. Ethernet

   C. AppleTalk

   D. Thicknet

   E. None of the above

7. 10Base2 uses which type of cable?

   A. RG59

   B. RG62

   C. RG58

   D. UTP

8. When using 10Base2, you:

   A. Must terminate each end with 50-ohm terminators

   B. Must terminate each end with 75-ohm terminators

   C. Don't need to terminate UTP

9. 10Base-T is often referred to as:

   A. Thinnet

   B. Thicknet

   C. Twisted Pair (UTP)

   D. Ethernet

10. Which is not a protocol?

    A. TCP/IP

    B. NetBEUI

    C. AppleTalk

    D. ARP

    E. NFS

    F. Ethernet

11. Star topologies always require a hub, which means they:

    A. Use more wire than bus topologies

    B. Are easier to troubleshoot than ring topologies

C. Can bring the entire network down
   if the hub fails

D. Are easy to add new computers

E. All of the above ✓

12. SMP means:

A. Simultaneous Multi-Processing

B. Symmetric Multi-Processing

C. Simple Mail Protocol ╱

13. FDDI is a fiber-optic network based on
    which topology?

A. Star

B. Ring ╱

C. Bus

14. A gigabyte is:

A. 1×10^9

B. 10×10^9

C. 10×10^6

D. 1,073,741,824 bytes ╱

15. Web browsers communicate using:

A. HTML

B. FTP

C. HDLC

D. HTTP ╱

16. Which networking topology would be
    easiest to configure for a 10-workstation
    Windows peer-to-peer network.

A. NetBEUI ╱

B. IPX/SPX

C. TCP/IP

17. The OSI reference model has how many
    layers?

A. 2

B. 4

C. 10

D. 7 ╱

E. 5

18. RAID 0 is also known as:

A. Striping

B. Mirror set

C. Striping with parity ╱

D. None of the above

19. Which type of cable will operate at
    100 Mbs?

A. Category 3 cable

B. Category 5 cable ╱

C. Category 2 cable

D. 10BASE2

20. SQL is used to:

A. Access remote mail servers

B. Perform fast searches on web sites

C. Access databases ╱

D. Program mainframes

21. T1 service is:

A. 64 Kbps

B. 56 Kbps

C. 1 Mbps

D. 1.544 Mbps ╱

E. 1.024 Mbps

22. UTP is:

A. Universal Transaction Protocol

B. TCP/IP protocol

C. A type of wiring ✓

D. A signaling method over Ethernet

23. Why do bridges provide better network performance than repeaters?

    A. Because they analyze packets and only forward them on required ports. ✓

    B. They use faster hardware than repeaters.

    C. They ignore bad input signals.

24. Which channel is data carried on over ISDN?

    A. The A channel

    B. The B channel ✓

    C. The C channel

    D. The D channel

25. Which network access method does LocalTalk use?

    A. CSMA/CD

    B. CSMA/CA ✓

    C. Token passing

    D. AppleTalk

26. Which network access method does ArcNet use?

    A. CSMA/CD

    B. CSMA/CA

    C. Token passing ✓

    D. AppleTalk

27. Which network access method does Ethernet use?

    A. CSMA/CD ✓

    B. CSMA/CA

    C. Token passing

    D. AppleTalk

28. CSMA/CA networks are typically slower than CSMA/CD networks because:

    A. There are more collisions on CSMA/CA networks.

    B. CSMA/CA networks must wait a random amount of time before transmitting on the media.

    C. CSMA/CA networks must wait for a token before transmitting on the cable.

    D. CSMA/CA networks use twisted-pair cable and CSMA/CD networks use coaxial cable.

29. NetWare networks use which protocols?

    A. IPX/SPX

    B. NetBEUI

    C. TCP/IP

    D. None of the above

30. Which is not a routable protocol?

    A. IP

    B. IPX

    C. AppleTalk

    D. NetBEUI

    E. None of the above

31. ATM networks can easily switch and route packets because:

    A. All packets are a fixed size.

    B. Packrets are variable in size, making switching more effective for small packets.

    C. ATM packets do not have headers that require decoding.

32. Token Ring networks determine who gets the token based on:

    A. Who is ready to transmit data

    B. Synchronized network timers

    C. Random back-off timers

    D. NIC address

33. WANs are typically slower than LANs because:

1

A. WANs have more hops than LANs, thus the network signal must be processed by each hop.

B. WANs typically use public switching networks to cover great distances.

C. WAN hardware technology is years behind LAN technology.

34. Which topology is easiest to troubleshoot?

A. Star topology

B. Ring topology

C. Bus topology

35. NetBEUI was invented by IBM to be used:

A. In small workgroup-type networks

B. In large networks containing mainframes

C. In OS/2 networks to compete with Windows NT

36. A star network is more expensive to set up than a bus network because:

A. Star hubs are very expensive.

B. Star networks require expensive connectors at the end of each cable.

C. Star-based NICs are more expensive than bus-based NICs.

D. Star networks require much more cable than bus networks.

37. When several hubs are interconnected in the star network, it is referred to as:

A. Star bus topology

B. An intranet

C. Switched network

38. Which topology is a passive topology?

A. Star

B. Ring

C. Bus

39. As signals travel over long distances, they become weaker. This is referred to as:

A. Signal to noise ratio

B. Attenuation

C. 3db point

40. A device that regenerates signals, allowing for greater distances between devices in a LAN without regard to packet information, is a:

A. Bridge

B. Router

C. Switching hub

D. Repeater

41. Logically, the star topology sends data like which topology?

A. Bus

B. Mesh

C. ArcNet

D. Ring

42. In a correctly terminated 10Base2 network, if you remove a T connector from any computer on the network and measure the resistance of the bus between the center conductor and the shield, you should measure about:

A. 50 ohms

B. 75 ohms

C. 100 ohms

D. 25 ohms

43. In a bus network, if one computer is not able to communicate with any other computer on the network, but all other computers communicate fine, what is the most likely cause of the problem?

A. The terminator closest to the computer is not communicating.

B. The segment of cable that connects the noncommunicating computer to its nearest neighbor is defective.

C. The NIC board in the computer is not communicating

D. The length of cable for the network exceeds maximum length.

44. One computer in an ArcNet network is having problems communicating with other computers on the network. You have changed the NIC card, the cable connecting to the hub, and the port on the hub. What is the most likely cause of the problem?

   A. The length of cable to the hub.

   B. The type of cable is wrong. ArcNet uses RG62.

   C. The connector on the computer motherboard where the NIC is plugged in.

   D. The network address of the NIC is a duplicate address.

45. You are the network administrator for a small company that has grown steadily over the years. You have a 10Base-T network; with each new employee, you add a new connection. Your network currently has 150 computers connected to it, and you are getting complaints about how slow the network is at certain times of the day. You test the network at lunch and find no problems. What is the most likely cause of the network slowdown?

   A. The network servers are overloaded.

   B. You have exceeded the maximum cable length for your 10Base-T network, which causes intermittent problems.

   C. You have too many hubs on the network, which causes delays.

   D. Your large network is susceptible to network traffic.

1.1   Answers and Explanations: Practice Problems

1. **C**   Collision Sense Multiple Access, a type of access method.

2. **B**   CSMA/CD, the CD stands for collision detect.

3. **G**   All of the above items are forms of media.

4. **C**   DataPoint Corporation of San Antonio, Texas invented ArcNet in 1977.

5. **B**   False. Token ring networks use tokens for media access.

6. **D**   10Base5 is also called thicknet. An easy way to remember this is thicknet can carry signals about 500 meters, while thinnet can carry signals about 200 meters. Thus 10Base5 and 10Base2.

7. **C**   10Base2 uses 50-ohm RG58 coaxial cable.

8. **A**   You must terminate each end of a 10Base2 bus with 50-ohm terminators.

9. **C**   10Base-T uses standard twisted pair, and the T stands for twisted pair.

10. **F**   Ethernet is a physical network not a protocol.

11. **E**   All the statements are characteristics of the star topology.

12. **B**   Symmetric Multi-Processing. This is the type of multi-processing employed by Windows NT when more than one processor is present.

13. **B**   FDDI employs the ring technology. The signal passes through each computer in the ring.

14. **D**   This is 2 raised to the 20th power. Another standard for a gigabyte is $1024 \times 1024 \times 1000 = 1,058,576,000$.

15. **D**   HTTP, or Hypertext Transfer Protocol, is the method in which web pages are transmitted.

1

16. **A** NetBEUI was designed for small networks, thus configuration is automatic. TCP/IP requires assigning an IP address to each computer on the network. IPX/SPX is designed for Novell networks.

17. **D** The Open Systems Interconnection (OSI) reference model has seven layers.

18. **A** Raid level 0 refers to disk striping. Other popular implementations are Raid level 1, called disk mirroring, and Raid level 5, called disk striping with parity.

19. **B** Category 5. Remember that as the number gets larger, the cable can support higher data rates and the expense also rises.

20. **C** Structured Query Language (SQL) is used to communicate with databases.

21. **D** T1 service operates at 1.544 Mbps.

22. **C** UTP stands for Unshielded Twisted Pair.

23. **A** Bridges can intelligently look at packets and only retransmit them on required ports. Repeaters do not look at incoming data, so they must retransmit on all ports.

24. **B** ISDN has three channels: 2B+D. Data is carried on the B channels.

25. **B** LocalTalk employs collision-avoidance access.

26. **C** ArcNet was the first commercial token-passing network.

27. **A** Ethernet employs collision-detection access.

28. **B** CSMA/CA networks are typically slower than CSMA/CD because CSMA/CA network must wait a random amount of time before transmitting on the media.

29. **A** NetWare uses the IPX/SPX suite of protocols.

30. **D** NetBEUI, invented by IBM, is not a routable protocol.

31. **A** All packets in an ATM network are 53 bytes and are called cells. Fixed-size packets are easier to design hardware and allocate buffers for.

32. **D** Network Interface Card IDs determine the order of token passing.

33. **B** A WAN is typically slower than a LAN due to the cost of high-speed transmission equipment required for long distances. Phone lines are typically used for WANs.

34. **A** The star is easiest to troubleshoot because the bad connection can be found by unplugging links from the hub.

35. **A** NetBEUI, an extension to NetBIOS, was invented by IBM for small workgroup networks.

36. **D** Every connection in a star network must run back to the hub, which usually results in more wiring.

37. **A** Star bus topology.

38. **C** The bus topology is a passive topology.

39. **B** Attenuation.

40. **D** A repeater simply retransmits any incoming signals on any port to all other ports. Bridges, routers, and switching hubs analyze each packet at different levels of the OSI model to determine what to do.

41. **A** Logically, a star network is like a bus because each computer transmits to all computers.

42. **D** 25 ohms. This is because each end of the bus is terminated with 50 ohms between the center conductor and the shield. These 50-ohm terminators are parallel, which results in a resistance of 25 ohms.

43. **C** If there are any cable problems in a bus network then typically the entire network is down. Therefore, if a terminator is missing or the cable is too long or defective, the entire network would fail. The only choice left is the NIC board.

44. **D** In ArcNet networks, it is up to the system administrator to set the NIC ID. If duplicate IDs exist, one of the duplicated computers will not be able to access the network.

45. **D** Your 10Base-T network is a CSMA/CD-type network. As you add connections, you add network traffic. This traffic varies during the day. It can be heavy in the morning as all the computers log on and idle at lunch when most employees are not using the network. As traffic increases, so does the number of collisions causing the network to slow down. It is time to break this network into segments.

1.1   Key Words

Attenuation

Local Area Network (LAN)

Network

Network topology

Passive topology

Repeater

Stand-alone system

Thicknet

Thinnet

Transmission medium

Wide Area Network (WAN)

1.2 Compare File and Print Servers with Application Servers

A. Server-Based Networking

After a network is wired, there are several methods to effectively share network resources. A *peer-to-peer network* is the simplest network configuration that enables users to access each other's resources. As the network grows, it becomes necessary to dedicate computers specifically for resource sharing. A peer-to-peer network cannot handle the volume of requests that a large network generates.

When a network contains computers designated for management and sharing of resources, this is termed a *server-based network*. In many cases, these computers may have specialized hardware to perform that task, such as RAID controllers or Open PrePress Interface (OPI) spoolers.

1. Clients

In a server-based network, the users of the shared resources are termed *clients*. Client computers are typically less powerful computers than the network servers to which they are attached. Two types of client architecture are in use today, *thin clients* and *thick clients*.

- **Thin**—The thin client has very little hardware in the computer and typically consists of software, such as browsers, to access network servers. This type of client is receiving much press as the NetPC.

- **Thick**—The thick client, such as Windows 95 and Windows NT Workstation, is in wider use today. These computers execute programs in their own RAM and have local disks to store files.

2. File Servers

File servers are computers whose main task is to provide file sharing to computers on the network. These computers must handle multiple and simultaneous requests for file resources. These computers may also employ specialized hardware to increase reliability, speed, and capacity. Typically, this is accomplished with the help of *Redundant Arrays of Inexpensive Disks* (RAID).

There are six levels of RAID.

Level 0 Striping

Level 1 Disk mirroring

Level 2 Disk striping with ECC

Level 3 ECC stored as parity

Level 4 Disk striping with large blocks

Level 5 Disk striping with parity

Only three of the preceding levels are common today—levels 0, 1, and 5. All levels except level 0 (Striping) provide varying levels of fault tolerance.

- **Level 0 (Disk striping without parity)**—Employed for systems that require the fastest access without regard to redundancy. In this configuration, the disks are arranged to provide parallel access. If a file contains 4 sectors worth of data, then sectors 1 and 3 are stored on one disk while sectors 2 and 4 are on the other.

- **Level 1 (Disk mirroring)**—Employed when data redundancy and downtime is critical. In this method, when a write is issued to one disk, the other disk also receives the write. If one disk becomes defective, the other disk can take over without shutting down the computer.

- **Level 5 (Disk striping with parity)**—Provides faster access and better utilization of disks than level 1 as the number of disks increases. A parity sector is maintained across all disks and can be rebuilt if one disk fails.

Raid controllers contain specialized hardware to communicate with the disk arrays, thus offloading the main CPU.

The file sever must also provide security for all the files on the server. A common file server is Windows NT Server. Security is provided by limiting access to the shares and to the files.

When a disk or directory is shared, the administrator decides who can access the share. With Windows NT *New Technology File System* (NTFS), the administrator can grant or reject file and directory access to any user or group of users on the network.

File backup and maintenance are easier in a server-based network because only the file servers must be backed up.

3. Print Servers

Print servers are used to maintain a single printer or a group of printers across the network. A print server manages access to a shared printer, making it accessible to users at other network machines.

The print server usually incorporates a *spooler* that can accept jobs from clients much faster than the printer can print them. This quickly frees up the client machine because the client machine believes printing is complete. The spooler writes the job to the disk and sends the job to print when the printer is available. A *non-blocking spooler* can accept jobs from many clients in parallel.

Print servers can range from the spooler built into Windows NT to high-end Cluster Printing Systems, such as the MicroPress from T/R Systems. *High-end spoolers* provide high-speed image storage and management (OPI) that enables the clients to work with low-resolution representations of the actual images.

4. Application Servers

An *application server* runs all or part of an application on behalf of the client, then transmits the result to the client for further processing.

A common application server is a SQL database server. The client asks the SQL server to find a record, and the SQL server does all the work in locating the information, returning the desired record to the client.

B. Comparison Between File, Print, and Application Servers

Application servers run part or all of an application for clients, thus requiring a lot of CPU horsepower. File and print servers do not offload processing of client computers. They must service many requests from many computers in parallel, however, requiring large amounts of RAM and disk space.

1.2 Exercise

When you joined your company, there were 10 employees and a simple peer-to-peer network, which worked well. Your company has received a new contract and has just added 30 employees, all using email, word processing, printing capability, and access to the corporate database that is stored on your computer.

You must convince your boss to migrate from the peer-to-peer network to a client/server network. List the advantages of the server-based network and the equipment required for the migration.

1.2 Exercise Explanation

In this environment, you could install one server computer that acts as an application server as well as a file server and print server. The database stored on your local machine should be moved to the new file server and be maintained by a SQL application. You should show your boss the advantages of the security and speed of server applications, data reliability through server backups, and reduced administrative costs because only a single server needs to be maintained. Each user no longer needs to be concerned with sharing resources and setting security on the shared resources. Also show how easy it is to grow a server-based network versus a peer-to-peer network.

1.2   Practice Problems

1. Select the most appropriate configuration for a SQL server with 100,000 records.

    A. Pentium 100 processor, 64 MB RAM, RAID controller with 5 disks (4.3 GB 7200 rpm)

    B. Pentium 200 with MMX, 128 MB of RAM, 2 IDE disks (3.1 GB 5400 rpm)

    C. Pentium II 266 processor, 64 MB of RAM, 2 IDE disks (3.1 GB 5400 rpm)

    D. Pentium 100 processor, 128 MB RAM, 2 IDE disks (3.1 GB 5400 rpm)

2. Select the most appropriate configuration for a file server accessed by 200 computers.

    A. Pentium 100 processor, 64 B RAM, Raid controller with 5 disks (4.3 GB 7200 rpm)

    B. Pentium 200 with MMX, 128 MB of RAM, 2 IDE disks (3.1 GB 5400 rpm)

    C. Pentium II 266 processor, 64 MB of RAM, 2 IDE disks (3.1 GB 5400 rpm)

    D. Pentium 100 processor, 128 MB RAM, 2 IDE disks (3.1 GB 5400 rpm)

3. Select the most appropriate configuration for a print server accessed by 200 computers.

    A. Pentium 100 processor, 64 MB RAM, RAID controller with 5 disks (4.3 GB 7200 rpm)

    B. Pentium 200 with MMX, 128 MB of RAM, 2 IDE disks (3.1 GB 5400 rpm)

    C. Pentium II 266 processor, 64 MB of RAM, 2 IDE disks (3.1 GB 5400 rpm)

    D. Pentium 100 processor, 128 MB RAM, 2 IDE disks (3.1 GB 5400 rpm)

4. Your corporation has 10 executives that access the corporate web site for company news and stock prices only. What is the best type of client to service these executives?

    A. A thin client architecture

    B. A thick client architecture

    C. Windows 3.11

    D. Windows 95

5. A print server:

    A. Will make your printers run faster

    B. Will free up client computers faster when the client is printing

    C. Requires a lot of CPU horsepower to keep up with laser printers

6. A file server:

    A. Is more difficult to back up because the volume of data is much greater

    B. Requires the fastest available CPU to handle the large amount of file accesses

    C. Requires fast disks because the disk I/O is typically the bottleneck in file servers

7. Network administrators employ RAID to:

    A. Provide reliable storage for important information

    B. Make backups easier

    C. Help programmers eliminate bugs

8. The simplest method of protecting a single disk from failure is:

    A. RAID Level 0

    B. RAID Level 1

    C. RAID Level 5

9. Your company provides video streaming applications in which the data can easily be regenerated from CD-ROM. Which RAID level is best suited for this application?

    A. RAID Level 1

    B. RAID Level 0

    C. RAID Level 5

10. Your large network has five 24-ppm laser printers. Which is the best implementation to share the printers?

    A. Plug each printer into a separate parallel port on a print server.

    B. Simply provide a network connection for each printer.

    C. Install two network cards in your print server and put the five printers in a separate network along with the print server.

11. Which is not an example of client/server computing?

    A. A workstation application accessing a SQL database on a server

    B. A workstation application accessing the corporate mail server to find an address

    C. A terminal accessing a mainframe database

12. A database system utilizing SQL is an example of:

    A. A file server

    B. A print server

    C. An application server in a client/server architecture

13. Which is not true about a client/sever application?

    A. The client must have some processing power to take the load off the server.

    B. The server processes the database request and only sends the results across the network.

    C. The client must have as much processing power as the server to handle the responses from the server quickly, and not slow the server down.

14. The most common use of client/server networking is:

    A. Database servers

    B. Mail servers

    C. GroupWare

15. In a server-based network, what component of the operating system intercepts file and print requests and sends them out the network to the server?

    A. The interceptor

    B. The NDIS driver

    C. The redirector

    D. The OSI model

16. Which is not an advantage of storing applications on network servers instead of on the client's computer?

    A. Lower licensing cost

    B. Easier to upgrade

    C. Greater uptime because application is on the server

    D. Requires less disk space because the application is only installed on the server

17. Spooling a job means:

    A. Employing a special spool driver that transmits the print job to the network spooler

    B. Storing the job in memory or on disk until the physical printer is ready to accept the job

    C. Sending a print job across the network instead of printing on a local printer

18. Every time an employee of your company prints a job the output contains funny characters and numbers instead of what was intended. What is the most likely cause of this problem?

   A. The network card on the employee's computer is causing error, which accounts for the weird characters.

   B. The employee does not have the correct access to the printer.

   C. The print driver does not match the printer.

19. When setting up a client/server network, the server computer should be:

   A. More powerful than the client computers

   B. Less powerful than the client computers

   C. The same as the client computers

20. Clustering refers to:

   A. Installing servers in the same location forming clusters

   B. All the computers connected to a multi-port hub are considered a cluster

   C. Technology that enables a group of computers to appear as one high-speed computer to users on the network

21. SMP would be more important to which of the following?

   A. An application server running SQL

   B. A file server with hundreds of clients

   C. A print server controlling 30 printers

22. Network-aware applications:

   A. Provide file locking to prevent data from being corrupted by multiple users

   B. Must know the type of NIC installed to access the network

   C. Can only run over a network

23. PostScript is:

   A. A database-scripting language

   B. A method of writing efficient web pages

   C. A printer-description language

24. Windows NT Server has what levels of RAID built in?

   A. RAID level 0

   B. RAID level 1

   C. RAID level 2

   D. RAID level 5

   E. All of the above

25. A hot-swappable disk is:

   A. A disk that exactly mirrors another disk and can be exchanged with the other disk

   B. A disk that can be plugged or unplugged with power applied

   C. A disk that can be moved or tilted when spinning

1.2 Answers and Explanations: Practice Problems

1. **C** This is an application server that requires processing power more than anything else. Searching large databases is processor intensive. The most powerful processor in this group is the Pentium II 266.

2. **A** This is a large file server. Access speed and redundancy are the two most important aspects of a large file server. Here, a RAID controller is used to provide redundancy and to offload the system CPU to speed access.

3. **D** Print servers are not demanding on CPUs, so a less expensive Pentium 100

will do fine. The extra RAM and hard disks are used to spool files.

4. **A** For simple dedicated tasks, a thin client is the choice. The executives will not be required to learn how to get around in the operating system of a thin client.

5. **B** Print servers are non-blocking, which means they are always ready to accept data. If the printer is busy, the print server spools the incoming data to RAM or to the hard disk. This frees up the client computer faster because the client is not required to wait for the printer.

6. **C** The bottleneck on file servers is usually the disk, so increasing the bandwidth to the disks is of utmost importance.

7. **A** RAID provides reliable storage because the system can tolerate and recover from single disk failures.

8. **B** RAID level 1 provides disk mirroring, in which one disk exactly mirrors the other disk. If a disk fails, the other disk takes over.

9. **B** RAID level 0, striping with no parity, is the fastest of all RAID levels. Here the disks are accessed in parallel, and no parity calculations are required.

10. **C** The fastest method of supplying a printer with data is the network connection. However, if you plug the printers into the same network as the server and clients, the job must traverse the network twice—once from the client computer to the server and again from the server to the printer. This adds network traffic. If the printers are installed on their own network, then traffic is reduced and data is supplied to the printers in the fastest possible manner.

11. **C** In client/sever computing, both the client and the server share the task of processing. Terminals do not process data; they simply display data from the mainframe.

12. **C** This is the classic example of client/server computing in which the server is an application server.

13. **C** Clients usually do not require as much processing power as servers because the server must handle many requests from many clients.

14. **A** SQL database servers are the largest use of the client/server architecture in use today.

15. **C** It is the job of the redirector to redirect disk and print requests from the local machine to a server on the network.

16. **C** This is not true. If the server goes down, then all users of the application stored on the server cannot run the application.

17. **B** Spooling a job simply means storing the job somewhere until the printer is ready to accept the job. Spooling can occur locally or at the print server if one is used.

18. **C** This is a common problem when PostScript jobs are sent to PCL printers. If your printer is a PCL printer, then all users must have the correct PCL driver installed.

19. **A** The server computer must be more powerful than the clients because the server is performing most of the processing and handling multiple request from different clients.

20. **C** Clustering technology enables groups of computers to present themselves as one computer to the network. Clustering also refers to fault-tolerant computers—if one computer in a cluster fails, the other computer takes over without affecting any network connections.

21. **A** Having multiple processors is a big plus in SQL configurations. This enables the SQL server to handle requests in parallel.

22. **A** Network-aware applications must provide a mechanism to prevent data corruption when several users access data.

File locking is usually the method chosen by these applications.

23. **C**   PostScript, invented by Adobe Systems, is a very powerful Page Description Language (PDL) used for printing.

24. **A, B, D**   The three levels of RAID built into Windows NT are 0, 1, and 5—Striping without parity, mirroring, and striping with parity.

25. **B**   The term "hot swappable" refers to a component's capability to be swapped with power applied. This is a bonus in a RAID system. If a disk fails, another disk is hot swapped and the RAID controller rebuilds the new disk.

1.2   Key Words

Application server

Clients

File server

New Technology File System (NTFS)

Peer-to-peer network

Print server

Redundant Arrays of Inexpensive Disks (RAID)

Server-based network

Spooler

1.3 Compare User-Level Security with Access Permission Assigned to a Shared Directory on a Server

Two basic network security models are in use today, *password-protected shares* and *access permissions*. These two models are often referred to as *share-level security* and *user-level security*.

A. Password-Protected Shares

In the password-protected shares network security model, also referred to as *share-level security*, each shared resource is assigned a password. To access the resource, the user enters the correct password and is granted access to the resource. This method does not require user authentication.

The type of access can be controlled by the operating system; however, you cannot grant different levels of access to different users. Different operating systems expose different types of access to shares. Windows 95 is a good example of an operating system that implements share-level security.

B. Access Permissions

Access-permissions security (user-level access) is more advanced and flexible than password-protected shares. Rights are assigned on a user-by-user basis and authentication is employed. A user logs on to the network by supplying a user name and a password associated with the user name. The server validates the user name and password before access to any network resource is granted. The server or domain controller in this architecture must maintain a database of users and passwords.

Each resource in the network has permissions associated with it. After the user is validated, access to resources is granted based on permissions granted to that user. In user-level access configurations, it is easy to think of passwords being associated with users and permissions being associated with resources.

Windows NT employs *discretionary access control*. This is the capability to assign permissions at the discretion of the owner (or other authorized person).

Windows NT incorporates access-permissions security in two different models, the *workgroup model* and the *domain model*.

1. Workgroup Model

In the workgroup model, every server in the network maintains its own set of users and passwords in the Security Account Manager (SAM) database. Each time a user logs on, the Local Security Authority (LSA) validates the user name and password against the SAM database. Each server in a workgroup maintains its own SAM.

After a user is authenticated, an access token is created for that user. This token is used to determine the level of access to network resources for that user.

Each resource has an Access Control List (ACL) associated with it. This list identifies which groups or users have access to the object the ACL represents. The ACL consists of Access Control Entries (ACEs), which specify the permissions for a particular user or group.

Each ACE has an access mask, which defines all possible permissions for a particular user to that object. When a user attempts to access a network resource, Windows NT compares the security information in the user's access token with the ACE, and permission is either granted or denied.

This model is appropriate for workgroups consisting of few servers. As the number of servers grows, the amount of work to keep all the SAM databases up-to-date also grows.

2. Domain Model

The domain model maintains a single SAM database for the entire network. This database is maintained on a computer designated as the domain controller. All security validation works basically the same as the workgroup model, with the difference that the LSA must communicate with the domain controller to validate the user against the domain's SAM database.

3. Windows NT Groups and Permissions

As the number of users increases, the difficulty in maintaining permissions for these users also increases. Windows NT enables the system administrator to create groups of users and to apply permissions to the entire group.

The security of a network resource varies depending on the type of resource. For example, a Windows NT printer has four categories of security:

Full Control	Gives the user administrative control of the printer
Manage Documents	Allows a user to change the status of print jobs but not of printers
Print	Allows a user to print and to change the status of only his jobs
No Access	Means the user has no access to the printer

Permissions on NTFS directories under Windows NT are as follows:

Full Control	Gives all access to the directory including changing permissions
Read	Allows the user to read or to execute programs from the subdirectory
List	Allows viewing of file names and subdirectories under the current subdirectory
Add	Allows adding files or subdirectories
No Access	Denies all access to the subdirectory
Change	Allows reading, writing, deleting, and creating files and subdirectories
Add and read	Allows reading and creating files and subdirectories

The preceding directory permissions are only supported under the NTFS file system. If the disk is formatted with the FAT file system, directory permissions are not available. When a share is created under Windows NT, the following permissions are available:

Full Control	Gives all access to the directory including changing permissions
Read	Allows the user to read or to execute programs from the share or any subdirectory under the share
Change	Allows reading, writing, deleting, and creating files and subdirectories under the share
No Access	Denies all access to the share

The share permissions are available regardless of the type of file system on the disk (such as FAT or NTFS).

1.3   Exercise

You are a systems administrator for a small company that has one Windows NT file server. On this file server, there is a series of database files all under the same directory. Certain users in the company update the database, and other users only access the database. How can you allow certain users to modify the database while at the same time allow other users only read access to the database?

1.3   Exercise Explanation

There are two methods to accomplish this goal. The first method is to grant all users full control to the subdirectories and files on the disk. After this is done, a share is set up and access permissions to the share are set on a user-by-user basis. The other method is just the opposite, in which all users are granted access to the share, but subdirectory and file access is determined on a user-by-user basis. The most common approach today is the first approach.

1.3   Practice Problems

1. Windows for Workgroups employs which type of resource sharing architecture?

    A.   User-level security

    B.   Share-level security

    C.   Password-protected shares

    D.   Access permissions

2. User-level security is good for:

    A.   Large networks with more than 50 computers

    B.   Peer-to-peer networks with less than 10 computers

    C.   Networks that have many servers but few users

3. Which file system allows specific permissions for files and directories on Windows NT?

    A.   HPFS

    B.   NTFS

    C.   FAT

    D.   FAST FAT32

4. Which file system allows setting of permissions on disk shares?

    A.   NTFS

    B.   FAT

    C.   HPFS

    D.   All of the above

5. Discretionary access control means:

    A.   The operating systems employs ACLs.

    B.   The administrator decides who can or cannot log on to the server.

    C.   The owner of a resource decides who has access and the type of access to the resource.

6. Which operating system(s) implements discretionary control?

    A.   Windows 95

    B.   DOS

    C.   Windows NT

7. How many different modes of network operation does Windows NT server support?

    A.   1

    B.   2

    C.   3

    D.   4

8. In a Windows NT workgroup network, there are five Windows NT servers. How many SAM databases are there?

    A.   1

    B.   2

    C.   10

    D.   5

9. In a Windows NT domain network with five Windows NT servers, how many SAM databases are there?

    A.   1

    B.   2

    C.   10

    D.   5

10. In a Windows NT network with one server and nine clients, which networking model is easier to implement?

    A.   Windows NT workgroup

    B.   Windows NT domain

    C.   Windows NT trusted domain

11. The Windows NT SAM database is where:

    A.   User names and passwords are stored

B.   Disk-sharing information is stored

C.   Printer-sharing information is stored

12. In a peer-to-peer network, which network security model is used?

A.   User-level security

B.   Share-level security

C.   Password-protected shares

D.   Access permissions

13. ACE is an acronym for:

A.   Access control entity

B.   Access control entry

C.   Access control enabled

14. ACLs:

A.   Contain users' passwords

B.   Contain resource passwords

C.   Contain ACEs

15. In user-level access, network resources: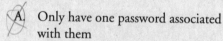

A.   Only have one password associated with them

B.   Have multiple passwords associated with them

C.   Have no passwords but have permissions associated with them

16. When a user logs on to Windows NT, who is responsible for authentication?

A.   The LSA

B.   The ACL administrator

C.   The SAM process

D.   The ACE generator

17. When a print server grants a user print access:

A.   That user can delete his own job

B.   That user can pause other jobs to allow clearing of paper jams

C.   That user can change the priority of other jobs from the console to allow his job to print sooner

18. Which type of access is not associated with directory shares?

A.   Read

B.   Change

C.   Add

D.   No Access

19. Which access is not associated with FAT directories?

A.   List

B.   Read

C.   Write

D.   Full Control

E.   No Access

F.   All the above

20. Which access is not associated with NTFS directories?

A.   List

B.   Read

C.   Write

D.   Full Control

E.   No Access

F.   None of the above

21. How many Primary Domain Controllers can exist in a Windows NT Domain?

A.   1

B.   2

C.   As many as the administrator wants, although each domain controller must run on a separate computer

22. In a Windows NT domain, the Local Security Authority must verify logins with:

   A. The local SAM database

   B. The ACL manager on the domain controller

   C. The remote SAM database on the domain controller

   D. The local LSA security database

23. One reason domains are easier to manage than workgroups with a large network is:

   A. Users can be combined into groups to minimize the number of changes required when security changes.

   B. There is only one SAM database for the entire network, requiring only one database to be updated.

   C. ACLs are automatically updated when users are added to the domain.

24. When a user attempts to print a job on a shared Windows NT printer, the user's access is verified:

   A. By checking the user's credentials against the SAM

   B. By checking the user's credentials in the local ACL

   C. By using the user's token and ACL for the share

25. In Windows NT, if you delete a user then add the user back in with the exact name and rights:

   A. His security is automatically recognized because the name is the same and all resources are updated.

   B. All security information is lost because each time a new user is created a unique security ID is created for that user.

26. You are a systems administrator. A user complains he gets access denied each time he attempts to read a shared NTFS directory. You look at the shares, and the user has Change access to the share. What is the most likely cause of this problem?

   A. The user's network card is defective.

   B. The user logged on to the network with the wrong password.

   C. You gave the user correct share permissions but forgot to give the user access to the NTFS directory.

   D. The server was in the process of coming up and was not ready to handle user requests.

27. To create a new subdirectory under an NTFS volume, what is the minimum level of access required?

   A. Full Control

   B. Write

   C. Read

   D. Change

   E. Add

1.3   Answers and Explanations: Practice Problems

1. **B, C**   Windows for Workgroups supports only the password-protected shares model, also called share-level security.

2. **A**   As a network grows larger, it is easier to manage user-level security than share-level security.

3. **B**   NTFS, New Technology File System, enables the user to apply permissions on files and directories on the Windows NT platform.

4. **D**   All disk architectures allow setting of permissions on shares.

5. **C**   In discretionary access control systems, the owner (usually the creator) of

an object decides the type of access granted to users of the object.

6. **C** Windows NT employs discretionary access control to all objects in the system.

7. **B** Windows NT supports the workgroup model and the domain model of server networking.

8. **D** In the Windows NT workgroup model, each computer maintains its own SAM database.

9. **A** The Windows NT domain model has only one SAM database for the entire domain. This database is located on the Primary Domain Controller (PDC) and is replicated on any Backup Domain Controllers.

10. **A** The Window NT workgroup model is easier to set up than the domain model. In small networks, the Windows NT workgroup model is easy to maintain because the number of users is small.

11. **A** The Security Account Manager (SAM) database is where user names and passwords are stored.

12. **B** Peer-to-peer networks implement share-level security. There is not a database of users in the peer-to-peer network architecture.

13. **B** An ACE is simply an entry in the access control list (ACL) for an object under Windows NT. The ACE contains access information about a user or group for this object.

14. **C** The access control list (ACL) is a collection of ACEs.

15. **C** In user-level access, network users have passwords and resources have permissions.

16. **A** The Local Security Authority (LSA) is responsible for logon authentication in the Windows NT operating system.

17. **A** Print access only allows the user to modify his job.

18. **C** Add access is not associated with directory shares. Add access is a security attribute for disk files and directories under NTFS.

19. **F** Directory permissions cannot be individually set on FAT directories or files.

20. **C** There is no such permission as Write access under Windows NT.

21. **A** In a Windows NT domain, there is only one domain controller; however, there may be several backup domain controllers.

22. **C** In the domain model, the LSA communicates with the PDC to verify logons against the PDC SAM database.

23. **B** Updating one database each time a change occurs is much easier than updating every server on the network.

24. **C** Each time a user logs on, the user is given a token. This token is used each time the user attempts to access any resources. The token is used to identify the user's entry in the ACL for the share.

25. **B** Each time a user or group is created, a unique Security Identifier (SID) is assigned. If you delete a user and then add the user back, a different SID is created for the user; thus, the rights the original user had are lost.

26. **C** Under NTFS, if you grant a user access to a share, it does not guarantee that the user can access directories or files. The user must also have permissions to gain file and directory access under NTFS.

27. **E** Add. This enables the user to create the subdirectories but does not grant access to any files.

1

1.3 Key Words

Access Control Entry (ACE)

Access Control List (ACL)

Access mask

Access permission security

Discretionary access control

Domain model

Share-level security

User-level security

Workgroup model

1.4 Compare a Client/Server Network with a Peer-to-Peer Network

All networks share some common elements, including:

Resources	Disks, printers, faxes, and other resources used by clients on the network
Servers	Machines that share local resources on the network
Clients	Machines that request and use shared resources
Media	The interconnection between networked computers

PC networks generally fall into one of these two categories:

- **Server-based network.** Consists of groups of user-oriented PCs (*clients*) that request and receive network resources from network servers.

  Included in these resources are file services, print services, e-mail, fax services, and application services.

- **Peer-to-peer network.** Consists of groups of user-oriented PCs that operate as equals (*peers*), sharing and using each other as resources.

  In a peer-to-peer network, each computer is responsible for its own security. A peer that shares and uses resources is essentially a server and a client. These networks work well with 10 or fewer computers.

When deciding which type of network to implement, several factors must be considered, including:

Number of computers

Cost

Security requirements

Administrative requirements

A. Peer-to-Peer Implementations

Peer-to-peer networks have several advantages over server-based networks:

Lower Cost

Easy to set up and install

Usually no dedicated network administrator is required

Users have control over their own resources and manage their own security

Simple cabling schemes are possible

Along with the advantages of the peer-to-peer network, there are several disadvantages:

Limited growth

No central organization

Weak security

Additional load on computers acting as clients and servers

B. Server-Based Implementations

Server-based networks include specialized high-performance computers dedicated to certain tasks, such as file servers, print servers, or application servers.

Advantages of the server-based network include:

Centralized management of a large number of users

Strong security that is centralized

Capability to grow

Capability to create redundant systems

Some disadvantages of the server-based architecture include:

More expensive to set up due to dedicated server hardware

More difficult to initially set up due to centralized management of users and resources

Usually requires a network administrator to manage the network

C. Windows Implementations

Windows operating systems implement both types of networking. Windows 95 and Windows NT Workstation implement peer-to-peer networks, while Windows NT Server is used to implement a server-based network that is scalable to thousands of computers and users.

1.4   Exercise

A small accounting firm consisting of 10 computer stations wants to install networking. The company is not large enough to justify the cost of a dedicated network administrator, but it keeps very sensitive accounting information about its clients, so security is very important. The computer operators are experienced at accounting software but not at other aspects of networking or computer support.

List the reasons for installing a peer-to-peer network. List the inadequacies of a peer-to-peer network in this scenario.

List the reasons for installing a server-based network. List the inadequacies of a server-based network in this scenario.

1.4 Exercise Explanation

Because there are only 10 computers and no network administrator, a peer-to-peer network is very attractive. A peer-to-peer network is cheaper to implement in this firm because no dedicated server is required. The peer-to-peer network is weak in providing adequate security for the client's information. A server-based network is an excellent choice for providing security. However, a dedicated server adds expense to the network.

1

1.4   Practice Problems

1. Windows 95 implements which type of networking?

    A. User-level security

    B. Peer-to-peer

    C. Server-based

2. Peer-to-peer networks are best for:

    A. Large networks with more than 50 computers

    B. Peer-to-peer networks with less than 10 computers

    C. Networks that have many servers but few users

3. Security in a peer-to-peer network:

    A. Is weak and centrally managed

    B. Is the responsibility of each user sharing resources

    C. Does not exist

    D. Requires a systems administrator to implement

4. Security in a server-based network:

    A. Is strong and centrally managed

    B. Is the responsibility of each user sharing resources

    C. Is easy to manage and does not require a system administrator

    D. None of the above

5. A Windows NT workgroup model in which each computer has a user is a:

    A. Peer-to-peer network

    B. Server-based network

    C. Application server

6. Windows NT domain model is a:

    A. Peer-to-peer network

    B. Server-based network

    C. Application server

7. If cost is the most important issue in deciding network architecture, which statement is correct?

    A. A peer-to-peer network it the best choice.

    B. A server-based network is the best choice.

    C. It depends on the number of computers and how they are to be used.

    D. The NT domain model is the best choice.

8. In a network with 20 users, one file server, and no network administrator, which is the best choice for the network?

    A. Windows NT Server domain model with Windows 95 clients

    B. Windows NT Server workgroup model with Windows 95 clients

    C. Windows 95 peer-to-peer network

    D. Window NT Workstation peer-to-peer network

9. What is the largest file size on a Windows NT Server disk?

    A. 1 gigabyte

    B. 4 gigabytes

    C. 1 exabyte

    D. 100 megabytes

10. What is the maximum number of characters in a Window NT Server file name?

    A. 8

    B. 12

    C. 64

    D. 128

    E. 255

11. How big is an exabyte?

    A. One million gigabytes

    B. 1×10^9 bytes

    C. 1×10^{32} bytes

    D. 1×10^{64} bytes

12. NT Server can distribute processing across several processors utilizing SMP. How many processors can be used effectively in a Windows NT 4.0 SMP system?

    A. 2

    B. 4

    C. 8

    D. 32

13. Your company has purchased 100 Pentium-based computers with 8 mega-bytes of RAM to serve as client computers in a Windows NT Server domain. Which is the best choice of client operating system for these computers?

    A. Window NT Workstation

    B. Windows NT Server for Workgroups

    C. Windows 95

    D. Windows 3.1

14. In which type of network does the computer act as a client and as a server?

    A. A Windows NT domain server network

    B. A peer-to-peer network

    C. A server-based network

15. In user-level access, network resources:

    A. Only have one password associated with them

    B. Have multiple passwords associated with them

    C. Have no passwords but have permissions associated with them

16. Which server-based oper supports the MIPs platfo

    A. Windows 95

    B. Windows NT Server

    C. Windows NT Server

17. Windows NT Server can support how many incoming RAS connections?

    A. 4

    B. 16

    C. 32

    D. 256

    E. 128

18. Minimum RAM requirements for servers are typically?

    A. 8 megabytes

    B. 16 megabytes

    C. 32 megabytes

    D. 128 megabytes

1.4 Answers and Explanations: Practice Problems

1. **B** Windows 95 implements a peer-to-peer networking scheme.

2. **B** Peer-to-peer is intended for networks consisting of 10 or fewer computers. As the number of computers increases, the demands placed on a peer-to-peer network make it difficult to use.

3. **B** Security in a peer-to-peer network is set by each user sharing his resources. There is no central security authority in a peer-to-peer network.

4. **A** Security in a server-based network such as the Windows NT domain is centrally managed. Here, there is one user database for the entire network.

5. **A** In Windows NT workgroup, each computer is responsible for its own resources. There are no dedicated servers, so this is the peer-to-peer model.

6. **B** The Windows NT domain model is a server-based networking architecture that is centrally managed by the Primary Domain Controller (PDC).

7. **A** Peer-to-peer networks are less expensive than server-based networks. There are not dedicated servers, and the operating systems are simpler and less expensive.

8. **B** Windows NT Server would manage the file server, and the clients would use Windows 95. With a dedicated server, this architecture is better than a simple peer-to-peer network.

9. **C** Windows NT uses 64-bit addressing for the file system. This allows a file as large as 1 raised to the power of 64 bytes, or 1 exabyte.

10. **E** Windows NT allows up to 255 characters in a file name.

11. **D** An exabyte is 1 raised to the power of 64 bytes.

12. **B** Windows NT 4.0 is optimized for up to four processors in the same system.

13. **C** Windows NT will not function with only 8 megabytes of memory, and Windows 3.1 is not a good client for network operating systems. Windows 95 was designed to be a networking client and will run with 8 megabytes of RAM.

14. **B** In a peer-to-peer network, each computer that shares resources is a server. It is also a client if it uses resources shared by other computers.

15. **C** User-level access networks have passwords for users and permissions for resources.

16. **C** Windows NT is the only multi-platform operating systems from Microsoft. Support for the MIPs platform was dropped from Windows NT 4.0, so the only operating system on the list is Windows NT 3.51.

17. **D** Windows NT Server can support up to 256 RAS connections.

18. **C** Having adequate RAM in a server is very important and can increase performance significantly. The minimum amount of RAM for servers is 32 megabytes.

1.4 Key Words

Peer-to-peer networking

Server-based networking

Peer

Client

1.5   Compare the Implications of Using Connection-Oriented Versus Connectionless Communications

The Network Layer of the OSI model determines the route a packet travels as it passes through routers from source to destination.

Communications between computers can be set up in two different manners:

- **Connection-Oriented**—These systems assume there will be communication errors between computers. With this in mind, these protocols are designed to make sure data is delivered in sequential order, error-free to its destination. TCP/IP is an example of connection-oriented protocol.

- **Connectionless-Oriented**—These systems assume data will reach its destination with no errors; thus, there is no protocol overhead associated with these systems. Without this overhead, these systems are typically very fast. User Datagram protocol is an example of connectionless-oriented protocol.

Connectionless-mode protocols work well in LAN environments in which the number of transmission errors is kept to a minimum. In a WAN environment in which the data must pass through multiple routers and errors are more frequent, these protocols do not perform as well. Sequential-packet delivery is not guaranteed in connectionless systems, so it is up to the higher-level protocols to assemble packets in the correct order as well as to handle errors.

A.   Connection-Oriented Mode

In connection-oriented mode, the path from source PC to destination PC is predetermined. This path can contain several links, which form a logical pathway called a *connection*. The nodes forwarding the data packet have the capability to track which packet is part of which connection. This enables the internal nodes to provide flow control as the data moves along the connection. If a node detects a transmission error, it requests the preceding node to retransmit the bad packet.

The nodes keep track of which packets belong to which connection, allowing several concurrent connections through the node.

B.   Connectionless-Oriented Mode

Connectionless-oriented mode does not incorporate all the internal control mechanisms found in connection-oriented mode. Error recovery is delegated to the source and destination nodes. These nodes acknowledge receipt of packets and retransmission of bad or lost packets. Connectionless-oriented mode is faster than connection-oriented mode because internal nodes only forward packets without tracking connections and handling errors.

In an error-prone environment with many links, the connectionless-oriented mode can actually be slower because the packet must be retransmitted from the source node instead of from internal nodes.

1.5   Practice Problems

1. What ISO layer determines the route a packet will take through a network?

   A. Data Link Layer

   B. Presentation Layer

   C. Network Layer

   D. Physical Layer

2. Which connection mode is faster when there are little or no errors?

   A. Connectionless-oriented mode

   B. Connection-oriented mode

3. In a LAN, which mode is most appropriate?

   A. Connectionless-oriented mode

   B. Connection-oriented mode

4. Which Internet protocol is connection-oriented?

   A. NetBEUI

   B. TCP/IP

   C. UDP/IP

   D. None of the above

5. Which Internet protocol is connectionless-oriented?

   A. NetBEUI

   B. TCP/IP

   C. UDP/IP

   D. None of the above

6. Which OSI layer facilitates transmission of data across a single link between nodes?

   A. Network Layer

   B. Physical Layer

   C. Application Layer

   D. Data Link Layer

7. Which mode puts the responsibility of reliable data delivery on the two end nodes?

   A. Connection-oriented

   B. Connectionless-oriented

   C. None of the above

8. Which mode is used in the global Internet?

   A. Connection-oriented mode

   B. Connectionless-oriented mode

   C. All of the above

9. Which mode guarantees packets will be delivered in sequence?

   A. Connection-oriented mode

   B. Connectionless-oriented mode

   C. None of the above

10. A connection is:

    A. A physical link between two computers on a LAN

    B. A remote dial-up link between a client and server

    C. A logical pathway between source and destination nodes

    D. A physical link between any two nodes in a link

11. Which mode enables concurrent connections through nodes in a network?

    A. Connection-oriented mode

    B. Connectionless-oriented mode

12. Which description is associated with connection-oriented mode protocols?

    A. Guaranteed delivery of packets

    B. Fast but unreliable

    C. Used for microwave communication links

    D. Used in wireless systems

13. Which description is associated with connectionless-oriented mode protocols?

   A. Fast but unreliable

   B. Used for microwave communication links

   C. Guaranteed delivery of packets

   D. Used in wireless systems

1.5 Answers and Explanations

1. **C** The Network Layer describes the process of routing a packet through a series of nodes to a destination elsewhere on the network.

2. **A** Connectionless-oriented mode is faster because there is no overhead for error handling.

3. **A** In a LAN there are very few errors so a connectionless-oriented mode is most appropriate.

4. **B** TCP/IP is a connection-oriented protocol. NetBEUI is not a member of the Internet protocol suite, and UDP/IP is connectionless-oriented.

5. **C** UDP/IP is a connectionless-oriented protocol. NetBEUI is not a member of the Internet protocol suite, and TCP/IP is a connection-oriented protocol.

6. **D** The Data Link Layer facilitates the transmission of data across a single link between two nodes.

7. **B** Connectionless-oriented mode does no error checking so the responsibility is up to the two end nodes communicating through the network.

8. **A** The global Internet is very complicated and very error-prone, thus connection-oriented protocols are used.

9. **A** Connection-oriented mode not only handles error recovery but also guarantees packets will be delivered in sequence.

10. **C** A connection is a logical pathway between source and destination nodes.

11. **A** Connection-oriented mode enables concurrent connections through nodes because this mode tracks each connection and examines all packets passing through the node.

12. **A** Connection-oriented mode guarantees all packets arrive error-free in correct sequence.

13. **A** Connectionless-oriented communications are not responsible for error detection or delivering packets in correct sequence. Without this overhead, this mode is faster but not reliable.

1.5 Key Words

Connectionless-oriented mode

Connection-oriented mode

1.6   Distinguish Whether SLIP or PPP Is Used as the Communications Protocol for Various Situations

These two protocols are used primarily for dial-up access. Serial Line Internet Protocol (SLIP) operates at the OSI Physical Layer while Point-to-Point Protocol (PPP) provides Physical Layer and Data Link Layer functionality. There are three protocols that can be used to access the Internet: SLIP, PPP, and CSLIP. CSLIP is a compressed form of SLIP. PPP is becoming the protocol of choice because it is faster and more reliable than SLIP or CSLIP. SLIP is still used on older systems that dial up to SLIP-supported hosts.

A.   Serial Line Internet Protocol (SLIP)

When using SLIP to connect to the Internet, the user must know the IP address assigned by the Internet Service Provider (ISP). SLIP does not provide any automated fashion to register IP addresses. If the address is dynamically assigned via Dynamic Host Configuration Protocol (DHCP), the user must assign the address manually or run a logon script. SLIP was originally implemented in 1984.

The simplicity of SLIP leads to the following disadvantages:

> Operator intervention is required during connection because SLIP cannot register IP addresses automatically.

> SLIP can only support one protocol at a time over a serial link.

> SLIP does not perform any error-checking for bad frames.

Windows NT supports the client end of SLIP; however, the server component of Remote Access Service (RAS) does not provide SLIP support.

B.   Point-to-Point Protocol (PPP)

The design goal of PPP, as referenced in RFC 1171, has three major components:

> A method for encapsulating datagrams over serial links

> An extensible Link Control Protocol (LCP)

> A family of Network Control Protocols (NCPs) for establishing and configuring different network layer protocols

A goal of PPP was to address the shortcomings of SLIP. The improvements implemented to achieve this goal include:

> The capability to dynamically negotiate IP addresses

> The addition of checksum error-checking for each frame

The capability to support multiple protocols over a single serial connection

The addition of NCPs to negotiate choices of network layer protocols

The addition of LCP to establish link options

PPP is a bit-oriented protocol that identifies the beginning and end of a packet with bit patterns referred to as flags. This characteristic of PPP was derived from the High Data Link Control (HDLC) protocol.

Including the beginning and end flag, the PPP packet can be as large as 1508 bytes with a maximum of 1500 data bytes.

1.6   Practice Problems

1. Your computer has remote access dial-up utilizing TCP/IP; however, automatic IP addressing is not supported. What dial-up protocol are you using?

   A. TCP/IP

   B. UDP/IP

   C. SLIP

   D. PPP

2. You want to run several protocols across your remote access communication link. Which dial-up protocol should you use?

   A. TCP/IP

   B. PPP

   C. SLIP

   D. UDP/IP

3. Which protocol was partially derived from HDLC?

   A. SLDC

   B. PPP

   C. SMB

   D. SLIP

4. PPP is which type of protocol?

   A. Bit-oriented protocol

   B. Byte-oriented protocol

   C. Character-oriented protocol

   D. Count-oriented protocol

5. Which part of PPP enables it to verify whether the line has a good enough quality connection to reliably support the connection?

   A. SLIP

   B. LCP

   C. NCP

   D. HDLC

6. Which dial-up protocol has a 2-byte CRC associated with each frame?

   A. SLIP

   B. PPP

   C. HDLC

   D. TCP/IP

7. PPPTP is:

   A. A higher-speed version of PPP

   B. A tunneling protocol that that uses PPP to establish a secure link to a remote LAN over the Internet

   C. An Internet protocol that used PPP for secure transactions such as banking and credit card usage

   D. A version of PPP that can employ multiple phone lines for a higher-speed connection

8. Which protocol operates only at the Physical Layer?

   A. PPP

   B. SLIP

   C. TCP/IP

   D. UDP/IP

9. Which dial-up protocol provides Data Link Layer functionality?

   A. PPP

   B. SLIP

   C. TCP/IP

   D. UDP/IP

10. Which protocol is typically found in older dial-up systems?

    A. SLIP

    B. PPP

    C. TCP

11. What is the most popular serial-link protocol?

   A. SLIP

   B. HDLC

   C. PPP

12. Which dial-up protocol does not support NetBEUI?

   A. SLIP

   B. PPP

   C. HDLC

13. Which dial-up protocol supports IPX?

   A. SLIP

   B. PPP

   C. SDLC

14. What is the purpose of DHCP?

   A. To allow easy access to web pages

   B. To assign standard addresses to web pages

   C. To enable users to share IP addresses so that a relatively small number of IP addresses can support many users

15. Which dial-up protocol is not used with DHCP?

   A. SLIP

   B. PPP

   C. HDLC

   D. TCP/IP

16. Multi-Link under Windows NT allows:

   A. SLIP connections utilizing multiple communications links in parallel

   B. PPP connections utilizing multiple communications links in parallel

   C. Multiple Internet protocols running across the same communications link

17. The CSLIP communication protocol is:

   A. A new form of SLIP to support faster modems

   B. A new form of SLIP to support features that are in PPP

   C. SLIP with compression

18. Which dial-up protocol employs the Logical Link Control (LLC) level error control?

   A. PPP

   B. SLIP

   C. CSLIP

19. LLC is a sublayer to which OSI level?

   A. Physical Layer

   B. Data Link Layer

   C. Network Layer

20. Which protocol provides physical device addressing at the Media Access Control (MAC) sublayer?

   A. PPP

   B. SLIP

   C. CSLIP

21. MAC is a sublayer to which OSI level?

   A. Physical Layer

   B. Data Link Layer

   C. Network Layer

22. Most ISDN links use which serial-link protocol?

   A. PPP

   B. CSLIP

   C. SLIP

   D. HDLC

1

23. AppleTalk is supported over which dial-up protocol?

   A. Ethertalk

   B. PPP

   C. SLIP

   D. CLSIP

24. How many information data bytes can be contained in a PPP packet?

   A. 256

   B. 1024

   C. 2048

   D. 1500

25. The first implementation of SLIP appeared in:

   A. 1984

   B. 1992

   C. 1970

   D. 1990

1.6 Answers and Explanations: Practice Problems

1. **C** SLIP does not support automatic IP addressing. This must be accomplished manually or via a script.

2. **B** One improvement of PPP over SLIP is the capability to transport multiple protocols over a single serial connection.

3. **B** PPP is one of many derivative protocols of High Level Data Link Control.

4. **A** Being a derivative of HDLC makes PPP a bit-oriented protocol with each frame beginning and ending with a flag character of 0x7e which is 6 "1" bits in a row.

5. **B** PPP uses an extensible Line Control Protocol (LCP) that establishes the link after it has determined the quality of the connection is sufficient to support a reliable connection.

6. **B** Because SLIP does not support error detection, and HDLC and TCP/IP are not dial-up protocols, PPP is the only choice left. The Frame Check Sequence field (FCS) or CRC consists of 16 bits prior to the ending flag character.

7. **B** Point-to-point tunneling protocol is a feature of NT enabling secure connections to remote LANs to be established across the Internet.

8. **B** SLIP operates only at the Physical Layer of the OSI model. This is one of the limitations addressed in designing the PPP protocol.

9. **A** PPP operates at the Data Link Layer as well as the Physical Layer of the OSI model.

10. **A** SLIP was developed before PPP; thus, it is found on older dial-up systems.

11. **C** With its added capabilities, PPP has overtaken SLIP as the most used dial-up protocol.

12. **A** SLIP only supports a single IP connection. HDLC is not a dial-up protocol and PPP supports NetBEUI.

13. **B** PPP supports IPX; SLIP does not. SDLC is not a dial-up protocol.

14. **C** Dynamic Host Configuration Protocol (DHCP) dynamically assigns IP addresses, enabling a few IP addresses to support a larger number of users than fixed IP addressing.

15. **A** SLIP does not support automatic IP addressing; PPP does.

16. **B** Multi-Link is a feature of Windows NT that enables pooling of serial communication links to achieve higher bandwidth connections utilizing PPP.

17. **C** Compressed Serial Line Internet Protocol (CSLIP) is a compressed version of the SLIP protocol.

18. **A** SLIP and CSLIP do not support error detection. PPP utilizes LLC for error control.

19. **B** LLC is one of two sublayers to the Data Link Layer of the OSI model.

20. **A** Because SLIP and CSLIP only implement the Physical Layer of the OSI model and MAC is a sublayer to the Data Link Layer, the only choice is PPP.

21. **B** MAC is a sublayer to the Data Link Layer of the OSI model.

22. **A** ISDN lines are popular for connecting LANs to the Internet. When connecting a LAN, multiple protocols must share the same dial-up link. PPP is the only dial-up protocol with this capability.

23. **B** PPP is the only dial-up protocol that supports multiple protocols across the same serial connection. AppleTalk is one of the protocols supported.

24. **D** There can be up to 1500 information bytes in a PPP packet. The total length of a PPP packet is 1508 if all information bytes are used.

25. **A** The first implementation of SLIP appeared in 1984, based on standards set forth by the Internet Engineering Task Force (IETF).

1.6 Key Words

Bit-oriented protocol

Flag

Remote Access Service (RAS)

Serial Line Internet Protocol (SLIP)

Point-to-Point Protocol (PPP)

CSLIP

1.7 Define the Communication Devices That Communicate at Each Level of the OSI Model

A. The OSI Model

The Open Systems Interconnection (OSI) model was developed by the International Standards Organization (ISO) to establish global standards for information exchange across networks. The model consists of seven layers.

- **Layer 1, the Physical Layer**—Consists of protocols that define communication on the network media.

- **Layer 2, the Data Link Layer**—Receives data frames from the Network Layer and packages these frames for the Physical Layer. The Data Link Layer packages raw data bits from the Physical into frames for the Network Layer. The Data Link Layer was improved by the IEEE 802 project to include two sublayers: Media Access Control (MAC) and Logical Link Control (LLC).

- **Layer 3, the Network Layer**—Determines the route packets take to reach their destination. It is the Network Layer that translates logical network addresses into physical addresses. If packets are too large to traverse a link in the route to the destination, it is the job of the Network Layer to break these packets into smaller ones.

- **Layer 4, the Transport Layer**—Ensures that packets are delivered in sequence error-free. The Transport Layer breaks large messages from the Session Layer into manageable packets to be sent out to the network.

- **Layer 5, the Session Layer**—Creates a virtual connection between two applications on separate computers. This virtual connection is called a *session*. The Session Layer maintains synchronization between applications by placing checkpoints in the data stream. It is this layer that performs the name recognition and security that enable the applications to communicate.

- **Layer 6, the Presentation Layer**—Defines the format used by applications to exchange data. In this sense, this layer is also called the *translator*. This layer is responsible for protocol conversion, data encryption, and data compression. This is where the redirector service operates.

- **Layer 7, the Application Layer**—The topmost layer of the OSI model. This layer exposes all the network services to the applications. When an application accesses the network, it is through this layer all actions are carried out.

B. Devices at each OSI Layer

1. The Physical Layer

The lowest layer of the OSI is the Physical Layer. Devices at this layer include hubs, transmitters, receivers, cables, connectors, and repeaters.

Repeaters simply regenerate weak incoming signals. Because no packet information is necessary to perform this task, repeaters reside at the Physical Layer. A repeater simply retransmits any frame it receives including frames with errors.

2. The Data Link Layer

The Data Link Layer adds information to each packet coming from the Network Layer. Thus, the Data Link Layer has knowledge of the packet structure and fields. Devices such as intelligent hubs, bridges, and Network Interface Cards (NICs) with associated drivers reside at this layer.

A *bridge* is a step up from repeater; the bridge can intelligently forward incoming packets. A bridge does not simply retransmit each frame out all ports. Instead, it only transmits the frame out the port leading to the next destination segment of the frame. To perform these functions, the bridge must build internal routing tables to determine the correct segment to send a packet.

3. The Network Layer

The Network Layer has the responsibility of determining the route a packet must take to reach its destination. Devices that accomplish this are routers, brouters, and gateways. Included in this layer are circuit, packet, and message switching.

Gateways perform protocol conversion by totally rebuilding the protocol stack between networks. Gateways can reside at the Network Layer OSI model. However, gateways typically reside at the Application Layer.

Routers and *brouters* are a step up from bridges. The router builds routing tables like the bridge, but the information available to the router enables it to pass packets through a chain of other routers and, in many cases, determine the best route. This is a vast improvement over determining the next segment a packet will take.

Brouters are a combination bridge and router that act as a bridge for nonroutable protocols.

4. The Higher Layers

The higher layers (Transport, Session, Presentation, and Application) typically reside in the computers that are communicating with each other across the network. The one exception is the gateway, which can span all layers.

1.7   Exercise

You are a systems administrator for a small company that has grown significantly over the years. You have seven 10Base-T hubs, each with 24 ports. You have just added a new 24-port hub and filled all the ports to support new sales and marketing staff. The network seems very sluggish, and you are receiving many complaints about network speeds. Your boss wants to know what is wrong and how you intend to fix the problem. He read an article about 100-megabit Ethernet and thinks this will solve the problem. What is the most likely cause of the problem and the real solution?

1.7   Exercise Explanation

Speed is not the problem with your network, and upgrading to 100 megabits may not help the problem. In fact, if the cabling is not at least category 5, upgrading can cause more problems than it solves. Your most likely problem is network traffic. You have over 190 computers on your 10Base-T network, all causing collisions. The simplest solution is to purchase a bridge and put each major department on a segment of the bridge. This will cut down on network traffic and solve your problem.

1.7   Practice Problems

1. The OSI Presentation Layer is named so because:

   A. It presents data to the user.

   B. It presents data to the application.

   C. It presents a uniform data format to the application layer.

   D. It does all of the above.

2. Which OSI layer includes cable and connectors?

   A. The Data Link Layer

   B. The Physical Link Layer

   C. The Connection Layer

   D. The Physical Layer

3. Which layer defines network topology?

   A. The Network Layer

   B. The Physical Layer

   C. The Data Link Layer

   D. The Physical Link Layer

4. Which layer is concerned with bits instead of frames?

   A. The Network Layer

   B. The Session Layer

   C. The Physical Layer

   D. The Data Link Layer

   E. None of the above

5. Which layer builds frames from received raw bits?

   A. The Data Link Layer

   B. The Physical Layer

   C. The Session Layer

   D. The Network Layer

6. IEEE 802 project provided enhancements to which OSI layer?

   A. The Data Link Layer

   B. The Application Layer

   C. The Session Layer

   D. The Physical Layer

   E. None of the above

7. The Media Access Control is a sublayer of which OSI layer?

   A. The Presentation Layer

   B. The Physical Layer

   C. The Session Layer

   D. The Data Link Layer

   E. The Application Layer

8. Which OSI layer determines the route a packet will take to reach its destination?

   A. The Route Layer

   B. The Presentation Layer

   C. The Data Link Layer

   D. The Network Layer

   E. The Physical Layer

9. Network interface cards and their associated drivers reside at which OSI layer?

   A. The Physical Layer

   B. The Data Link Layer

   C. The Network Layer

   D. None of the above

10. Which device can bridge non-routable protocols?

   A. Gateway

   B. Router

   C. Brouter

   D. Repeater

11. Which device tears down a frame and rebuilds it to accommodate a different protocol stack?

   A. Gateway

   B. Router

   C. Brouter

   D. Bridge

12. Which device resides at the OSI Network Layer?

   A. Bridge

   B. Router

   C. Gateway

   D. Repeater

13. Which device resides at the OSI Data Link Layer?

   A. Cable

   B. Bridge

   C. Repeater

   D. Router

14. Which device does not reside at the OSI Physical layer?

   A. Repeater

   B. Cable

   C. Connectors

   D. Bridge

15. Which device simply regenerates incoming signals?

   A. Repeater

   B. NIC

   C. Bridge

   D. Gateway

16. Which device does not build routing tables?

   A. Bridge

   B. Router

   C. Brouter

   D. Repeater

17. When a bridge cannot determine to which port to send a frame:

   A. It sends an error message back to the originator.

   B. It sends a request to the next bridge to find the correct port.

   C. It sends the frame out all ports.

18. Which OSI layer translates logical network addresses into physical addresses?

   A. The Network Layer

   B. The Data Link Layer

   C. The Session Layer

   D. The Presentation Layer

   E. The Application Layer

19. In which layer would you find a redirector?

   A. The Application Layer

   B. The Presentation Layer

   C. The Data Link Layer

   D. The Physical Layer

   E. The Network Layer

20. Which type of switching provides a dedicated path with well-defined bandwidth?

   A. Virtual switching

   B. Message switching

   C. Circuit switching

   D. Packet switching

   E. Physical switching

21. Which switching model treats each message as a separate entity?

   A. Virtual switching

   B. Message switching

C.   Circuit switching

D.   Packet switching

E.   Physical switching

22.   Which switching model breaks up the message into smaller components and routes the components to the destination address independently?

A.   Packet switching

B.   Virtual switching

C.   Circuit switching

D.   Message switching

E.   Physical switching

23.   Which layer enables two computers to establish, use, and tear down a communication channel?

A.   The Session Layer

B.   The Application Layer

C.   The Data Link Layer

D.   The Physical Connection Layer

24.   What layer performs compression and encryption?

A.   The Presentation Layer

B.   The Data Link Layer

C.   The Application Layer

25.   Which layer inserts checkpoints in the data stream between applications?

A.   The Data Link Layer

B.   The Physical Layer

C.   The Presentation Layer

D.   The Network Layer

E.   The Session Layer

26.   Which layer presents API calls to user programs?

A.   The Presentation Layer

B.   The Application Layer

C.   The Transport Layer

D.   The Data Link Layer

27.   Which layer is the only layer that can send information directly to its counterpart on another computer?

A.   The Network Layer

B.   The Application Layer

C.   The Data Link Layer

D.   The Physical Layer

E.   None of the above

28.   Which layer adds the Cyclic Redundancy Check (CRC) field to the data frame?

A.   The Physical Layer

B.   The Data Link Layer

C.   The Network Layer

D.   The Physical Link Layer

29.   Of the two sublayers comprising the Data Link Layer, which is lowest providing access to the NICs hardware?

A.   The Media Access Control (MAC) sublayer

B.   The Logical Link Control (LLC) sublayer

C.   The LAN Interface Control (LIC) sublayer

D.   None of the above

30.   What type of device is commonly used to interface personal computer networks to mainframes?

A.   Bridge

B.   Brouter

C.   Gateway

D.   SMA converter card

31.   Which is not a common characteristic of a gateway?

A.   They are task-specific.

B. They are expensive.

C. They are fast.

32. What is the device that typically resides at the Application Layer of the OSI model?

   A. Application programs

   B. Software-based router

   C. Brouter

   D. Gateway

33. Which communication device can actually use all seven layers of the OSI model?

   A. AppleTalk router

   B. Gateway

   C. Brouter

   D. Software-based router

34. Which communication device can be used to prevent broadcast storms?

   A. Gateway

   B. Bridge

   C. Repeater

   D. Router

35. Which of the following protocols will not work with routers?

   A. IPX

   B. IP

   C. AppleTalk

   D. DECnet

   E. NetBEUI

36. Which of the following is not a routing algorithm?

   A. Open Shortest Path First (OSPF)

   B. Routing Information Protocol (RIP)

C. NetWare Link Services Protocol (NLSP)

D. Microsoft Services Protocol (MSP)

37. There are two basic types of routers. They are:

   A. Fast and slow

   B. Static and dynamic

   C. Frame-based and packet-based

   D. Message-based and packet-based

38. Implementation of the OSI model is called:

   A. A protocol stack

   B. A gateway

   C. A communication network

   D. A networking protocol

39. Datagrams are associated with which OSI layer?

   A. The Network Layer

   B. The Presentation Layer

   C. The Application Layer

   D. The Data Link Layer

   E. The Transport Layer

1.7 Answers and Explanations: Practice Problems

1. **C** Many people confuse the Presentation Layer because it seems to present data to the user when in fact it presents a uniform data format to the Application Layer.

2. **B** The Physical Layer of the OSI model includes cables and connectors.

3. **B** The Physical Layer also defines network topology.

4. **C** The Physical Layer only recognizes bits. It transmits and receives bits. Higher layers recognize frames constructed by the Data Link Layer.

5. **A**   This is the job of the Data Link Layer. It packages received bits into frames to be passed to the Network Layer.

6. **A**   Two sublayers, the Media Access Control (MAC) and Logical Link Control (LLC), were added to the Data Link Layer.

7. **D**   As discussed in question 6, the MAC is a sublayer of the Data Link Layer.

8. **D**   The Network Layer determines network-wide routing. The Data Link Layer can route packets to the next segment but not across several segments.

9. **B**   Network interface cards and drivers operate at the Data Link Layer. They accept frames from higher layers and put the bits on the wire.

10. **C**   A brouter can bridge non-routable protocols.

11. **A**   The job of the gateway is protocol conversion. This is accomplished by tearing down the received packet and reforming it to match the destination protocol.

12. **B**   The router resides at the Network Layer. The router requires network configuration information to build internal network routing tables.

13. **B**   The bridge resides at the Data Link Layer and requires address information to pass the frame to the correct next segment.

14. **D**   The bridge resides at the Data Link Layer.

15. **A**   The repeater simply regenerates incoming signals to all ports without regard for the information in the frame. For this reason, the repeater resides at the Physical Layer.

16. **D**   The repeater has no knowledge of segments or routes; thus, it does not build routing tables.

17. **C**   If a bridge cannot determine the correct port to send a packet, it will send it out to all ports except the port it came in on.

18. **A**   The Network Layer translates logical network addresses into physical addresses.

19. **B**   The redirector is found at the Presentation Layer. This is an important component of many operating systems that make remote devices appear to be local.

20. **C**   In circuit switching, a dedicated physical path is established and maintained for the length of the communication session.

21. **B**   In message switching, also referred to as store and forward switching, each device receives a frame and waits until the next device in the chain is ready to receive it. Each frame is treated as a separate entity.

22. **A**   In packet switching, frames are broken down into individual smaller packets, each with source and destination address information. The packets can take separate routes to the destination. This has the advantage of changing routes when bandwidth loads become high on certain links.

23. **A**   After a communication channel is established between two computers, this is called a session. It is the job of the Session Layer to establish, use, and tear down sessions.

24. **A**   The Presentation Layer performs protocol conversion, data encryption, data translation, data compression, character-set conversion, and graphic-command expansion.

25. **E**   The Session Layer can insert checkpoints in the data stream between two computers to maintain synchronization.

26. **B**   The Application Layer interfaces to programs by exposing a set of network APIs.

27. **D** The Physical Layer is the only layer that can directly send information to its counterpart on another system. All other layers must pass data down the protocol stack to reach the other computer.

28. **B** The Data Link Layer builds a frame consisting of a header, data, and a trailer. The trailer contains a CRC to guarantee error-free transmissions.

29. **A** The MAC Layer communicates directly with the NIC.

30. **C** Gateways are employed to perform the protocol conversion required for personal computers to communicate with mainframes. One popular gateway is the SNA gateway.

31. **C** Gateways are task-specific, expensive, and usually slow. It requires a lot of CPU horsepower and RAM to provide protocol conversion.

32. **D** Gateways usually reside at the Application Layer but can span all layers of the OSI model.

33. **B** As previously stated, the gateway can span all layers of the OSI model and usually a dedicated server on the network.

34. **B** A bridge can be employed to prevent broadcast storms. This is because a bridge examines all frames and will not forward bad frames.

35. **E** NetBEUI is a non-routable protocol and will not be passed through a router.

36. **D** NetWare RIP and NLSP are routing algorithms used in NetWare networks. Internet RIP and NetWare RIP reside in the Network Layer of the OSI model. OPSF is similar to RIP but is more efficient and supports class of service. OPSF is replacing RIP in an effort to cut down the number of bottlenecks caused by RIP. MSP is not a routing protocol.

37. **B** Static and dynamic are the two types of routers in use today. In static routers, the routing tables must be manually input; in dynamic routers, the routing tables are built automatically.

38. **A** A protocol stack consists of layers of protocols, each communicating with the layer above and below it (thus the term stack).

39. **E** The datagram is associated with the Transport Layer. Datagrams are a component of Datagram Delivery Protocol (DDP) or AppleTalk.

1.7   Key Words

Application Layer

Bridge

Brouter

Data Link Layer

Gateway

Network Layer

Physical Layer

Presentation Layer

Session Layer

Transport Layer

Repeater

1.8 Define the Characteristics and Purpose of Media Used in IEEE 802.3 and IEEE 802.5 Standards

A. The 802 Project

As networks became popular, the IEEE began the 802 project in February 1980 to define certain LAN standards. The name of the project (802) comes from the year and month the project was started. Project 802 focused on the physical aspects of networking relating to cabling and data transmission on the cable. These specifications fall into the bottom two layers (Physical and Data Link) of the OSI mode. There are 12 categories contained in the 802 standards:

802.1	Internetworking
802.2	Logical Link Control (LLC)
802.3	Carrier-Sense Multiple Access with Collision Detection (CSMA/CD) or Ethernet
802.4	Token Bus LAN
802.5	Token Ring LAN
802.6	Metropolitan Area Network (MAN)
802.7	Broadband Technical Advisory Group
802.8	Fiber-Optic Technical Advisory Group
802.9	Integrated Voice/Data Networks
802.10	Network security
802.11	Wireless networks
802.6	Demand Priority Access LAN, 100BaseVG-AnyLAN

B. 802.3 Carrier-Sense Multiple Access with Collision Detection (CSMA/CD) or Ethernet

Xerox Corporation developed Ethernet in late 1970. In 1980, DIX (or DEC), Intel, and Xerox began to jointly publicize this network. The implementation was a baseband network that employed CSMA/CD as the media access control mechanism. In a *baseband system*, a single signal carried on a cable can use all available bandwidth of the cable.

In 1985, version II of the network was released and Project 802 chose this version of Ethernet as the basis for the 802.3 standard. The two versions of Ethernet are for the most part interchangeable, with the main difference being the network packet header.

When computers employ the CSMA/CD or Ethernet signaling method, the following sequence of events occurs:

1

1. The computer listens to the wire and waits until there is no traffic.

2. The computer transmits its data onto the wire. At this time, no other computer on the network can transmit until the data reaches its destination and the cable is traffic free.

3. If the computer sending the data detects a collision (caused by two computers sending data at the same time), the computer stops transmitting, waits a random amount of time, and retries by returning to step 1.

This method of media access puts several limitations on Ethernet. The main limitations include the total distance of any two nodes on the network, the number of repeaters between any two nodes, and segment lengths between any two nodes.

Different cables have different characteristics. The two important characteristics to Ethernet are *impedance* and *propagation delay.*

Propagation delay is the amount of time it takes a signal to travel through a medium. Propagation delay of RG58 cable is typically .66 times the speed of light, which is about 299,792,458 meters per second. If the time to propagate the signal end-to-end of the network is greater than the amount of time required to transmit a frame, collisions may not be detected. This is called a *late collision.*

The time it takes a repeater to regenerate the signal must also be considered. The propagation and attenuation characteristics of different Ethernet cabling schemes cause the rules to change based on the type of cabling used.

Ethernet cabling comes in the following forms:

10Base2	Segments up to 185 meters (sometimes rounded up to 200) and referred to as thinnet. Uses RG58U cable of 50-ohms, which is about ¼-inch thick.
10Base5	Segments up to 500 meters and referred to as thicknet. Uses RG6, which is about ½-inch thick.
10Base-F	Segments up to 2,000 meters, incorporating fiber optic cable.
10Base-T	Segments up to 100–150 meters are generally accepted; however, the maximum signal loss must not exceed 11.5db. This cabling scheme incorporates Unshielded Twisted Pair (UTP).
10Broad36	Segments up to 3,600 meters in a dual-cable configuration. This is a broadband configuration.

There are also rules governing the number of repeaters and cable segments between any two nodes on the network. This is commonly referred to as the *5-4-3 rule.* There can be no more than five repeated segments, no more than four repeaters, and only three of the five cable segments can be populated.

This can be a problem on 10Base-T networks in which several hubs may be cascaded because hubs count as repeaters.

C.   802.5 Token Ring

The 802.5 token ring network is physically cabled as a star network, but it is logically a ring. Wiring each connection back to a central hub (Multistation Access Unit, or MAU) creates the physical star; however, the logical ring must be maintained when equipment is added or removed from the network. The hub, or MAU, contains a "collapsed ring." If a workstation falls off the network, the MAU immediately bypasses that particular workstation, maintaining the logical ring.

This topology is intended for commercial and light industrial usage. IBM made this commercially possible with the introduction of a 4 Mbit/sec token ring network in the mid-1980s.

Tokens are small frames passed logically around the network from one workstation to another. When a workstation wants to transmit, it must wait for the token. The workstation can acquire the token by changing 1 bit in the token, which changes the token into the start-of-frame field for a data frame. The workstation can then transmit the rest of the frame. No other workstation transmits at this time because only one workstation owns the token. The frame makes the round trip of the network and, when it returns to the transmitting workstation, it is changed back into a token. The token is then passed to the next workstation downstream.

As the number of workstations on the network increases, the efficiency of the token ring topology increases. This is because there are no collisions to contend with. The round-robin architecture gives all workstation equal opportunity to access the media. A priority scheme is implemented, however, that enables a workstation to request future use of the token.

Each workstation has a unique Medium Access Control (MAC) address, and one workstation on the network takes the job of the *active monitor* by transmitting a *claim token.* It is the job of the active monitor to look for errors, bad frames, and workstations that are malfunctioning. If the active monitor fails, the other workstations on the network arbitrate to determine which workstation becomes the next active monitor.

The 802.5 specification does not describe cabling techniques for token ring.

1.8   Exercise

A company with 50 workstations has hired you as a consultant to network the computers that have been stand-alone until now. You notice that each office has RG59 coaxial cable and 6-pair UTP cable terminating in a central room. The company wants an easy-to-manage network at the lowest cost. What type of network would you recommend?

1.8   Exercise Explanation

At first you might be tempted to use the coaxial cable; however, RG59 is 75 ohms and Ethernet uses RG58, which is 50 ohms. The best choice is 10Base-T because the UTP cable is in place, and the components to implement a 10Base-T solution are inexpensive. A token ring solution would be much more expensive.

1.8   Practice Problems

1. Which company invented Ethernet?

   A. Digital Equipment Corporation (DEC)

   B. Intel

   C. Datapoint

   D. Xerox

2. Which company invented 4 Mbit/sec token ring?

   A. Datapoint

   B. Xerox

   C. IBM

   D. Intel

3. Which 802 protocol describes Ethernet?

   A. 802.1

   B. 802.3

   C. 802.5

   D. 802.2

4. Which 802 protocol describes token ring Media Access Control?

   A. 802.1

   B. 802.3

   C. 802.5

   D. 802.2

   E. None of the above

5. What is the maximum number of segments between any two nodes on an 802.3 network?

   A. 2

   B. 5

   C. 3

   D. 4

6. What is the maximum number of repeaters between any two nodes on an 802.3 network?

   A. 2

   B. 5

   C. 3

   D. 4

   E. None of the above

7. What is a MAC address on an Ethernet network?

   A. A logical address that identifies the workstation

   B. An address assigned by the system administrator

   C. A workstation's logical domain address

   D. A physical address assigned by the system administrator

   E. A physical address assigned by the NIC manufacturer

8. In IBM token ring, how are tokens claimed?

   A. They are not passed on until the transmitting workstation has put its frame on the wire.

   B. They are converted to a start-of-frame for a packet.

   C. They are converted to a claim token.

   D. They are converted to an acknowledge token.

9. CSMA/CD networks have total length restrictions between the furthest nodes on a network because:

   A. Attenuation degrades the signal

   B. Impedance changes as the cable length increases

C. Propagation delays

D. None of the above

10. What is the difference between baseband networks and broadband networks?

A. Broadband networks are WAN; baseband are LAN.

B. Broadband networks carry several channels on a single cable; baseband only caries one.

C. Broadband networks operate at higher bit rates than baseband networks.

D. All of the above.

11. What is the difference between an Ethernet frame and an 802.3 frame?

A. The length of the Ethernet frame is much larger than the 802.3 frame.

B. The length of the 802.3 frame is much larger than the Ethernet frame.

C. 802.3 uses LLC to distinguish multiple clients and has a length field; Ethernet uses a 2-byte field to distinguish multiple client protocols.

12. What is the size of an 802.3 MAC address?

A. 16 bits

B. 8 bits

C. 64 bits

D. 48 bits

13. How many bits of the MAC address determine the manufacturer?

A. 8

B. 12

C. 16

D. 24

14. What is the CRC used for?

A. To denote the end of frame

B. To denote the beginning of frame

C. Address resolution on Ethernet

D. To detect errors that occurred during transmission

15. Token Ring is a physical:

A. Bus network

B. Ring network

C. Star network

16. As the number of active nodes increases, what network topology is favorable?

A. Ethernet

B. Token Ring

C. 10Base2

D. 10Base5

17. What is the maximum end-to-end distance between nodes in a 10BASE2 network?

A. 200 meters

B. 2,000 meters

C. 185 meters

D. 200 feet

18. What is the maximum end-to-end distance between nodes in a 10Base5 network?

A. 250 meters

B. 5,000 meters

C. 500 meters

D. 500 feet

19. What is the maximum bit rate in 10Base-F network?

A. 10 Mbits/sec

B. 100 Mbits/sec

C. 2.4 Mbits/sec

D. 4 Mbits/sec

20. What is the hub called in a token ring network?

A. Multi-station access unit

B. Hub

C. Central hub

D. Bridge

E. Router

21. To increase the distance of a 10Base2 network to more than 2.5 kilometers, which device should be used?

A. Repeater

B. Bridge

C. Passive HUB

D. Active HUB

22. Which topology employs RG58 coaxial cable?

A. Token Ring

B. 10Base2 Ethernet

C. 10Base5 Ethernet

D. 10Base-T Ethernet

E. None of the above

23. Which cable is used in thicknet?

A. RG58U coaxial cable

B. RG6 coaxial cable

C. RG59 coaxial cable

D. UTP cable

24. How many tokens can exist on a token ring topology at the same time?

A. 1

B. 2

C. Number of workstations/2

25. How many active monitors are on a token ring network?

A. 1

B. 2

C. Up to 8

26. The speed electronic signals travel through cable is:

A. Faster than the speed of light

B. Same as the speed of light

C. Slower than the speed of light

27. Propagation delay is:

A. Signal attenuation due to long cable lengths

B. The amount of time it takes a signal to travel through a medium

C. Reflections caused by poorly terminated systems

1.8 Answers and Explanations: Practice Problems

1. **D** Xerox invented Ethernet in 1970.

2. **C** IBM invented 4 Mbit/sec token ring in the mid-1980s.

3. **B** IEEE 802.3 describes the Ethernet protocol.

4. **C** IEEE 802.5 describes token ring media access.

5. **B** Remember the 5-4-3 rule, in which 5 is the maximum number of repeated segments, 4 is the maximum number of repeaters, and 3 is the maximum number of segments of the 5 that can be populated.

6. **D** Four, as in the 5-4-3 rule.

7. **E** The MAC address is a permanent address assigned by the manufacturer to each NIC separately.

8. **B** A single bit is changed in the token, and it becomes the start-of-frame sequence.

9. **C** Propagation delays are the finite amount of time it takes an electronic signal to travel through cabling. This delay must be less than the amount of time it takes to put a frame on the wire or collisions could be missed.

10. **B** Broadband systems assign carrier frequencies to different channels allowing multiple channels to use the same medium. In baseband systems, a single signal has full use of the medium.

11. **C** There are very minor differences between the Ethernet frame and the 802.3 frame. The differences are the method used to distinguish protocols.

12. **D** A MAC address consists of six bytes, which make 48 bits.

13. **D** Of the six bytes, three are used to define the manufacturer.

14. **D** The Cyclic Redundancy Check, or CRC, is used to verify the integrity of each frame.

15. **C** Token Ring is a physical star because each workstation is connected to a central hub.

16. **B** As the number of active nodes increases, the number of collisions increases in an Ethernet topology. Token ring does not suffer from this problem; thus, it is favored as the number of active nodes increases.

17. **C** 10Base2 specifies the maximum distance between endpoints as 185 meters.

18. **C** 10Base5 specifies the maximum distance between endpoints as 500 meters.

19. **A** Even though fiber can handle much higher bit rates, this version of Ethernet is 10 Mbits/sec.

20. **A** In token ring, the hub is called the Multi-station Access Unit, or MAU.

21. **B** A bridge must be used to segment the network. This is because 2.5 kilometers is the maximum end-to-end distance for the network. A repeater will not help.

22. **B** 10Base2 uses 50-ohm RG58 cable.

23. **B** RG6 coaxial cable is used in thicknet. The cable is so named because it is ½-inch thick.

24. **A** Only one token can exist on a token ring network.

25. **A** Only one active monitor can exist on a token ring network. The active monitor is usually the workstation with the lowest MAC address.

26. **C** Electronic signals are always slower than the speed of light. Cables have propagation delay specifications. RG58 is .66, which means signals travel .66 times the speed of light.

27. **B** Propagation delay is the amount of time it takes a signal to travel through a medium.

1.8 Key Words

5-4-3 rule

10Base2

10Base5

10Base-F

10Base-T

10Broad36

Active monitor

Hub

Impedance

Late collision

Medium Access Control address

Propogation delay

1.9   Explain the Purpose of NDIS and Novell ODI Network Standards

1

A.   Reason for Low-Level Standards

In the late 1980s, as the number of companies manufacturing Network Interface Cards increased, so did the complexity of developing protocol stacks to support these cards. The capability to bind several protocol stacks to one NIC also became important.

Before the late 1980s, layers 3 and 4 of the OSI model were tightly coupled with proprietary implementations of the Media Access Control (MAC) interface sublayer. This made it very difficult for multiple vendors to support all the operating systems on the market.

NDIS and ODI accomplished these goals by allowing the higher levels of the protocol stack to be independent of the NIC. This was accomplished by providing a standard interface.

B.   NDIS

Microsoft and 3Com jointly developed Network Device Interface Specification (NDIS) in 1989. This standard defined an interface between the MAC sublayer and higher layers of the OSI model. The two goals of NDIS are:

- To provide a vendor-neutral boundary between the transport protocols and the NIC driver. This enables the protocol stack to function with any NDIS-compliant adapter driver.

- To define a binding methodology, enabling multiple protocols to share the same NIC. In addition, NDIS allows binding one protocol to multiple NICs.

Non-Windows NT implementations of NDIS include a "protocol manager" (PROTMAN), which binds the different protocols with the MAC layer. It is the job of the protocol manager to route incoming packets from the MAC layer to the correct protocol stack. Under Windows NT, the PROTMAN is not required. Binding is accomplished through information in the Registry and a small wrapper around the NDIS code.

C.   ODI

Open Data-Link Interface (ODI) was jointly developed by Novell and Apple Computer Corporation and was released in 1989. The goals of ODI are similar to the goals of NDIS in providing a seamless integration between the Data Link Layer and the Transport Layers of the protocol stack. Before ODI there was dedicated IPX, which only allowed one protocol IPX to utilize a NIC. This became a major limitation as the number of different protocol stacks increased.

ODI consists of three main components:

Protocol Stacks

Multiple Link Interface Drivers (MLIDs)

Link Support Layer (LSL)

1. Protocol Stacks

The *protocol stack* component consists of the Transport and Network Layer of the OSI model. It is the protocol stack that acts as the interface to the Application Layers.

The protocol stacks package data from the Presentation and Application Layers, then provides network functionality by routing the packets to their destination. Multiple ODI protocol stacks can coexist on a single system. To distinguish media frames, two IDs are used—the stack ID and the protocol ID.

2. Multiple Link Interface Drivers (MLID)

The MLID has two basic functions: to build and strip media headers off of packets, and to send and receive packets at the Physical Layer. To accomplish these tasks the MLID consists of three modules:

- **Media Support Module (MSM)**—Performs initialization functions independent of the media. This module also builds the configuration table (information about the hardware and driver) based on information obtained from the Hardware Specific Module (HSM). It is the MSM that handles I/O requests such as reset, enabling and disabling promiscuous mode, and shutdown.

- **Topology Specific Module (TSM)**—Provides support for specific media types. This module builds the MAC headers, collects statistics depending on the type of media, and manages the Event Control Block. The Event Control Block is a mechanism for passing data between OSI modules.

- **Hardware Specific Module (HSM)**—Directly controls the hardware. This module resets the hardware and is responsible for moving packets on and off the NIC. This is the module developed by vendors.

The only part of the MLID that vendors must develop is the HSM, which requires less effort than developing the entire protocol stack.

3. Link Support Layer (LSL)

The LSL is the packet router in the ODI protocol. It is instrumental in keeping the other layers independent of each other. It routes incoming and outgoing packets.

1.9   Exercise

You work for a small company that has slowly migrated from Novell to Windows NT. There is a Novell server on the network, but it is not used by anyone because the newer Windows NT servers are faster and larger. One user wants to copy an old file off of the Novell server but cannot see the server from his machine. What is the most likely cause of the problem?

1.9   Exercise Explanation

You probably have one of two situations. Either there is no IPX driver installed on the Windows NT machine, or the IPX protocol stack is not bound to the NIC.

1.9 Practice Problems

1. Which companies developed NDIS?

    A. Microsoft and Digital Equipment Corporation (DEC)

    B. Microsoft Intel

    C. Microsoft and 3Com

    D. Novell and Apple

2. Which companies developed ODI?

    A. Apple and Novell

    B. Microsoft and Novell

    C. Novell and 3Com

    D. Apple and Microsoft

3. ODI is a replacement for which protocol?

    A. Dedicated IPX

    B. 802.3

    C. 802.5

    D. NDIS 2.0

4. What is the name of the module that manages bindings in NDIS systems?

    A. The binder

    B. The binding manager

    C. The protocol manager

    D. The NDIS binding layer (NBL)

    E. None of the above

5. Which Microsoft operating system does not incorporate the binding module?

    A. Windows for Workgroups

    B. Windows 95

    C. Windows NT 3.51

    D. All of the above

6. The NDIS specification includes which layer(s) of the OSI model?

    A. 1

    B. 1 and 2

    C. 2

    D. 2 and 3

    E. All of the above

7. How many protocols can dedicated IPX support on a NIC?

    A. 1

    B. 2

    C. 4

    D. One per installed NIC

8. MLIDs are a component of which protocol?

    A. NDIS

    B. ODI

    C. Neither

9. The PROTMAN is used by which protocol?

    A. NDIS

    B. ODI

    C. Neither

10. Which protocol routes packets in a round-robin fashion to determine the correct protocol stack?

    A. NDIS

    B. ODI

    C. Neither

11. Which protocol supports 802.3 frames?

    A. NDIS

    B. ODI

    C. Both

12. Which is not a difference between NDIS 2.0 and NDIS 3.0?

    A. NDIS 3.0 implements a C-call interface.

    B. NDIS 3.0 is multi-processor safe.

C. NDIS 3.0 drivers are 32-bit drivers.

D. NDIS 3.0 supports quality of service.

13. Under Windows NT, where is protocol binding information maintained?

A. By the protocol manager

B. In the file ndis.ini

C. In the file sys.ini

D. In the Registry

14. Which is not a goal for NDIS and ODI?

A. To support multiple protocols on same NIC

B. To define common interface to make driver development easier

C. To define a common set of lower-level protocols that both Microsoft and Novell would jointly support

1.9   Answers and Explanations: Practice Problems

1. **C**   Microsoft and 3Com in 1989.

2. **A**   Apple and Novell developed ODI and released it in 1989.

3. **A**   Novell replaced dedicated IPX with ODI in release 4.0 of NetWare.

4. **C**   NDIS systems use the protocol manager to bind protocol stacks.

5. **C**   Windows NT 3.51 maintains binding information in the Registry and does not use the protocol manager.

6. **C**   NDIS includes the Data Link Layer of the OSI module, specifically the MAC sublayer.

7. **A**   A limitation of dedicated IPX is the capability to support only 1 protocol.

8. **B**   MLIDs are the interface drivers that build and strip media headers in the ODI protocol.

9. **A**   PROTMAN is the protocol manager under NDIS in Windows systems.

10. **A**   NDIS routes packets in a round-robin fashion. This is why it is important to have the most-used protocol first in the binding order.

11. **C**   Both protocols support Ethernet.

12. **D**   NDIS 3.0 does not support quality of service.

13. **D**   Windows NT maintains the protocol binding information in the Registry.

14. **C**   Microsoft and Novell developed separate low-level protocols working with other companies, not each other.

1.9   Key Words

Hardware Specific Module (HSM)

Link Support Layer (LSL)

Media Support Module (MSM)

Multiple Link Interface Drivers (MLID)

Network Device Interface Specification (NDIS)

Open Data-Link Interface (ODI)

Protocol manager (PROTMAN)

Practice Exam: Standards and Terminology

1. CSMA of CSMA/CD is:

    A. Collision Sense Media Access

    B. Copper System Media Access

    C. Collision Sense Multiple Access

    D. Complete Signal Media Access

2. Which media access network tries to detect collisions instead of avoiding collisions.

    A. AppleTalk

    B. ArcNet

    C. CSMA/CD

    D. CSMA/CA

3. 10Base5 is also called:

    A. Thinnet

    B. Ethernet

    C. AppleTalk

    D. Thicknet

4. When using 10Base2, you

    A. Must terminate each end with 50-ohm terminators

    B. Must terminate each end with 75-ohm terminators

    C. Don't need to terminate UTP

    D. Must terminate each connection with 75-ohm terminators

5. The OSI reference model has how many layers?

    A. 2

    B. 8

    C. 7

    D. 4

6. Which type of cable will operate at 100 Mbs?

    A. 10Base2

    B. Category 2 cable

    C. Category 5 cable

    D. Category 3 cable

7. Why do bridges provide better network performance than repeaters?

    A. They analyze packets and only forward them on required ports.

    B. They use faster hardware than repeaters.

    C. They simply regenerate the signal.

    D. They are active versus passive devices.

8. Which network access method does Ethernet use?

    A. CSMA/CD

    B. CSMA/CA

    C. Token passing

    D. AppleTalk

9. NetWare networks use which protocols?

    A. NetBEUI

    B. IPX/SPX

    C. TCP/IP

    D. NDIS

10. How many levels of RAID are there?

    A. 1

    B. 5

    C. 6

    D. 4

11. Which is not an example of client/server computing?

    A. A workstation application accessing a SQL database on a server

    B. A workstation application accessing the corporate mail server to find an address

    C. A terminal accessing a mainframe database

    D. A workstation using a proxy server to access the Internet

12. User-level security is good for:

    A. Large networks with more than 50 computers

    B. Peer-to-peer networks with less than 10 computers

    C. Networks that have many servers but few users

    D. Systems that are not networked

13. In a peer-to-peer network, which network security model is used?

    A. User-level security

    B. Share-level security

    C. Password-protected shares

    D. Access permissions

14. In user-level access, network resources

    A. Only have one password associated with them

    B. Have multiple passwords associated with them

    C. Have different passwords based upon desired access

    D. Have no passwords but have permissions associated with them

15. Which connection mode is faster when there are little or no errors?

    A. Connectionless-oriented mode

    B. Connection-oriented mode

16. You want to run several protocols across your remote access communication link. Which dial-up protocol should you use?

    A. TCP/IP

    B. PPP

    C. SLIP

    D. UDP/IP

17. Which dial-up protocol is typically found in older dial-up systems?

    A. SLIP

    B. PPP

    C. TCP

    D. UDP

18. What is the purpose of DHCP?

    A. To allow easy access to web pages

    B. To assign standard addresses to web pages

    C. To enable users to share IP addresses so that a relatively small number of IP addresses can support many users

    D. To allow first time users access to the Internet without an IP address

19. The OSI Presentation Layer is named so because:

    A. It presents data to the user.

    B. It presents data to the application.

    C. It presents a uniform data format to the Application layer.

    D. It presents packets to the Data Link Layer.

20. Which OSI layer is the only layer that can send information directly to its counterpart on another computer?

    A. The Network Layer

    B. The Application Layer

    C. The Data Link Layer

    D. The Physical Layer

21. What type of device is commonly used to interface personal computer networks to mainframes?

    A. Bridge

    B. Brouter

    C. Gateway

    D. SMA converter card

22. Which 802 protocol describes Ethernet?

    A. 802.1

    B. 802.3

    C. 802.5

    D. 802.2

23. Which 802 protocol describes Token Ring media access control?

    A. 802.1

    B. 802.3

    C. 802.5

    D. 802.2

24. What is a MAC address on an Ethernet network?

    A. A logical address that identifies the workstation

    B. A physical address assigned by the NIC manufacturer

    C. A workstation's logical domain address

    D. A physical address assigned by the system administrator

25. CSMA/CD networks have total length restrictions between the furthest nodes on a network because:

    A. Attenuation degrades the signal.

    B. Impedance changes as the cable length increases.

    C. Propagation delays.

    D. Emissions from signals cause interference.

Answers and Explanations: Practice Exam

1. **C** Collision Sense Multiple Access. A type of media access method.

2. **C** CSMA/CD. The CD stands for collision detect.

3. **D** Thicknet, because the coaxial cable (RG6) used to implement 10Base5 is about ½-inch in diameter.

4. **A** You must terminate each end of a 10Base2 bus with 50-ohm terminators.

5. **C** The OSI model has seven layers.

6. **C** Category 5 cable will operate at 100Mbs. As the number increases, so does the quality of the cable.

7. **A** A bridge has the capability to read the destination address of a frame and only forward the frame to the required ports, thus cutting down on traffic and collisions. This increases network performance.

8. **A** Ethernet employs collision detection access.

9. **B** Novell, along with Apple, invented IPX/SPX in 1989; these protocols are used in Novell NetWare networks.

10. **C** There are six levels of RAID, commonly referred to as RAID Level 0–RAID Level 5.

11. **C** In client/sever computing, both the client and the server share the task of processing. Terminals do not process data; they simply display data from the mainframe.

12. **A** As a network grows larger, it is easier to manage user-level security than share-level security.

13. **B** Peer-to-peer networks implement share-level security. There is not a database of users in the peer-to-peer network architecture.

14. **D**   In user-level access, network users have passwords and resources have permissions.

15. **A**   Connectionless-oriented mode is faster because there is no overhead for error handling.

16. **B**   One improvement of PPP over SLIP is the capability to transport multiple protocols over a single serial connection.

17. **A**   SLIP was developed before PPP; thus, it is found on older dial-up systems.

18. **C**   Dynamic Host Configuration Protocol (DHCP) dynamically assigns IP addresses, enabling a few IP addresses to support a larger number of users than fixed IP addressing.

19. **C**   Many people confuse the Presentation Layer because it seems to present data to the user when, in fact, it presents a uniform data format to the Application Layer.

20. **D**   The Physical Layer is the only layer that can directly send information to its counterpart on another system. All other layers must pass data down the protocol stack to reach the other computer. Other layers have virtual connections.

21. **C**   Gateways. This is because protocol conversion is usually required to communicate with mainframe computers.

22. **B**   IEEE 802.3 describes the Ethernet protocol.

23. **C**   IEEE 802.5 describes token ring media access.

24. **B**   The MAC address is a permanent address assigned by the manufacturer to each NIC separately.

25. **C**   For detection methods to work correctly, the propagation delay must be less than the amount of time it takes to put a packet on the wire.

CHAPTER 2

Planning

2.1 Selecting the Appropriate Media for Various Situations

Media choices include:

    Coaxial cable

    Twisted-pair cable

    Fiber-optic cable

    Wireless communications

Situational elements include:

    Cost

    Distance limitations

    Number of nodes

On any network, the various entities must communicate through some form of media; this includes cables, light, and radio waves. Transmission media enable computers to send and receive messages but do not guarantee the messages will be understood—that function is left to the upper-layer protocols.

A. Transmission Media Types

The most common type of LAN media is *copper cable*—*twisted-pair* and *coaxial.* The next most popular type of LAN connection media is *fiber-optic cable,* which has two major types—*single mode* and *multimode.* Wireless media (which is, in a sense, no media at all) is also gaining popularity.

Cable Type	Description
Twisted-pair	Similar to the cabling used to connect your telephone to the wall outlet
Network coaxial	Similar to the cable used to connect your television set to the cable TV outlet
Fiber-optic	Consists of a number of glass or high-grade plastic optical strands surrounded by a tough outer wrapping
Wireless transmissions	Uses radio waves or light to transmit data

B.   Characteristics of Transmission Media

Each type of transmission media has special characteristics that make it suitable for a specific type of service:

Cost

Installation requirements

Bandwidth

Band usage (baseband or broadband)

Attenuation

Electromagnetic interference

1. Bandwidth

Bandwidth refers to the measure of the capacity of a medium to transmit data.

Data transmission rates frequently are stated in terms of the bits that can be transmitted per second. An Ethernet LAN theoretically can transmit 10 million bits per second (bps) and has a bandwidth of 10 megabits per second (Mbps).

The bandwidth that a cable can accommodate is determined in part by the cable's length. A short cable generally can accommodate greater bandwidth than a longer cable, which is one reason all cable designs specify maximum lengths for cable runs. Beyond those limits, the highest-frequency signals can deteriorate, and errors begin to occur in data signals.

2. Band Usage

Two ways to allocate the capacity of transmission media are:

- **Baseband:** Devotes the entire capacity of the medium to one communication channel. Most LANs function in baseband mode.

- **Broadband:** Enables two or more communication channels to share the bandwidth of the communications medium.

These are both illustrated in Figure 2.1.1.

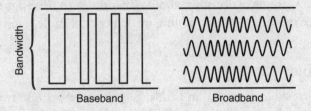

Figure 2.1.1 Baseband and broadband transmission modes.

Multiplexing enables broadband media to support multiple data channels. Multiplexing makes sense under a number of circumstances:

- **When media bandwidth is costly:** High-speed leased lines are expensive. If a leased line has sufficient bandwidth, multiplexing can enable the same line to carry mainframe, LAN, voice, video conferencing, and other data types.

- **When bandwidth is idle:** Many organizations have installed fiber-optic cable that is used only to partial capacity. With proper equipment, a single fiber can support hundreds of megabits— or even a gigabit or more—of mixed voice, video, and data.

- **When large amounts of data must be transmitted through low-capacity channels:** Multiplexing techniques can divide the original data stream into several lower-bandwidth channels, each of which can be transmitted through a lower-capacity medium. The signals then can be recombined at the receiving end.

Demultiplexing refers to recovering the original separate channels from a multiplexed signal. Multiplexing and demultiplexing are performed by a *multiplexor* (also called a *MUX*), which usually has both capabilities.

3. Attenuation

Attenuation is a measure of how much a transmission medium weakens a signal. Attenuation measurements always specify the frequency used to make the measurement because attenuation varies with frequency. As a rule, the higher the frequency, the greater the attenuation. Attenuation is one of the major factors limiting cable lengths that can be used in networks. Too much attenuation weakens a signal to the point where a station might not be able to distinguish it from background electrical noise.

4. Electromagnetic Interference

Electromagnetic interference (EMI) is electrical background noise that distorts a signal carried by a transmission medium. EMI makes it harder for a station listening to a medium to detect valid data signals on it. Some network media are more susceptible to EMI than others. Fiber-optic cable is generally considered immune to all forms of EMI.

Crosstalk is a special kind of EMI caused by having wires next to each other carrying data and "leaking" some of their data signals as EMI. Crosstalk is of particular concern in high-speed networks that use copper cables because there are typically many individual cables in close proximity to each other.

C. Cable Media

You need to know how to make decisions about network transmission media. The following sections discuss three types of network cabling media: coaxial cable, twisted-pair cable, and fiber-optic cable.

1. Coaxial Cable

Coaxial cable, the first cable type used in LANs, gets its name because two conductors share a common axis. It is most frequently referred to as *coax*. Figure 2.1.2 shows what this looks like.

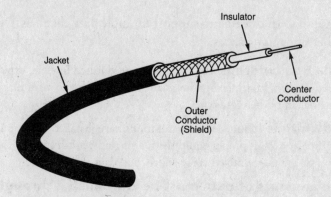

Figure 2.1.2 The structure of coaxial cable consists of four main components.

The components of a coaxial cable are:

- **Center conductor:** Usually solid copper wire, although it is sometimes made of stranded wire.

- **Outer conductor (shield):** Forms a tube surrounding the center conductor. It can consist of braided wires, metallic foil, or both. The outer conductor serves as a ground and also protects the inner conductor from EMI.

- **Insulator:** Keeps the outer conductor spaced evenly with the inner conductor.

- **Jacket:** Non-conductive encasement that protects the cable from damage.

> All copper cables have a characteristic measurement called *impedance*, which is measured in ohms. Impedance is a measure of the apparent resistance to an alternating current. You must use a cable that has the proper impedance in any given situation.

There are two types of coaxial cable:

- **Thinnet:** A light and flexible cabling medium that is inexpensive and easy to install. Thinnet is similar enough to some members of the RG-58 family of cables, which also have a 50-ohm impedance, that one is sometimes substituted for the other. Thinnet is approximately .25 inches (6 mm) in thickness. Thinnet cable can reliably transmit an Ethernet signal for 185 meters (about 610 feet).

- **Thicknet:** Thicknet is thicker than Thinnet and is approximately 0.5 inches (13 mm) in diameter. Because it is thicker and does not bend as readily as Thinnet, Thicknet cable is harder to work with. A thicker center core and better shielding means that Thicknet can carry signals a longer distance than Thinnet. Thicknet can transmit an Ethernet signal approximately 500 meters (1,650 feet).

Thicknet cable is sometimes called *Standard Ethernet*. Thicknet can be used to connect two or more small Thinnet LANs into a larger network.

Thicknet is also more expensive than Thinnet. Some Thicknet cabling is durable enough that it can be installed outside, running from building to building—although doing so can create ground loops and act as a conduit for lightning damage. Electrical surge protectors should be used when a Thicknet segment is used to connect buildings.

a. Coaxial Characteristics

You should be familiar with the installation, cost, bandwidth, and EMI resistance characteristics of coaxial cable:

- **Installation:** Coaxial cable is reasonably easy to install because the cable is robust and difficult to damage. In addition, connectors can be installed with inexpensive tools and a bit of practice. The device-to-device cabling approach that coax uses can be difficult to reconfigure when new devices cannot be installed near an existing cable.

  Coaxial cable can be installed in either of two configurations: daisy-chain (from device to device—Ethernet) and star (ARCnet). Both of these are shown in figure 2.1.3.

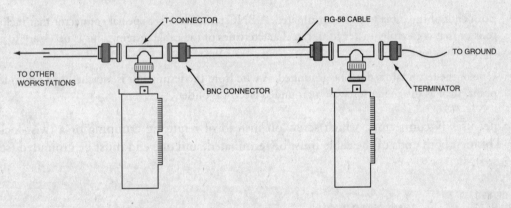

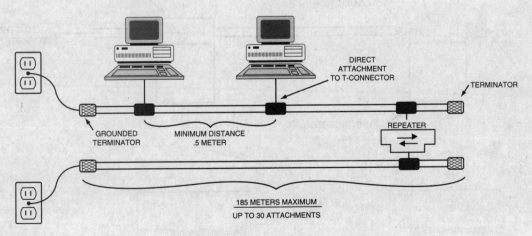

Figure 2.1.3 Coaxial cable wiring configurations—the top illustration is the daisy-chain configuration and the bottom illustration is the star configuration.

- **Cost:** The coaxial cable used for Thinnet falls toward the low end of the cost spectrum, whereas Thicknet is among the more costly options.

- **Bandwidth:** LANs that employ coaxial cable typically have a bandwidth between 2.5 Mbps (ARCnet) and 10 Mbps (Ethernet).

- **EMI Characteristics:** All copper media are sensitive to EMI, although the shield in coax makes them fairly resistant. Coaxial cables, like other copper cables, radiate a portion of their signal, and electronic eavesdropping equipment can detect this radiated signal.

b. Connectors for Coaxial Cable

The most common connector used with coaxial is the *Bayonet-Neill-Concelman* (BNC). BNC connectors and Thinnet cabling have the following characteristics:

- A BNC T-connector must be used to connect the network interface card in the PC to the network. The T-connector attaches directly to the network board. (See figure 2.1.3 to see an illustration of a BNC T-connector.)

- BNC cable connectors attach cable segments to the T-connectors.

- A BNC barrel connector connects two Thinnet cables.

- Both ends of the cable must be terminated. A BNC terminator is a special connector that includes a resistor that is carefully matched to the characteristics of the cable system. This is necessary to arrest signal reflections.

- One of the terminators must be grounded. A wire from the terminator is attached to a grounded point, such as the center screw of a grounded electrical outlet.

Thicknet uses N-connectors, which screw on instead of requiring crimping or a twist-lock. As with Thinnet, both ends of the cable must be terminated, and one end must be grounded (see fig. 2.1.4).

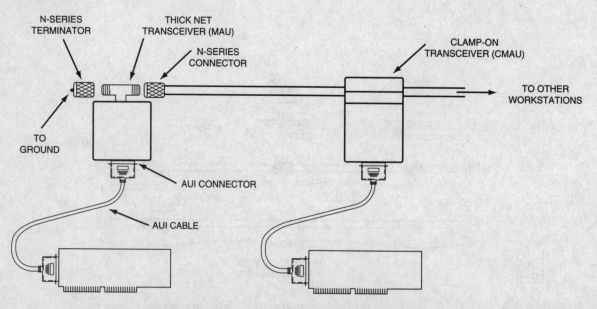

Figure 2.1.4 Connectors and cabling for Thicknet.

Workstations don't connect directly to the cable with Thicknet. Instead, a *transceiver* is attached to the Thicknet cable. This transceiver has a port for an *Attachment Unit Interface,* or *AUI connector,* an *AUI cable* (also called a *transceiver cable* or a *drop cable*) connects the workstation to the Thicknet medium. Transceivers can connect to Thicknet cables in two ways:

- Transceivers can be connected if you cut the cable and use N-connectors and a T-connector on the transceiver.

- The more common approach is to use a clamp-on transceiver, which has pins that penetrate the cable without the need for cutting it. These are frequently referred to as *vampire taps.*

2. Twisted-Pair Cable

Twisted-pair cable has become the dominant cable type for all new network designs that employ copper cable. Twisted-pair cable is inexpensive to install and offers the lowest cost-per-foot of any cable type.

A basic twisted-pair in a cable consists of two strands of copper wire that are twisted together and used to carry a single signal (see fig. 2.1.5). This twisting reduces the sensitivity of the cable to EMI and also reduces the tendency of the cable to radiate radio frequency noise that interferes with nearby cables and electronic components. This is because the radiated signals from the twisted wires tend to cancel each other out.

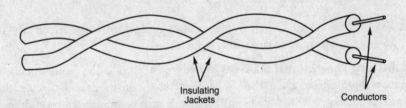

Insulating
Jackets

Conductors

Figure 2.1.5 Twisted-pair cable.

Twisting also controls the tendency of the wires in the pair to cause EMI in each other. Whenever two wires are in close proximity, the signals in each wire tend to produce noise, called *crosstalk,* in the other. Twisting the wires in the pair reduces crosstalk in much the same way that twisting reduces the tendency of the wires to radiate EMI.

a. Shielded Twisted-Pair (STP) Cable

Shielded twisted-pair cabling consists of one or more twisted pairs of wire enclosed in a foil wrap and woven-copper shielding. Figure 2.1.6 shows IBM Type 1 cabling, the first cable type used with IBM Token Ring. Early LAN designers used shielded twisted-pair cable because the shield reduces the tendency of the cable to radiate EMI and thus reduces the cable's sensitivity to outside interference.

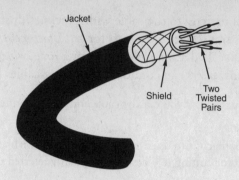

Figure 2.1.6   A shielded twisted-pair cable.

The shield is connected to the ground portion of the electronic device to which the cable is connected. A *ground* is a portion of the device that serves as an electrical reference point, and it usually is connected to a metal stake driven into the ground. A properly grounded shield minimizes signals getting into or out of the cable.

Various types of STP cable exist; some shield each pair individually and others shield several pairs. Each cable type is appropriate for a given kind of installation.

Because so many different types of STP cable exist, stating precise characteristics for STP is difficult. The following list offers some general guidelines:

- **Cost:** STP cable costs more than thin coaxial or unshielded twisted-pair cables. STP is less costly, however, than thick coax or fiber-optic cable.

- **Installation:** Different network types have different installation requirements. One major difference is the connector used. IBM Token Ring uses a unisex data connector (the connectors are both male and female), which can be installed with such common tools as a knife, a wire stripper, and large pliers.

  STP cable tends to be rather bulky. IBM Type 1 cable is approximately $1/2$-inch (13 mm) in diameter. Therefore, cable paths fill up quickly when using STP cables.

- **Capacity:** STP cable has a theoretical capacity of over 500 Mbps, although no common technologies exceed 155 Mbps with 100-meter cable runs. The most common data rates for STP cable are 4 and 16 Mbps, which are the data rates for token ring networks.

- **Attenuation:** All varieties of twisted-pair cable have attenuation characteristics that limit the length of cable runs. Different STP cable types have different attenuation characteristics.

- **EMI Characteristics:** The shield in STP cable results in good EMI characteristics for copper cable, compared to coaxial cable. This is one reason STP might be preferred to unshielded twisted-pair cable. As with all copper cables, STP is sensitive to interference and vulnerable to electronic eavesdropping.

- **Connectors for STP:** AppleTalk and token ring networks can be cabled using UTP cable and RJ-45 connectors (see fig. 2.1.7), but both networks originated as STP cabling systems. For STP cable, AppleTalk employs a DIN-type connector. IBM Token Ring networks use the IBM Data Connector (see fig. 2.1.8).

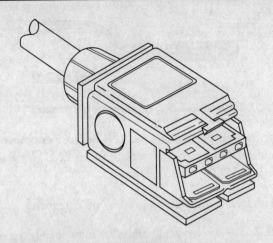

Figure 2.1.7   Connectors used with STP cable.

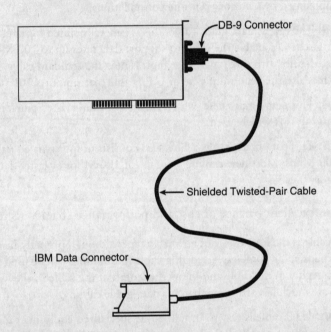

Figure 2.1.8   A PC ready to connect to a token ring network.

b. Unshielded Twisted-Pair (UTP) Cable

Unshielded twisted-pair cable doesn't incorporate a braided shield into its structure (see fig. 2.1.9). The characteristics of UTP are similar in many ways to STP, however, differing primarily in attenuation and EMI. Several twisted pairs can be bundled together in a single cable. These pairs typically are color coded.

Telephone systems typically use UTP cabling. Network engineers can sometimes use existing UTP telephone cabling (if it is of a high enough quality to support network communications) for network cabling.

Figure 2.1.9 A multipair UTP cable.

UTP cable is a latecomer to high-performance LANs because engineers only recently solved the problems of managing radiated noise and susceptibility to EMI. Now all new copper-based cabling schemes are based on UTP.

UTP cable is available in five standardized grades, or categories:

- **Category 1 and 2:** These voice-grade cables are suitable only for voice and for low data rates (below 4 Mbps). The growing need for data-ready cabling systems has caused Category 1 and 2 cable to be supplanted by Category 3 for new installations.

- **Category 3:** The lowest data-grade cable, this is generally suited for data rates up to 10 Mbps. Some encoding schemes enable the cable to support data rates up to 100 Mbps. Category 3, which uses four twisted-pairs with three twists per foot, is now the standard cable used for most telephone installations. It is also the minimum type of UTP cable that supports 10Base-T.

- **Category 4:** This data-grade cable, which consists of four twisted pairs, is suitable for data rates up to 16 Mbps but isn't widely used.

- **Category 5:** This data-grade cable, which also consists of four twisted pairs, is suitable for data rates up to 100 Mbps. Most new cabling systems for 100 Mbps or faster data rates are designed around Category 5 cable.

UTP cable offers an excellent balance of cost and performance characteristics:

- **Cost:** UTP cable is the least costly of any cable type, although properly installed Category 5 tends to be fairly expensive. In some cases, existing cable in buildings can be used for LANs, but you need to verify the category of the cable and know the length of the cable in the walls. Distance limits for voice cabling are much less stringent than for data-grade cabling.

- **Installation:** UTP cable is easy to install. Some specialized equipment might be required, but the equipment is low in cost and can be mastered with very little practice. Properly designed UTP cabling systems can be reconfigured to meet changing requirements easily.

  Category 5 cable has stricter installation requirements than lower categories of UTP. Special training is recommended for dealing with Category 5 UTP.

- **Capacity:** The data rates possible with UTP have pushed up from 1 Mbps, past 4 and 16 Mbps, to the point where 100-Mbps data rates are now common.

- **Attenuation:** UTP cable shares similar attenuation characteristics with other copper cables. UTP cable runs are limited to a few hundred meters, with 100 meters as the most frequent limit.

- **EMI Characteristics:** Because UTP cable lacks a shield, it is more sensitive to EMI than coaxial or STP cables. The latest technologies make it possible to use UTP in the vast majority of situations, provided that reasonable care is taken to avoid electrically noisy devices such as motors and fluorescent lights. UTP usually is not suitable for electrically noisy environments such as factories, where very high-powered tools and equipment can radiate EMI significant distances.

- **Connectors for UTP:** The most common connector used with UTP cables is the *8-pin modular plug/jack* (commonly called an *RJ-45 connector*). These connectors are easy to install on cables and are also extremely easy to connect and disconnect. They have eight pins and look like a common RJ-11 telephone jack (see fig. 2.1.10). They are slightly different sizes and don't work together because of the different pin-outs.

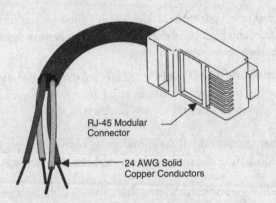

RJ-45 Modular Connector

24 AWG Solid Copper Conductors

Figure 2.1.10   An 8-pin modular connector.

3. Fiber-Optic Cable

Fiber-optic cable is the ideal cable for data transmission. This type of cable accommodates extremely high bandwidths, presents no problems with EMI, and supports durable cables and cable runs as long as several kilometers. Two disadvantages of fiber optic cables are cost and installation difficulty.

The center conductor of a fiber-optic cable is a fiber that consists of highly refined glass or plastic designed to transmit light signals. The fiber is coated with a cladding that reflects signals back into the fiber to reduce signal loss. A plastic sheath protects the fiber (see fig. 2.1.11).

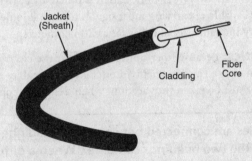

Jacket (Sheath)

Cladding

Fiber Core

Figure 2.1.11   A fiber-optic cable.

A fiber-optic network cable consists of two strands that are enclosed in plastic sheaths—one strand sends and the other receives. Two types of cable configurations are available:

- **Loose:** Incorporates a space between the fiber sheath and the outer plastic encasement; this space is filled with a gel or other material.
- **Tight:** Contains strength wires between the conductor and the outer plastic encasement.

In both cases, the plastic encasement must supply the strength of the cable, while the gel layer or strength wires protect the delicate fiber from mechanical damage.

Optical fiber cables don't transmit electrical signals. Instead, the data signals must be converted into light signals. Light sources include:

- **Laser:** The purity of laser light makes lasers ideally suited to data transmissions because they can work at long distances and high bandwidths. Lasers are expensive light sources and are used only when their special characteristics are required.

- **Light-emitting diode (LED):** LEDs are inexpensive and produce a relatively poorer quality of light than lasers. LEDs are suitable for less-stringent applications, such as 100 Mbps or slower LAN connections that extend less than two kilometers.

The end of the cable that receives the light signal must convert the signal back to an electrical form. Several types of solid-state components can perform this service.

As with all cable types, fiber-optic cables have their share of advantages and disadvantages.

- **Cost:** The cost of the cable and connectors has fallen significantly in recent years, but fiber-optic cable is still the most expensive cable type to install. The electronic devices required to use it are significantly more expensive than comparable devices for copper cable.

- **Installation:** Greater skill is required to install fiber-optic cable than to install most copper cables. Improved tools and techniques have reduced the training required. Still, fiber-optic cable requires greater care because the cables must be treated fairly gently during installation.

- **Capacity:** Fiber-optic cable can support very high data rates (into the terabits per second) even with long cable runs. Although UTP cable runs are limited to less than 100 meters with 100-Mbps data rates, certain types of fiber-optic cables may be able to carry a 100 Mbps signal for 20 kilometers.

- **Attenuation:** Attenuation in fiber-optic cables is much lower than in copper cables. Multimode fiber-optic cables are capable of carrying most signals for two kilometers, while single-mode fiber-optic cables may carry the same signal for as far as 20 kilometers.

- **EMI Characteristics:** Because fiber-optic cables don't use electrical signals to transmit data, they are totally immune to electromagnetic interference. The cables also are immune to a variety of electrical effects that must be taken into account when designing copper cabling systems.

When electrical cables are connected between two buildings, the ground potentials (voltages) between the two buildings can differ. When a difference exists, current flows through the grounding conductor of the cable—even though the ground is supposed to be electrically neutral and no current should flow.

When current flows through the ground conductor of a cable, the condition is called a *ground loop*. Ground loops can result in electrical instability and various other types of anomalies.

Because it is immune to electrical effects, fiber-optic cable is the best cable to use when connecting networks in different buildings.

Because the signals in fiber-optic cable are not electrical in nature, they cannot be detected by the electronic eavesdropping equipment that detects electromagnetic radiation. Therefore, fiber-optic cable is the best choice for high-security networks.

4. IBM Cabling

IBM uses its own separate names, standards, and specifications for network cabling and cabling components. These IBM cabling types roughly parallel standard forms used elsewhere in the industry.

IBM uses a unique, unisex connector—any two of these connectors can be connected together.

Table 2.1.1   IBM Cabling Types

Cable Type	Description	Comment
Type 1	Shielded twisted-pair (STP)	Two twisted-pairs of 22 AWG[1] wire in braided shield
Type 2	Voice and data	Two twisted-pairs of 22 AWG wire for data and braided shield, and two twisted-pairs of 26 AWG for voice
Type 3	Voice	Four solid UTP pairs; 22 or 24 AWG wire
Type 4	Not defined	
Type 5	Fiber-optic	Two 62.5/125-micron multimode fibers
Type 6	Data patch cable	Two twisted pairs of 26 AWG wire, dual foil, and braided shield
Type 7	Not defined	
Type 8	Carpet grade	Two twisted pairs of 26 AWG wire with shield for use under carpets
Type 9	Plenum grade	Two twisted pairs, shielded (see previous discussion of plenum-grade cabling)

1. The AWG designation in this table stands for the American Wire Gauge standard, a specification for wire gauges. The higher the gauge, the thinner the wire.

5. Comparison of Cable Media

When comparing cabling types, remember that the characteristics you observe depend highly on the implementations.

Some comparisons between cable types are fairly involved. Although fiber-optic cable is costly on a per-foot basis, for example, you can construct a fiber-optic cable that is many kilometers in length. To build a copper cable many kilometers in length, you would need to install repeaters and/or bridges at several points along the cable to amplify the signal. These repeaters could easily exceed the cost of a fiber-optic cable run.

Table 2.1.2   Comparison of Cable Media

Cable Type	Cost	Installation	Capacity	Range	EMI
Coaxial Thinnet	<STP	Inexpensive/ easy	10 Mbps typical	185 m	<sensitive than UTP
Coaxial Thicknet	>STP <Fiber	Easy	10 Mbps typical	500 m	<sensitive than UTP
Shielded Twisted-Pair (STP)	>UTP <Thicknet	Fairly easy	16 Mbps typical, up to 500 Mbps	100 m typical	<sensitive than UTP
Unshielded Twisted-Pair (UTP)	Lowest	Inexpensive/ easy	10 Mbps typical, up to 100 Mbps	100 m typical	Most sensitive
Fiber Optic	Highest	Expensive/ difficult	100 Mbps typical	10s of kilo-meters	Insensitive

D.   Wireless Media

All signals transmitted between computers consist of some form of electromagnetic (EM) wave-form, ranging from radio frequencies up through infrared light and microwave.

You can subdivide wireless networking technology into three basic types, corresponding to three basic networking scenarios:

- **Local Area Networks (LANs):** Occasionally, you will see a fully wireless LAN; more typi-cally, however, one or more wireless machines will function as members of a cable-based LAN. A LAN with both wireless and cable-based components is called a *hybrid.*

- **Extended local networks:** A wireless connection serves as a backbone between two LANs. For instance, a company with office networks in two nearby but separate buildings could connect those networks using a wireless bridge.

- **Mobile computing:** A mobile machine connects to the home network using cellular or satellite technology.

1. Reasons for Wireless Networks

Wireless networks are especially useful for the following situations:

- **Spaces where cabling would be impossible or inconvenient:** These include open lobbies, inaccessible parts of buildings, older buildings, historical buildings where renovation is prohibited, and outdoor installations.

- **People who move around a lot within their work environment:** Network administrators, for instance, must troubleshoot a large office network. Nurses and doctors need to make rounds at a hospital.

- **Temporary installations:** These situations include any temporary department set up for a specific purpose that soon will be torn down or relocated.

- **People who travel:** Many employees now travel outside the work environment and need instantaneous access to network resources.

2. Wireless Communications with LANs

It is often advantageous for a network to include some wireless nodes. Typically, though, the wireless nodes will be part of what is otherwise a traditional, cable-based network.

An *access point* is a stationary transceiver connected to the cable-based LAN that enables the cordless PC to communicate with the network. The access point acts as a conduit for the wireless PC.

You can classify wireless LAN communications according to transmission method. The four most common LAN wireless transmission methods are:

- **Infrared transmission:** Similar to a television with a remote control that transmits pulses of infrared light carrying coded instructions to a receiver on the TV, this technology has also been adapted to network communication. Four varieties of infrared communications are:

    Broadband optical telepoint: This method uses broadband technology. Data transfer rates in this high-end option are competitive with those for a cable-based network.

    Line-of-sight infrared: Transmissions must occur over a clear, line-of-sight path between transmitter and receiver.

    Reflective infrared: Wireless PCs transmit toward a common central unit, which then directs communication to each of the nodes.

    Scatter infrared: Transmissions reflect off floors, walls, and ceilings until (theoretically) they finally reach the receiver. Because of the imprecise trajectory, data transfer rates are slow. The maximum reliable distance is around 100 feet.

    Infrared transmissions typically are limited to within 100 feet. Within this range, however, infrared is relatively fast. Infrared's high bandwidth supports transmission speeds of up to 10 Mbps.

    Infrared devices are insensitive to radio-frequency interference, but reception can be degraded by bright light. Because transmissions are tightly focused, they are fairly immune to electronic eavesdropping.

- **Laser transmission**: High-powered laser transmitters can transmit data for several thousand yards when line-of-sight communication is possible. Lasers can be used in many of the same situations as microwave links without requiring an FCC license. For indoor LANs, laser light technology is rarely used, but it is similar to infrared technology.

- **Narrow-band radio transmission:** In narrow-band radio communications (also called *single-frequency radio*), the range is better than infrared, effectively enabling mobile computing over a limited area. Neither the receiver nor the transmitter is required to be in a direct line of sight. The signal can bounce off walls, buildings, and even the atmosphere; but heavy walls, such as steel or concrete enclosures, can block the signal.

- **Spread-spectrum radio transmission:** Spread-spectrum radio transmission is a technique originally developed by the military to solve several communication problems. Spread-spectrum improves reliability, reduces sensitivity to interference and jamming, and is less vulnerable to eavesdropping than single-frequency radio.

As its name suggests, spread-spectrum transmission uses multiple frequencies to transmit messages. Two techniques employed are *frequency hopping* and *direct-sequence modulation.*

Frequency hopping switches (*hops*) between several available frequencies (see fig. 2.1.12), staying on each frequency for a specified interval of time. The transmitter and receiver must remain synchronized during a process called a *hopping sequence* in order for this technique to work. The range for this type of transmission is up to two miles outdoors and 400 feet indoors. Frequency hopping typically transmits at up to 250 Kbps, although some versions can reach as high as 2 Mbps.

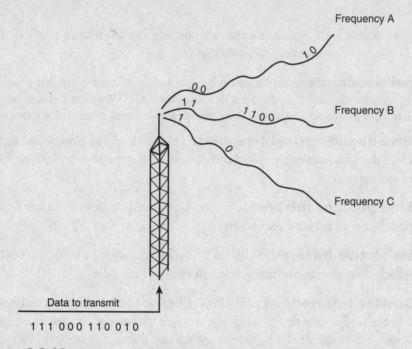

Figure 2.1.12   Frequency hopping employs various frequencies for a specific time period.

Direct-sequence modulation breaks original messages into parts called *chips* (see fig. 2.1.13), which are transmitted on separate frequencies. To confuse eavesdroppers, decoy data also can be transmitted on other frequencies. The intended receiver knows which frequencies are valid and can isolate the chips and reassemble the message. Eavesdropping is difficult because the correct frequencies are not known, and the eavesdropper cannot isolate the frequencies carrying true data. Because different sets of frequencies can be selected, this technique can operate in environments that support other transmission activity. Direct sequence modulation systems operating at 900 MHz support bandwidths of 2–6 Mbps.

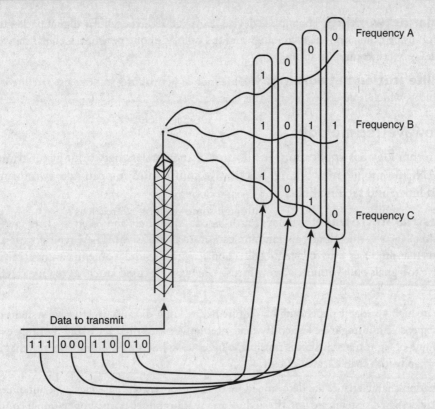

Figure 2.1.13 Direct-sequence modulation.

3. Wireless Bridging

Wireless technology can connect LANs in two different buildings into an extended LAN. This capability is, of course, also available through other technologies (such as a T1 line or a leased line from a telephone provider), but depending on the conditions, a wireless solution is sometimes more cost effective. A wireless connection between two buildings also provides a solution to the ground-potential problem.

A *wireless bridge* acts as a network bridge, merging two local LANs over a wireless connection. Wireless bridges typically use spread-spectrum radio technology to transmit data for up to three miles. (Antennae at each end of the bridge should be placed in an appropriate location, such as a rooftop.) A device called a *long-range wireless bridge* has a range of up to 25 miles.

4. Mobile Computing

Mobile computing is a growing technology that provides almost unlimited range for traveling computers by using satellite and cellular phone networks to relay the signal to a home network. Mobile computing typically is used with portable PCs or personal digital assistant (PDA) devices.

Three forms of mobile computing are:

- **Packet-radio networking:** The mobile device sends and receives network-style packets via satellite. Packets contain a source and destination address, and only the destination device can receive and read the packet.

- **Cellular networking:** The mobile device sends and receives cellular digital packet data (CDPD) using cellular phone technology and the cellular phone network. Cellular networking provides very fast communications.

- **Satellite station networking:** Satellite mobile networking stations use satellite microwave technology, which is described later in this chapter.

5. Microwave Technology

Microwave technology has applications in all three of the wireless networking scenarios: LAN, extended LAN, and mobile networking. Microwave communication can take two forms: terrestrial (ground links) and satellite links.

- **Terrestrial microwave:** Employs Earth-based transmitters and receivers. Uses low-gigahertz range frequencies, which limits all communications to line-of-sight. These typically use a parabolic antenna that produces a narrow, highly directional signal. A similar antenna at the receiving site is sensitive to signals only within a narrow focus. The highly focused antennas require careful adjustment.

  Costs are highly variable depending on requirements. Long-distance microwave systems can be quite expensive but might be less costly than alternatives with their recurring monthly expenses. When line-of-sight transmission is possible, a microwave link is a one-time expense that can offer greater bandwidth than a leased circuit.

  Attenuation characteristics are determined by transmitter power, frequency, and antenna size. Properly designed systems are not affected by attenuation under normal operational conditions. Rain and fog, however, can cause attenuation of higher frequencies.

  Because microwave signals are vulnerable to electronic eavesdropping, signals transmitted through microwave are frequently encrypted.

- **Satellite microwave:** Relay transmissions through communication satellites that operate in geosynchronous orbits 22,300 miles above the earth. Satellites orbiting at this distance remain located above a fixed point on earth.

  Earth stations use parabolic antennas (satellite dishes) to communicate with satellites. These satellites then can retransmit signals in broad or narrow beams, depending on the locations intended to receive the signals.

  Because no cables are required, satellite microwave communication is possible with most remote sites and with mobile devices. This enables transmission with ships at sea and motor vehicles.

  The distances involved in satellite communication result in an interesting phenomenon: Because all signals must travel 22,300 miles to the satellite and 22,300 miles when returning to a receiver, the time required to transmit a signal is independent of distance. It takes as long to transmit a signal to a receiver in the same state as it does to a receiver a third of the way around the world. The time required for a signal to arrive at its destination is called *propagation delay*. The delays commonly encountered with satellite transmissions range from 0.5 to 5 seconds.

  Attenuation characteristics depend on frequency, power, and atmospheric conditions. Microwave signals are sensitive to electronic eavesdropping, so signals transmitted through microwave frequently are encrypted.

2.1   Exercise

Go to a local computer store that sells networking equipment and ask to see their selection of network cards and cables. Write down their prices for each of the different major technologies offered, and pay attention to any recommendations they make about material selection.

Use this information to calculate the materials cost of installing transmission media to support a 40-computer office with 10Base-T versus 100Base-T. Assume average cable length to a hub is 50 feet, and make sure you get category ratings (Category 3 for 10 Mbps, Category 5 for 100 Mbps) for all equipment.

Next, assume that you have been directed to install IBM type 1 cabling because this will be a token ring network. Calculate the materials cost of installing type 1 STP for this 40-station network and using IBM data connectors to terminate it.

2.1   Exercise Explanation

Sample calculation (fictitious pricing):

Average cable length	= 50 feet
Cost per foot of cable	= $0.20
Number of cables	= 40
Connectors	= $0.90

Total materials cost = cable + connectors

Cable	= (number of cables × average cable length × cost per foot)
	= (40 × 50 ft. × 0.2)
	= $40

Connectors	= 2 × number of cables
	= 2 × 40
	= $80

Total materials cost = $40 + $80

Total materials cost = $120

Note that the cost of tools and skilled labor is extremely variable. It's not uncommon for a cabling company to charge in excess of $100 per cable installed.

2.1 Practice Problems

1. When installing a network, you must heed the distance limitations on the cable because the primary limiting factor for data transmission in a very long cable is:

   A. Crosstalk

   B. Collisions

   C. Attenuation

   D. EMI

2. *Baseband* is:

   A. A method for transmitting one signal at a time through the network medium

   B. The lowest (base) frequency a signal requires for transmission

   C. The network adapter requirement for wireless networks

   D. A method for transmitting multiple signals at a time through the network medium

3. When would you consider the use of multiplexing on your network?

   A. With typical 56k, T-1, or T-3 leased lines

   B. When a station has more than one network adapter installed

   C. In order to overcome cable length limitations

   D. When the server receives two signals simultaneously

4. The bandwidth presented to a device when using time-division multiplexing (TDM) is determined by:

   A. The network utilization

   B. The protocol

   C. The channel capacity

   D. The programmed configuration in the MUX

5. The use of fixed-time divisions to multiplex a given channel is known as:

   A. Synchronous TDM

   B. FDM

   C. Channel multiplexing

   D. ATM

6. In a multiplexing environment in which efficient line utilization is most important, what is used?

   A. Repeaters

   B. A transmission control MUX

   C. Capacity sensitive allocation units

   D. Stat-TDM

7. Typical LAN cable is made of:

   A. Aluminum

   B. Plenum

   C. Platinum

   D. Copper

8. Due to extreme signaling requirements, the data transmissions to your space probe operate very slowly. This application can be classified as:

   A. Time Division Multiplexing (TDM)

   B. High bandwidth

   C. Low bandwidth

   D. Baseband

9. Most common LANs operate in:

   A. Baseband mode

   B. Frequency transmission mode

   C. Multiplex mode

   D. Broadband mode

10. You are experiencing some transmission troubles on your network and suspect crosstalk. Crosstalk occurs:

    A. From such interferences as lightning

    B. When the network cables are installed to close to telephone wires

    C. When the multiplex time slots are not synchronized

    D. From adjacent wires

11. You will use BNC-style connectors to connect:

    A. Transceivers to AUI ports

    B. 10Base-T cable segments

    C. Thick coax cable segments

    D. Thin coax segments

12. The thickness of Thicknet cabling is due to:

    A. Increased shielding around the wires

    B. The superior insulation

    C. The number of outer conductors

    D. A thicker core cable

13. In deciding which type of network to install, you consider that one of the benefits of Thicknet over Thinnet is:

    A. Lower cost

    B. Easier to use

    C. Increased bandwidth for Ethernet

    D. Longer transmission distances

14. You are experiencing signaling problems on your coax-based LAN. A protocol analyzer indicates that signals keep bouncing back. What did you forget to install?

    A. A T connector

    B. An impedance reducer

    C. A terminator

    D. An RJ-45 type jack

15. Which type of connectors will you need with Thicknet?

    A. T-connectors

    B. RJ-45 type jacks

    C. RJ-11 type jacks

    D. N-connectors

16. Vampire taps are:

    A. Used to connect Thinnet networks to a Thicknet cable

    B. A type of transceiver

    C. Used to connect a transceiver to the cable in Thicknet networks

    D. All of the above

17. Coax cable consists of two conductors. The outer conductor:

    A. Transmits data

    B. Insulates the inner conductor from damage

    C. Serves as the ground or shield

    D. Is for voice communication

18. You are troubleshooting a Thinnet LAN. Which of the following cable lengths that you found is/are legal?

    A. 150 meters

    B. 200 meters

    C. 500 meters

    D. All of the above

19. You are troubleshooting a Thicknet LAN. Which of the following cable lengths that you found is/are legal?

    A. 150 meters

    B. 200 meters

    C. 500 meters

    D. All of the above

2

20. You are designing an Ethernet LAN. Which of the following is true of Thicknet?

   A. It has higher bandwidth than Thinnet.

   B. It has lower bandwidth than Thinnet.

   C. It has the same bandwidth as Thinnet.

   D. It can only transmit as 2.5 Mbps.

21. You are designing an Ethernet network wired with Category 5 twisted-pair copper cable:

   A. The cables used consist of only two wires.

   B. The cables used consist of two pairs of wires.

   C. The cables used consist of four pairs of wires.

   D. The cables used don't need to connect to a hub.

22. UTP cables should not run over or next to fluorescent lights due to:

   A. Crosstalk

   B. EMI

   C. Transmission resonance

   D. Luminary distortion

23. The twisting feature of twisted-pair copper cable is important for:

   A. Amplifying the transmission

   B. Reducing cable diameter

   C. Strengthening the cable

   D. Canceling crosstalk

24. The shielding in shielded twisted-pair (STP) cable:

   A. Is necessary to meet fire code regulations

   B. Is for grounding and shielding purposes

   C. Is to prevent crosstalk

   D. Is to keep out dust

25. Transmission speed is important to your particular network needs, and you need to choose the appropriate cable. The highest standard data rate for UTP is:

   A. 4 Mbps

   B. 10 Mbps

   C. 16 Mbps

   D. 100 Mbps

26. Twisted-pair cable is the most common LAN cable due to:

   A. Its low cost

   B. Ease of installation

   C. High availability of compatible network components

   D. All of the above

27. The most common STP cable used in networks is:

   A. IBM type 1

   B. IBM type 2

   C. TP-PMD

   D. Category 5

28. One of the disadvantages in STP:

   A. Is the short cable limitations

   B. Is that data transmission is limited to 16 Mbps

   C. Is its thickness

   D. Is the poor EMI characteristics

29. While wiring a LAN, you must limit your UTP cable length to:

    A. 100 meters

    B. 150 meters

    C. 200 meters

    D. 250 meters

30. EMI characteristics are not as good for UTP as they are for STP because:

    A. UTP uses a thinner cable wire.

    B. UTP has no outer shielding.

    C. UTP has four pairs of wire; STP only has two pairs.

    D. UTP connectors cause resonance interference.

31. The two strands in fiber-optic cabling are necessary for:

    A. Redundancy

    B. Crosstalk elimination

    C. Multiplexing signal strength

    D. Transmission and reception

32. Signal loss in fiber-optic cable is mostly a problem with which of the following?

    A. Data-to-light translation devices

    B. Cable-to-cable connections

    C. Lasers

    D. Light-emitting diodes

33. Fiber-optic cables provide which of the following?

    A. The least expensive network cable

    B. The highest transmission rates

    C. The most simple to install

    D. The most damage resistant

34. In order for electronic data to be transmitted via fiber optic cable:

    A. The data must be converted to light signals.

    B. A laser must be used.

    C. Special network couplers must be used.

    D. Manchester encoding must be used.

35. One benefit of fiber-optic cable is:

    A. Lower installation cost

    B. Error recovery features

    C. Better security

    D. Lower network equipment costs

36. An allowable cable length for multimode fiber-optic cable carrying a full duplex 10 Mbps Ethernet signal would be:

    A. 2 km

    B. 5 km

    C. 10 km

    D. 20 km

37. Two disadvantages of fiber-optic cable are:

    A. Limited capacity and EMI interference

    B. Short cable limits and cost

    C. Installation and degradation over time

    D. Cost and installation

38. Fiber-optic cables come in two types. They are:

    A. Full duplex and half duplex

    B. Single mode and asynchronous

    C. Laser and LED

    D. Single mode and multimode

39. In using fiber-optic cable, a faster transmission is achieved with:

    A. LEDs

    B. Radio frequency beams

    C. Lasers

    D. Electrical transmissions

40. A disadvantage of fiber-optic cable over copper cable is that:

    A. Fiber-optic cables are more durable.

    B. Fiber-optic cables don't work with the most common type of network, Ethernet.

    C. Fiber-optic cables can work over much longer distances than copper cables.

    D. Fiber-optic cables are more expensive than copper cables.

41. A standard, cabled LAN that includes some wireless components is known as:

    A. A hybrid LAN

    B. A point-to-point LAN

    C. A wireless LAN

    D. A spread-spectrum LAN

42. Wireless computers typically connect through:

    A. The frequency transmission conduit

    B. Infrared radio frequencies

    C. An access point cabled to a regular LAN

    D. Mobile computing

43. Laser, infrared, and radio transmissions are used:

    A. In fiber-optic cables

    B. In wireless networks

    C. In most small LANs

    D. Only in very large networks

44. Scatter infrared transmission:

    A. Doesn't need a transceiver

    B. Has shorter transmission distances than other forms of infrared

    C. Has longer transmission distances than other forms of infrared

    D. Works best out of doors

45. Radio, laser, and _____ are the most common means of wireless LAN transmission.

    A. Satellite

    B. Infrared

    C. LEDs

    D. Transmission beam

46. Wireless laser transmission has an advantage over other wireless technologies in that:

    A. It doesn't require an FCC license.

    B. It doesn't require line-of-sight.

    C. It requires a line-of-sight between the transmitter and the receiver.

    D. It is much less expensive to install.

47. A technical obstacle to using satellites for data traffic is:

    A. The expense

    B. The long latency

    C. The speed limitations

    D. Unavailable from remote areas

48. Satellite communications are done via:

    A. Laser

    B. Infrared

    C. Radio

    D. Microwave

49. You need to build a wireless network, and security is your dominant concerns. Which of the following transmission methods is the most secure?

    A. Infrared

    B. Laser

    C. Radio

    D. Spread spectrum

50. When planning a line-of-sight wireless connection between adjacent buildings, important considerations are (select three):

    A. Resistance to weather conditions

    B. Data throughput, or speed

    C. Technology used

    D. Monthly line costs

2.1 Answers and Explanations: Practice Problems

1. **C** Attenuation is the limiting factor for data transmission in very long cables. The longer the cable, the weaker the signal at the end.

2. **A** Baseband signaling only allows for transmitting one signal at a time through the same physical network medium.

3. **A** Multiplexing is used with typical 56k, T-1, or T-3 leased lines. A T-1 carries 24 multiplexed DS-0s, while a T-3 carries 24 multiplexed T-1s.

4. **D** The bandwidth presented by a Time Division MUX (TDM) is controlled by the MUX's configuration.

5. **A** Synchronous TDM is another name for using fixed-time divisions to multiplex a given channel.

6. **D** Stat-TDM can use a line more efficiently than a fixed TDM configuration.

7. **D** Most network cables are made of copper. Less frequently, plastic or glass is also used for fiber-optic cables.

8. **C** Low bandwidth is a descriptive term used for low-speed transmissions. The line between high and low bandwidth varies depending on the context in which it is used.

9. **A** Most common LANs, including token ring, FDDI, and Ethernet over 10Base-T, 10Base2, and 10ase5, all use baseband signaling.

10. **D** Crosstalk is the electromagnetic interference from adjacent wires in a pair or bundle of cables.

11. **D** BNC connectors are only used with thin coax (10Base2) segments

12. **D** The thicker core contributes most of the thickness of Thicknet (10Base5) cable

13. **D** A single Thicknet cable segment supports Ethernet data transmission over 500 meters, or more than twice the distance of Thinnet cabling. Thicknet is more expensive and harder to work with than Thinnet, and they both run at the same speed of 10 Mbps.

14. **C** A terminator is used with coax cabling to match the cable's impedance, which has the effect of keeping signals from being reflected and bouncing back.

15. **D** N-connectors are used with Thicknet.

16. **C** Vampire taps are used to connect a station to the cable in Thicknet networks. They are a way of connecting to the Thicknet without cutting it.

17. **C** The outer conductor in a coaxial cable serves as the ground or shield.

18. **A** Thinnet cable can support cable segments of up to 185 meters, so the only correct choice in this example is 150 meters.

19. **D** Thicknet cable can support cable segments of up to 500 meters, so all the choices listed are correct.

20. **C**   Both Thicknet and Thinnet are used with the 10 Mbps variety of Ethernet, so they can be said to have the same bandwidth in that context.

21. **C**   Category 5 cables by always consist of four pairs of wires.

22. **B**   The ballast in fluorescent lights can generate enough EMI to distort data signals, so installers of network cables need to avoid them.

23. **D**   Twisting the cables of each pair together has the effect of canceling crosstalk between them.

24. **B**   The shield used in STP is used for grounding and shielding purposes.

25. **D**   100 Mbps is the speed Category 5 cabling is tested at, and it is the highest standard data rate for UTP.

26. **D**   Twisted-pair cable is the most common LAN cable installed today due to its low cost, its ease of installation, and the high availability of compatible network components.

27. **A**   IBM type 1 cabling is the most common type of STP used in data networks. It is only commonly used for token ring networks.

28. **C**   STP is one of the thickest types of network cabling, which makes it more expensive and harder to work with.

29. **A**   100 meters is the maximum allowed length for standard UTP cables.

30. **B**   UTP is more susceptible to EMI because it has no outer shielding like STP (or coaxial cable) does.

31. **D**   In a fiber-optic data cable, one strand is used for transmitting and the other strand is used for receiving.

32. **B**   The most dramatic signal loss in a fiber optic environment happens at the connectors.

33. **B**   Fiber-optic cables support the highest data transmission rates available, with theoretical bandwidth of many gigabits per second.

34. **A**   Before transmitting any data through a fiber-optic cable, the data must be converted to light.

35. **C**   Fiber-optic cable is very difficult to eavesdrop on compared to copper cables, and so it is more secure.

36. **A**   Multimode fiber can generally carry a 10 Mbps signal for 2 km before attenuation becomes a problem.

37. **D**   The two major drawbacks of fiber-optic cable are its relatively expensive cost and the requirement for skilled installers to polish the cable ends and to make the connections.

38. **D**   The two different types of fiber-optic cables are single mode and multimode. The transmitters used on single mode cables are usually lasers, while the transmitters on multimode cables are typically LEDs.

39. **C**   Although both lasers and LEDs are used for different types of fiber-optic transmissions, lasers can turn on and off much more rapidly and so are used for high-speed data transmissions.

40. **D**   Fiber-optic cables are typically more expensive than copper cables, although they work over longer distances and potentially higher speeds than copper cables.

41. **A**   A LAN that has both wireless and standard cabled components is called a hybrid LAN.

42. **C**   Most wireless devices connect to the rest of the network through an access point cabled to a regular LAN.

43. **B**   Laser, infrared, and radio frequency transmissions are all commonly used in wireless networks.

44. **B** Scatter infrared technologies have shorter transmission distances than other forms of infrared.

45. **B** Infrared is one of the most common types of wireless communication.

46. **A** Laser-based wireless communications don't require an FCC license, but radio and microwave may require one.

47. **B** Because the signal has to travel over 44,000 miles, the long latency (half a second or more) can be unbearable for interactive traffic like Telnet, and it will seriously limit the throughput of non-interactive traffic.

48. **D** Satellite transmissions are done via microwave, in which each earth station uses a small parabolic antenna.

49. **D** Spread spectrum is the most secure of the options presented because its frequency-hopping makes it hard to eavesdrop on.

50. **A, B, C** The only choice that should not be a consideration is the monthly line charge, because in a wireless environment there are no line charges.

2.1   Key Words

Access point

Attenuation

AUI

Bandwidth

Baseband

Broadband

Category 5

Coaxial cable

Crosstalk

Data transmission rate

Direct sequence modulation

EMI (Electromagnetic interference)

FDM

Fiber-optic

Frequency hopping

Impedance

Infrared

Laser

Laser transmission

LED (Light-emitting diode)

Microwave transmission

Mobile computing

Multiplexing

Mux: multiplexor

N-connector

Narrow-band radio transmission

Plenum-grade cable

Propagation delay

PVC cable

RG-58

RJ-45

Shield

Spread-spectrum radio transmission

STP

T-connector

TDM

Terminator

Terrestrial microwave

Thicknet

Thinnet

Transceiver

Transmission media

UTP

Vampire tap

Wireless

Wireless bridging

2

2.2   Selecting the Appropriate Topology for Various Token Ring and Ethernet Networks

A.   Access Methods

An *access method* is a set of rules governing how the network nodes share the transmission medium. The rules for sharing among computers are similar to the rules for sharing among humans—they both boil down to a pair of fundamental philosophies: *first come, first serve* and *take turns*. These two philosophies define the two most important types of media access methods:

Access Method	Description
Contention	*Contention* means that the computers are contending for use of the transmission medium. Any computer in the network can transmit at any time (*first come, first serve*).
Token passing	The computers take turns using the transmission medium (*take turns*).

1. Contention

On contention-based networks, the nodes have equal transmission priority. Any computer can transmit at any time. When several computers attempt to transmit at the same time, a collision occurs. When a network gets extremely busy, most attempts to transmit result in collisions and little effective communication can take place.

Characteristics of Contention

The characteristics of contention are:

- It is the most popular media access control method on LANs (used in Ethernet).
- It is a simple protocol that can operate with inexpensive network software and hardware.
- Unless traffic levels consistently exceed about 30 percent of bandwidth, contention works well.
- It provides good performance at low cost.
- *Probabilistic*: A computer's chance of being permitted to transmit cannot be predicted.
- Collisions occur at unpredictable intervals, and no computer is guaranteed the capability to transmit at any given time.
- Collisions increase in frequency as more computers use the network. When too many computers use the network, collisions dominate network traffic, and relatively few frames are transmitted on the first try.

Mechanisms such as Ethernet's random back-off are usually put into place to minimize the effects of collisions.

- **Carrier sensing:** Each computer listens to the network before attempting to transmit. If the network is busy, the computer refrains from transmitting until the network quiets down.

- **Collision detection:** Computers continue to listen to the network as they transmit. If a computer detects another signal that interferes with the signal it's sending, it stops transmitting. Both computers then wait a random amount of time and attempt to retransmit.

Carrier detection and carrier sensing used together form the protocol used in all types of Ethernet: *Carrier Sense Multiple Access with Collision Detection (CSMA/CD)*. CSMA/CD limits the size of the network to the round-trip time of its smallest data frame (2,500 meters for thicknet). At longer distances, the collision detection mechanisms don't work—a node at one end can't sense when a node at the other end is sending data until too late in the transmission for the datalink to handle the back-off and retransmission.

Apple's LocalTalk network uses the protocol *Carrier Sense Multiple Access with Collision Avoidance (CSMA/CA)*. Collision avoidance uses additional techniques to further reduce the likelihood of collisions. In CSMA/CA, each computer signals a warning that says it is *about* to transmit data, and then the other computers wait for the broadcast. This increases order and reduces collisions, but it also increases the network traffic and system load.

Demand Priority

Demand priority is an access method used with the 100-Mbps 100VG-AnyLAN standard. Although demand priority is officially considered a contention-based access method, demand priority is considerably different from the basic CSMA/CD Ethernet. In demand priority, network nodes are connected to hubs, and those hubs are connected to other hubs. Contention, therefore, occurs at the hub. (100VG-AnyLAN cables can actually send and receive data at the same time. 100VG-AnyLAN cabling uses four twisted pairs in a scheme called *quartet signaling*.) Demand priority provides a mechanism for prioritizing data types.

---

2. Token Passing

Token passing utilizes a frame called a *token*, which circulates around the network. A computer that needs to transmit must wait until it receives the token. When the computer is finished transmitting, it passes the token frame to the next station on the network.

Token-passing methods can use station priorities and other methods to prevent any one station from monopolizing the network. Because each computer has a chance to transmit each time the token travels around the network, each station is guaranteed a chance to transmit at some minimum time interval.

Networks That Employ Token Passing Access Control

Token Ring	The most common token-passing standard, embodied in IEEE standard 802.5
IEEE standard 802.4	Implemented infrequently; defines a bus network that also employs token passing
FDDI	A 100-Mbps fiber-optic network standard that uses token passing and rings in much the same manner as 802.5 token ring

3. Comparing Contention and Token Passing

Token passing is more appropriate than contention under the following conditions:

- **When the network is carrying time-critical data:** Because token passing results in more predictable delivery, token passing is called *deterministic*.

- **When the network experiences heavy utilization:** Token-passing networks cannot become gridlocked due to excessive numbers of collisions.

- **When some stations should have higher priority than others:** Some token-passing schemes support priority assignments.

As an access-control mechanism, token passing appears to be clearly superior to contention. You find, however, that Ethernet—by far the dominant LAN standard—has achieved its prominence while firmly wedded to contention access control.

Token passing requires a variety of complex control mechanisms for it to work well. The necessary hardware is considerably more expensive than the hardware required to implement the much simpler contention mechanisms. The higher cost of token passing networks is difficult to justify unless special features are required.

Because token-passing networks are designed for high reliability, building network diagnostics and troubleshooting capabilities into the network hardware is common. These capabilities increase the cost of token-passing networks.

Conversely, although token-passing networks perform better than contention-based networks when traffic levels are high, contention networks exhibit superior performance under lighter loading conditions. Passing the token around (and other maintenance operations) eats into the available bandwidth.

B. Physical and Logical Topologies

A topology defines the arrangement of nodes, cables, and connectivity devices that make up the network. Two basic categories form the basis for all discussions of topologies:

Physical topology	Describes the actual layout of the network transmission media
Logical topology	Describes the logical pathway a signal follows as it passes among the network nodes

> The term *topology*, as used in Microsoft's test objectives for the Networking Essentials exam, applies not to the physical and logical topology archetypes describe in this section but to the complete network specifications (such as 10BASE-T or 10BASE5) described in the "Ethernet" and "Token Ring" sections of this chapter.

1. Bus Topologies

A *bus physical topology* is one in which all devices connect to a common, shared cable (sometimes called the *backbone*). This is shown in figure 2.2.1.

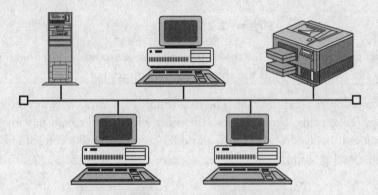

Figure 2.2.1   A bus physical topology.

The bus topology is ideally suited for networks that use contention-based access methods. Ethernet, the most common contention-based network architecture, typically uses a bus as its physical topology. Bus networks send all signals throughout the entire cable plant immediately.

2. Ring Topologies

Ring topologies are wired in a circle. Each device incorporates a receiver and a transmitter and serves as a repeater that passes the signal on to the next device in the ring in one direction only (see fig. 2.2.2). Because the signal is regenerated at each device, signal degeneration is low and longer distances are generally supported.

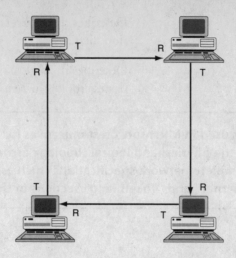

T = TRANSMIT
R = RECEIVE

Figure 2.2.2   A ring topology.

Ring topologies are ideally suited for token-passing access methods. The token passes around the ring, and only the node that holds the token can transmit data.

Ring physical topologies are quite rare. The ring topology is almost always implemented as a logical topology. Token ring, for example—the most widespread token-passing network—always arranges the nodes in a physical star (with all nodes connecting to a central hub) but passes data in a logical ring (see fig. 2.2.3).

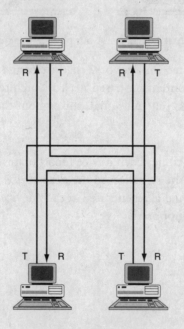

T = TRANSMIT

R = RECEIVE

Figure 2.2.3   A logical ring configured in a physical star.

3. Star Topologies

Star topologies require that all devices connect to a central hub. The hub receives signals from other network devices and routes the signals to the proper destinations. Star hubs can be interconnected to form *tree* or *hierarchical* network topologies.

A *star physical topology* is often used to implement a bus or ring logical topology. A *star physical topology* means that the nodes are all connected to a central hub (see fig. 2.2.4). The path the data takes among the nodes and through that hub (the logical topology) depends on:

The design of the hub

The design of the cabling

The hardware and software configuration of the nodes

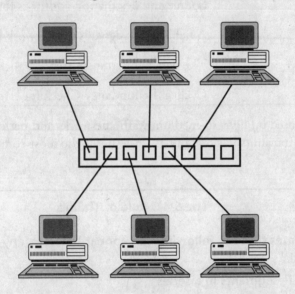

STAR

Figure 2.2.4 A star topology.

C.   Ethernet Topologies

Ethernet is a very popular local area network architecture based on the CSMA/CD access method. In common usage, the term *Ethernet* refers to original Ethernet (or Ethernet II, the latest version) as well as the earlier IEEE 802.3 standards.

Ethernet networks, depending on the particular variety, typically operate at 10, 100, or 1000 Mbps using baseband transmission. Each of the IEEE 802.3 specifications specifies which cable types it supports.

> The name of each Ethernet topology begins with a number (10 or 100). That number specifies the transmission speed for the network. For instance, 10Base5 is designed to operate at 10 Mbps, and 100Base-X operates at 100 Mbps.

Ethernet networks transmit data in small units called *frames*. The size of an Ethernet frame can be anywhere between 64 and 1,518 bytes. Eighteen bytes of the total size are taken up by frame overhead, such as the source and destination addresses, protocol information, and error-checking information.

Sections in a Typical Ethernet II Frame

Preamble	A field that signifies the beginning of the frame
Addresses	Source and destination addresses for the frame
Type	A field that designates the network layer protocol
Data	The data being transmitted
CRC	Cyclical Redundancy Check for error checking

Ethernet generally is used on light-to-medium traffic networks and performs best when a network's data traffic transmits in short bursts. Ethernet is the most commonly used network standard.

> ### The 5-4-3 Rule of Thumb
>
> The 5-4-3 rule states that the following can appear between any two nodes in the Ethernet network:
> - Up to 5 cable segments in a series
> - Up to 4 concentrators or repeaters
> - Up to 3 segments of cables that contain nodes (This really only applies to coaxial cables because UTP and fiber are always implemented in a point-to-point fashion.)

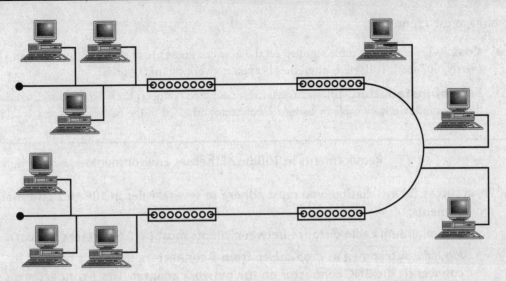

Figure 2.2.5   The 5-4-3 rule: 5 segments on a LAN, 4 repeaters, and 3 segments that contain nodes.

1. 10Base2

The 10Base2 cabling topology (Thinnet) uses the network interface card's on-board transceiver to translate the signals to and from the rest of the network (see fig. 2.2.6). Thinnet cabling uses BNC T-connectors that directly attach to the network adapter. Each end of the cable should have a terminator, and you must use a grounded terminator on one end.

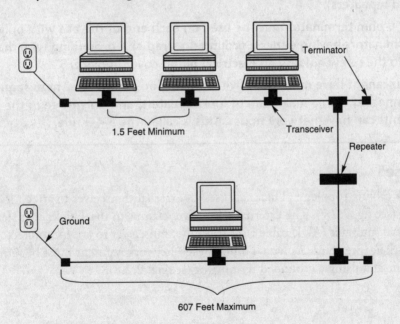

Figure 2.2.6   Two segments using 10Base2 cabling.

Reasons to use Thinnet:

- **Cost:** When any given cable segment on the network doesn't have to be run further than 185 meters (607 feet), 10Base2 is often the cheapest network cabling option.

- **Ease of installation:** 10Base2 is relatively simple to connect. Each network node connects directly to the network cable by using a T-connector attached to the network adapter.

Requirements in 10Base2 Ethernet Environments

For a successful installation, you must adhere to several rules in 10Base2 Ethernet environments:

- The minimum cable distance between clients must be 0.5 meters (1.5 feet).
- *Pig tails*, also known as *drop cables*, from T-connectors shouldn't be used to connect to the BNC connector on the network adapter. The T-connector must be connected directly to the network adapter.
- You cannot exceed the maximum network segment limitation of 185 meters (607 feet).
- The entire network cabling scheme cannot exceed 925 meters (3,035 feet) in its longest path.
- The maximum number of nodes per network segment is 30 (this includes clients and repeaters).
- A 50-ohm terminator must be used on each end of the bus with only one of the terminators having either a grounding strap or a grounding wire that attaches it to the screw holding an electrical outlet cover in place.
- You cannot have more than five segments on a network. These segments can be connected with a maximum of four repeaters, and only three of the five segments can have network nodes. This is called the 5-4-3 rule.

---

2. 10Base5

The 10Base5 cabling topology (Thicknet) uses an external transceiver to attach to the network adapter card (see fig. 2.2.7). The external transceiver clamps to the Thicknet cable. An Attachment Universal Interface (AUI) cable runs from the transceiver to a DIX connector on the back of the network adapter card. As with Thinnet, each network segment must be terminated at both ends, with one end using a grounded terminator (see fig. 2.2.8).

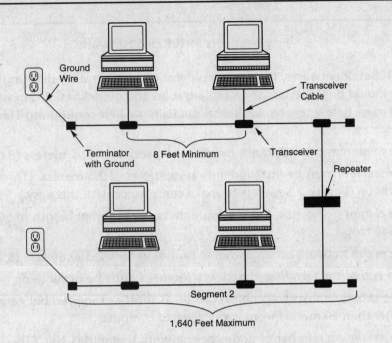

Figure 2.2.7 Two segments using 10Base5 cabling.

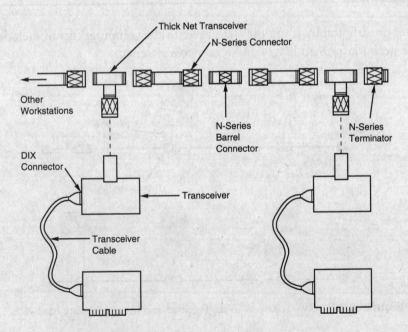

Figure 2.2.8 Components of a Thicknet network.

The primary advantage of 10Base5 is its capability to exceed the cable restrictions that apply to 10Base2. 10Base5 does pose restrictions of its own, however, which you should consider when installing or troubleshooting a 10Base5 network.

Requirements in 10Base5 Networks

As with 10Base2 networks, the first consideration when troubleshooting a 10Base5 network should be the established cabling rules and guidelines. Along with the 5-4-3 rule, you must follow several additional guidelines when configuring Thicknet networks, such as:

- The minimum cable distance between transceivers is 2.5 meters (8 feet).
- Transceivers must be installed only at multiples of 2.5 meters. (Thicknet has marks on it every 2.5 meters to make compliance with this easy.)
- You cannot go beyond the maximum network segment length of 500 meters (1,640 feet).
- The entire network cabling scheme cannot exceed 2,500 meters (8,200 feet).
- One end of the terminated network segment must be grounded.
- Drop cables (transceiver cables) can be as short as required but cannot be longer than 50 meters from transceiver to computer.
- The maximum number of nodes per network segment is 100. (This includes all repeaters.)

The length of the drop cables (from the transceiver to the computer) is not included in measurements of the network segment length and total network length.

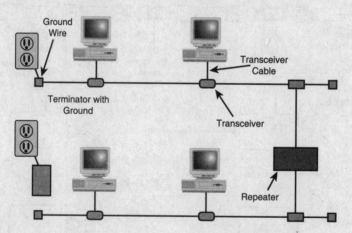

Figure 2.2.9   Two segments using Thicknet and the appropriate hardware.

3. 10Base-T

The trend in wiring Ethernet networks is to use unshielded twisted-pair (UTP) cable. 10Base-T, which uses UTP cable, is one of the most popular implementations for Ethernet. It is based on the IEEE 802.3 standard. 10Base-T supports a data rate of 10 Mbps using baseband transmission.

10Base-T cabling is wired in a star topology (see fig. 2.2.10). The nodes are wired to a central hub, which serves as a multiport repeater. A 10Base-T network functions logically as a linear bus. The hub repeats the signal to all nodes, and the nodes contend for access to the transmission medium as if they were connected along a linear bus. The cable uses 8 pin modular (RJ-45 type) connectors, and network adapter cards often have an RJ-45 type jack built into the back of the card.

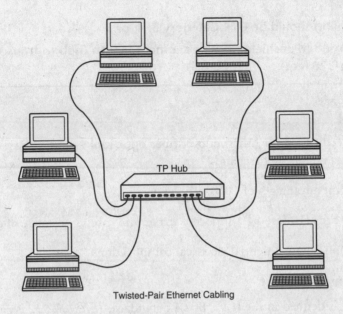

Twisted-Pair Ethernet Cabling

Figure 2.2.10   A 10Base-T network.

10Base-T segments can be connected by using coaxial or fiber-optic backbone segments. Some hubs provide connectors for Thinnet and Thicknet cables (in addition to 10Base-T UTP-type connectors).

By attaching a 10Base-T transceiver to the AUI port of the network adapter, you can use a computer setup for Thicknet on a 10Base-T network.

The star wiring of 10Base-T provides several advantages, particularly in larger networks:

- **The network is more reliable and easier to manage:** 10Base-T networks use a *concentrator* (a centralized wiring hub). These hubs are "intelligent" in that they can detect defective cable segments and shut them down.

- **You can design and build your LAN one segment at a time:** This capability makes 10Base-T more flexible than other LAN cabling options.

- **10Base-T is also relatively inexpensive to use:** In some cases, existing data-grade phone cable can be used for the LAN.

- **Star-based networks are significantly easier to troubleshoot and repair than bus-wired networks:** With a star network, a problem node can be easily isolated from the rest of the network.

Requirements for a 10Base-T Network

The requirements for a 10Base-T network are:

- The maximum number of computers on a single collision domain is 1,024. (Practical considerations such as traffic volume usually keep it to a much smaller number.)
- The cabling should be UTP Category 3, 4, or 5.
- The maximum unshielded cable segment length (hub to transceiver) is 100 meters (328 feet).

---

4. 10Base-FL

10Base-FL is a specification for Ethernet over fiber-optic cables. The 10Base-FL specification calls for a 10 Mbps data rate using baseband.

The most important advantages of 10Base-FL are:

Long cabling runs (10Base-FL supports a maximum cabling distance of about 2,000 meters)

The elimination of any potential electrical complications

5. 100VG-AnyLAN

100VG-AnyLAN is defined in the IEEE 802.12 standard. *IEEE 802.12* is a standard for transmitting Ethernet and token ring packets (IEEE 802.3 and 802.5) at 100 Mbps. 100VG-AnyLAN is sometimes called 100Base-VG. The "VG" in the name stands for voice grade.

100VG-AnyLAN's demand priority access method provides for two priority levels when resolving media access conflicts.

100VG-AnyLAN uses a *cascaded star* topology, which calls for a hierarchy of hubs (see fig. 2.2.11). Computers are attached to *child hubs*, and the child hubs are connected to higher-level hubs called *parent hubs*.

The maximum length for the two longest cables attached to a 100VG-AnyLAN hub is 250 meters (820 ft). The specified cabling is Category 3,4, or 5 twisted pair or fiber optic. 100VG-AnyLAN is compatible with 10Base-T cabling.

Both 100VG-AnyLAN and 100Base-X can be installed as a plug-and-play upgrade to a 10Base-T system.

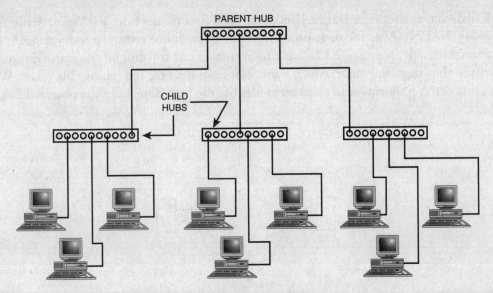

Figure 2.2.11 A cascaded star topology.

6. 100Base-X

100Base-X uses a star bus topology similar to 10Base-T's. 100Base-X provides a data transmission speed of 100 Mbps using baseband.

Cabling Specifications for the 100Base-X Standard

100Base-TX	Two twisted pairs of Category 5 UTP or STP
100Base-FX	Fiber-optic cabling using 2-strand cable
100Base-T4	Four twisted pairs of Category 3, 4, or 5 UTP

100Base-X is sometimes referred to as *Fast Ethernet.* Like 100VG-AnyLAN, 100Base-X provides compatibility with existing 10Base-T systems (that were properly cabled) and thus enables plug-and-play upgrades from 10Base-T.

D. Token Ring

Token ring uses a token-passing architecture that adheres to the IEEE 802.5 standard. The topology is always physically a star, but token ring uses a logical ring to pass the token from station to station. Each node must be attached to a concentrator called a *multistation access unit (MSAU or MAU).* The MSAU is used to bypass token ring stations that are not active.

Although 4-Mbps token ring network interface cards can run only at that data rate, 16-Mbps cards can be configured to run at 4 or 16 Mbps. All cards on a given ring must run at the same rate.

Each node acts as a repeater that receives tokens and data frames from its *Nearest Active Upstream Neighbor* (NAUN). After the node processes a frame, the frame transmits it downstream to the next attached node (see fig. 2.2.12). Each frame makes one trip around the entire ring and then returns to the originating node, which removes it from the ring and releases the token. Workstations that detect problems send a *beacon* to identify the fault domain of the potential failure.

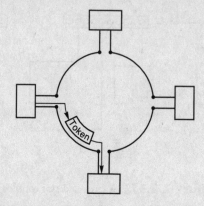

Figure 2.2.12 Operation of a token ring.

1. Token Ring Cabling

Traditional token ring networks use twisted-pair cable. The following is a list of standard components and cables used in token ring networks:

- **Type 1**

  A braided shield surrounds two twisted pairs of solid copper wire.

  Type 1 is used to connect terminals and distribution panels or to connect between different wiring closets that are located in the same building.

  It uses two STPs of solid-core 22 AWG wire for long, high data-grade transmissions within the building's walls.

  It is the most popular transmission medium for token ring.

  A token ring network using Type 1 STP cabling can support up to 260 computers.

- **Type 2**

  Type 2 uses a total of six twisted pairs: two are STPs (for networking) and four are UTPs (for telephone systems).

  It is used for the same purposes as Type 1, but enables both voice and data cables to be included in a single cable run.

- **Type 3**

  Type 3 is used as an alternative to Type 1 and Type 2 cable because of its reduced cost.

  It has unshielded twisted-pair copper with a minimum of two twists per inch.

It has four UTPs of 22 or 24 AWG solid-core wire for networks or telephone systems.

It cannot be used for 16-Mbps token ring networks.

Type 3 is used primarily for long, low data-grade transmissions within walls. Signals don't travel as fast as with Type 1 cable because of the lack of shielding.

The maximum cabling distance (according to IBM) is 45 meters (about 148 feet). Some vendors specify cabling distances of up to 150 meters (500 feet).

Type 3 uses RJ-11 or RJ-45 connectors. (Media filters, if necessary, can convert the network adapter to RJ-11 or RJ-45 format.)

- **Patch cable**

  Patch cable connects MSAUs.

  Typically IBM Type 6 cables come in standard lengths of 8, 30, 75, or 150 feet. (A Type 6 cable consists of two shielded 26-AWG twisted-pairs.) You can also get patch cables in custom lengths.

  It is used to extend the length of Type 3 cables or to connect computers to MSAUs.

  You need to have an IBM connector at each end.

- **Adapter cable**

  You should have an IBM data connector at one end and a nine-pin connector at the other end.

  You can connect client and server network adapters to other network components that use IBM data connectors.

- **MSAU**

  MSAU is a central cabling component for IBM Token Ring networks.

- **8228 MSAU**

  This is the original wiring hub developed by IBM for Token Ring networks.

  Each 8228 has 10 connectors, eight of which accept cables to clients or servers.

  RI (ring in) and RO (ring out) connectors are used to connect multiple 8228s to form larger networks.

  It has mechanical devices that consist of relays and connectors. Their purpose is to switch clients in and out of the network.

  Each port is controlled by a relay powered by a voltage sent to the MSAU from the client.

  When an 8228 is first set up, each of these relays must be initialized with the setup tool that is shipped with the unit.

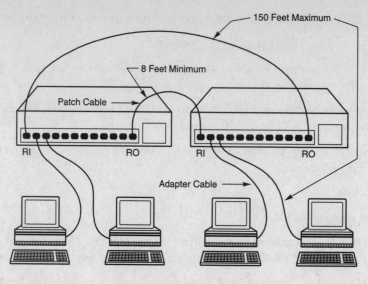

Token Ring Cabling

Figure 2.2.13 An example of a network cabling several clients and MSAUs. The distances noted are based on the rules for the small movable cabling system.

When you connect a token ring network, make sure you:

1. **Initialize each port in the 8228 MSAU by using the setup tool shipped with the MSAU.**

2. **If you're using more than one MSAU, connect the RO port of each MSAU with the RI port of the next MSAU in the loop. Complete the loop so that the MSAUs form a circle or ring.**

---

2. Passing Data on Token Rings

A frame called a *token* perpetually circulates around a token ring. The computer that holds the token has control of the transmission medium.

The actual process of passing data on a token ring is as follows:

1. The Active Monitor generates the token.

2. A computer in the ring captures the token.

3. If the computer has data to transmit, it holds the token and transmits a data frame. A token ring data frame contains the fields listed in table 2.2.1.

4. Each computer in the ring checks to see if it is the intended recipient of the frame.

5. When the frame reaches the destination address, the destination PC copies the frame to a receive buffer, updates the frame status field of the data frame (see step 2), and puts the frame back on the ring.

6. When the computer that originally sent the frame receives it from the ring, it acknowledges a successful transmission, takes the frame off the ring, and places the token back on the ring.

Table 2.2.1 Token Ring Data Frame Fields

Field	Description
Start delimiter	Marks the start of the frame
Access control	Specifies the priority of the frame; also specifies whether the frame is a token or a data frame
Frame control	Media Access Control information
Destination address	Address of receiving computer
Source address	Address of sending computer
Data	Data being transmitted
Frame check sequence	Error-checking information (CRC)
End delimiter	Marks the end of the frame
Frame status	Tells whether the destination address was located and whether the frame was recognized

3. The Beaconing Process

Beaconing is the strategy token ring networks use to auto-configure themselves and to resolve soft errors (ones that don't require administrator intervention).

The first station that is powered-up on a token ring network automatically becomes what is called the *active monitor station*. The primary responsibility of the active monitor station is to generate the token and to detect if the token gets lost. Any time the token is lost, the active monitor generates a new token.

The active monitor also sends out an Active Monitor Present frame every seven seconds, which starts the *Neighbor Notification process*. The Neighbor Notification process tells each station its Nearest Active Upstream Neighbor (NAUN). After each station announces itself to its next active downstream neighbor, the announcing station becomes the nearest active upstream neighbor (NAUN) to the downstream station (see fig. 2.2.14).

If a station detects a ring configuration change or an error, or doesn't receive one of its expected seven-second announcements from its upstream neighbor, it attempts to notify the network of the lack of contact from the upstream neighbor. It sends a message out onto the network ring, which includes:

The sending station's network address

The receiving NAUN's network address

The beacon type

From this information, the stations on the ring can determine which station might be having a problem and then can attempt to fix the problem without disrupting the entire network. This process is known as *autoreconfiguration*. If autoreconfiguration proves unsuccessful, manual correction becomes necessary.

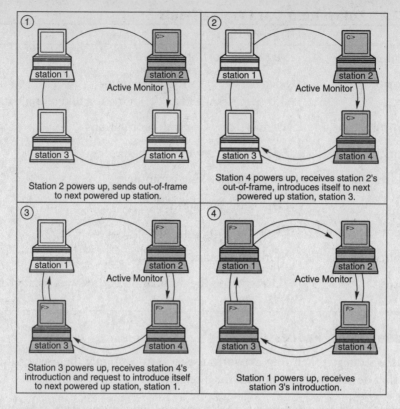

Figure 2.2.14 A token ring network utilizing the beaconing process.

2.2 Exercise

Go online and use a web browser to read through the Ethernet Home Page maintained by Charles Spurgeon at http://wwwhost.ots.utexas.edu/ethernet/ethernet-home.html and the Token Ring Design Rules from South Hills Datacom at http://jmazza.shillsdata.com/tech/tr/design_rules.

2.2 Practice Problems

1. In a CSMA/CD network, access to the transmission medium is:

    A. Deterministic

    B. Unlikely

    C. Always available to all stations

    D. Probabilistic

2. A difference between the contention-based and the token-passing access methods is that:

    A. Contention-based networks can run efficiently at very high utilization.

    B. Token-passing networks can run efficiently at very high utilization.

    C. A station can begin transmitting at any time on a contention based network.

    D. Token-passing networks are always faster than contention based networks.

3. The most common access method used is:

    A. Contention based

    B. Token passing

    C. Logical bus

    D. Physical star

4. Token passing is a _____ access method.

    A. CSMA/CD

    B. Simple to implement

    C. Primitive

    D. Deterministic

5. Under light loads, contention-based networks:

    A. Are more efficient than token passing networks

    B. Are less efficient than token passing networks

    C. Have many collisions

    D. Perform poorly with typical office applications

6. Under heavy traffic loads, token passing networks:

    A. Perform worse than contention based networks

    B. Perform better than contention based networks

    C. Have many collisions

    D. Stop exhibiting deterministic behavior

7. Ring topologies are usually implemented:

    A. As a star-wired physical bus

    B. As a physical ring, with one end station directly connected to other end stations

    C. As a physical star, but a logical ring

    D. As a logical bus, but wired as a physical star

8. Star topologies can be used with (choose two):

    A. Logical busses

    B. Physical busses

    C. Logical rings

    D. Physical rings

2

9. A central hub is required when using:

    A. A contention-based access method

    B. A token-passing access method

    C. A physical ring

    D. A physical star

10. Wiring your building in a physical star enables you to support (select all correct answers):

    A. networks that use a logical bus

    B. networks that use a logical ring

    C. networks that use CSMA/CD

    D. networks that use token passing

11. In an Ethernet network, access to the transmission medium is:

    A. Deterministic

    B. Unlikely

    C. Always available to all stations

    D. Probabilistic

12. You have a small office with four computers you want to connect together. None of the computers are more than 50 feet from the others. What type of network will be least expensive to install?

    A. Ethernet using 100Base-TX

    B. Ethernet using 10Base5

    C. Ethernet using 10Base2

    D. Ethernet using 10Base-T

13. You need to connect two Ethernet repeaters that are 200 meters apart. An appropriate cable choice would be:

    A. Thinnet

    B. Thicknet

    C. 10Base-T

    D. Unshielded Twisted Pair (UTP)

14. You are designing the Ethernet network for a new office building that will hold several hundred computer users on several floors. What type of Ethernet should you use to minimize your total cost of ownership?

    A. 10Base5 (Thicknet)

    B. 10Base2 (Thinnet)

    C. 10Base-F (fiber-optic)

    D. 10Base-T (UTP)

15. Your office is very dynamic, with existing users needing to move their computers frequently. Which type of Ethernet best accommodates this environment?

    A. 10Base5 (Thicknet)

    B. 10Base2 (Thinnet)

    C. 10Base-F (fiber-optic)

    D. 10Base-T (UTP)

16. You are moving into a new building, where the previous tenant had used Category 3 data-grade wiring for the telephone system. What type of Ethernet enables you to reuse that cabling for your network?

    A. 10Base5 (Thicknet)

    B. 10Base2 (Thinnet)

    C. 10Base-F (fiber-optic)

    D. 10Base-T (UTP)

17. You need to design a new network for a client who is concerned that they might need to upgrade from a 10 Mbps network to a 100 Mbps network. What type of Ethernet would you recommend they install?

    A. 10Base5 (Thicknet)

    B. 10Base2 (Thinnet)

    C. 10Base-F (fiber-optic)

    D. 10Base-T (UTP)

18. You need to connect offices on both sides of a very large manufacturing facility to an Ethernet network. The cable will have to pass some very electrically noisy devices, and will have to be over 500 meters long. What type of Ethernet would you recommend be installed for the connection between the two offices?

    A. 10Base5 (Thicknet)

    B. 10Base2 (Thinnet)

    C. 10Base-F (fiber-optic)

    D. 10Base-T (UTP)

19. What type of Ethernet is an easy upgrade from 10Base-T if you have Category 5 wiring installed?

    A. 10Base5

    B. 100Base-TX

    C. 100Base-T4

    D. 100Base-FX

20. You are called in to troubleshoot a coax-based Ethernet network. You see that they have four repeaters in the network data path between some stations. This:

    A. Will always create problems

    B. Always breaks the 5-4-3 rule

    C. May break the 5-4-3 rule if there are computers on more than three segments

    D. Is never a problem

21. All token ring networks must use which of the following physical topology layouts?

    A. Bus

    B. Hybrid

    C. Star

    D. Ring

22. The MAU serves what purpose?

    A. A means of generating a token

    B. Letting stations join and leave the network

    C. Initiating NIC tests when no one claims the token

    D. All of the above

23. Standard token ring speeds are:

    A. 10 and 100 Mbps

    B. 1 and 4 Mbps

    C. 4 and 16 Mbps

    D. 16 and 32 Mbps

24. A signal on a token ring network indicating a problem is called:

    A. A beacon

    B. A warning

    C. A network failure frame

    D. A broadcast frame

25. What port of a token ring MAU is connected to what port on a second MAU?

    A. RO to RI

    B. RO to RO

    C. RI to RI

    D. Master to slave

26. How many computers can be used on the same ring when using IBM type 1 cabling and 8228 MSAUs?

    A. None, this is an illegal configuration

    B. 72

    C. 128

    D. 260

2

27. How many computers can be used on the same ring when using IBM type 1 cabling and 8228 MSAUs?

    A. None, this is an illegal configuration

    B. 72

    C. 128

    D. 260

28. What is the primary duty of the Active Monitor in a token ring network?

    A. To monitor the (T_ANYTOKEN) timer

    B. To generate the token for the ring

    C. To notify each station when it is that station's turn to transmit

    D. To remove faulty computers from the network

29. On token rings, beacons happen:

    A. Whenever a station sends a frame

    B. Every seven seconds

    C. When a station joins or leaves a ring

    D. Only when there is a hard error requiring administrator intervention

30. Token ring uses an access arbitration method that can be considered:

    A. Deterministic

    B. Stochastic

    C. Probabilistic

    D. Simple

2.2 Answers and Explanations: Practice Problems

1. **D** In a CSMA/CD network, access to the network is probabilistic because any station can transmit any time, and overlapping transmissions are handled by making the stations perform a random back-off before retransmitting.

2. **B** Token-passing networks can run much more efficiently at very high utilization because the access method they use doesn't degrade under heavy loads the way contention based networks do.

3. **A** The most common network access method is Ethernet, which is contention-based (CSMA/CD).

4. **D** Token passing is a deterministic network access method because each station is guaranteed an opportunity to transmit in its turn.

5. **A** Under light network traffic loads, contention-based networks are more efficient than token-passing networks because the contention-based networks don't have all the overhead associated with token passing and maintenance.

6. **B** Under heavy traffic loads, token-passing networks typically perform better than contention-based networks because they do not use any more bandwidth arbitrating access with a heavy load than they do with a light load.

7. **C** Most ring topologies are implemented as a physical star, but as a logical ring. Token ring is the best example of this.

8. **A, C** Both logical bus topologies and logical ring topologies are frequently implemented using a physical star topology.

9. **D** A hub is required when using a physical star topology, in which all the cables in the star connect to the hub.

10. **A, B, C, D** Star wiring (with high-grade UTP) is generally the preferred way of cabling buildings for networks because it offers the most flexibility.

11. **A** Ethernet networks guarantee access to the transmission medium via a probabilistic scheme. Stations do not always have access to begin transmitting because they may sense another station is already transmitting (the Carrier Sense part of CSMA/CD).

12. **C** Ethernet using 10Base2 is the least expensive cabling option to install for small networks (in which the total cable length is under 185 meters) because it only needs one relatively inexpensive cable and no repeaters or hubs.

13. **B** Thicknet is the only choice listed that would work for Ethernet at 200 meters. STP is not standardized for Ethernet, and both Thinnet and 10Base-T are limited to less than 200 meters.

14. **D** The star wiring that 10Base-T uses is inexpensive and much easier to trouble-shoot and maintain than coaxial wiring like Thicknet or Thinnet.

15. **D** 10Base-T (UTP) is the best choice when computers move frequently because a single cable can be moved without affecting other users.

16. **D** 10Base-T is compatible with Categories 3, 4, and 5 of unshielded twisted-pair (UTP) wiring.

17. **D** 10Base-T is clearly the best choice here because the same cable plant can be used if they need to migrate to 100Base-T, 10Base-T is much less expensive than 10Base-F, and many newer networking devices can support both 10 Mbps and 100 Mbps speeds.

18. **C** 10Base-F using fiber-optic cable supports distances of up to 2,000 meters and is completely resistant to electrical noise.

19. **B** 100Base-TX and 10BASE-T can both use Category 5 copper wiring, and 100Base-TX is 10 times faster than 10Base-T.

20. **C** The 5-4-3 rule only allows four repeaters in the path if there are computers on no more than three of the cable segments.

21. **C** All token ring networks use a star physical topology even though they have a ring logical topology.

22. **B** The MSAU enables stations to join and leave the network dynamically. The stations themselves are responsible for the token.

23. **C** Standard token ring networks operate at either 4 Mbps or 16 Mbps. All stations on the same ring must be configured for the same speed.

24. **A** Stations begin to beacon when they detect a problem or certain types of changes in the network.

25. **A** When connecting two token ring MSAUs, the Ring Out (RO) of one always goes to the Ring In (RI) of the other.

26. **D** The classic IBM design using model 8228 MSAUs and type 1 STP cabling supports up to 260 computers on a ring.

27. **B** The classic IBM design using model 8228 MSAUs and type 3 UTP cabling supports up to 72 computers on a ring.

28. **B** The primary job of the active monitor is to generate the token for the ring.

29. **C** One of the common causes for self-correcting beacons is a station joining or leaving the ring.

30. **A** Because each station gets a turn to transmit when the token arrives, token rings are considered deterministic.

2.2   Key Words

Beacon	MAU
Bus	MSAU
Carrier detection	Patch cable
Carrier sensing	Physical topology
Contention	Repeater
CRC	RI
CSMA/CA	Ring
CSMA/CD	RO
Ethernet	Star
Frame	Token
IEEE standard	Token ring
Logical topology	Topology

2.3 Selecting the Appropriate Network and Transport Protocols for Various Token Ring and Ethernet Networks

Protocols include:

> DLC
>
> AppleTalk
>
> IPX
>
> TCP/IP
>
> NFS
>
> SMB

A. Transport Protocols

The *OSI reference model* is a standard describing the activities at each level of a protocol stack. The OSI reference model is useful primarily as a conceptual tool for understanding protocol layering. Although some protocols have been designed in strict conformance with the OSI reference model, full OSI compliance hasn't become popular.

Protocols are real implementations of the conceptual rules defined in the OSI reference model. Some protocols and protocol suites existed before the OSI reference model was published and can be matched only very loosely to the seven-layer model.

1. Packets and Protocols

Protocols describe the way in which network data is encapsulated in packets on the source end, sent via the network to a destination and then reconstructed at the destination into the appropriate file, instruction, or request. Breaking network data into packet-sized chunks provides smoother throughput because the small packets don't tie up the transmission medium as a larger unit of data might. Also, packets simplify the task of error detection and correction. Each file is checked separately for errors, and if an error is discovered, only that packet (instead of a whole file) must be retransmitted.

Table 2.3.1   Parts of a Packet[1]

Part	Function
Header	The header signifies the start of the packet and contains a bundle of important parameters, such as the source and destination address and time/synchronization information.
Data	This portion of the packet contains the original data being transmitted.
Trailer	The trailer marks the end of the packet and typically contains error-checking (Cyclical Redundancy Check, or CRC) information.

1. The exact composition of a network packet depends on the protocols you're using.

As the data passes down through the protocol layers, each layer performs its prescribed function, such as interfacing with an application, converting the data format, or adding addressing and error-checking parameters. Actual protocol stacks don't often comply exactly with the OSI model—some, in fact, predate the OSI model—but the concepts and terminology used in the OSI model are nevertheless useful for describing protocol functions.

When the packet reaches the transmission medium, the network adapter cards of all computers on the network segment examine the packet, checking the packet's destination address (see fig. 2.3.1). If the destination address matches the computer's hardware address, the network adapter interrupts the processor, and the protocol layers of the destination system process the incoming packet.

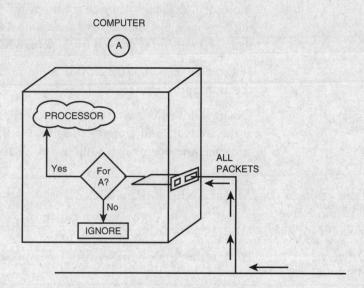

Figure 2.3.1   The network adapter card checks whether the packet's destination address matches the PC's address.

2. Protocols and Protocol Layers

Many of the addressing, error-checking, retransmission, and acknowledgment services most commonly associated with networking take place at the Network and Transport OSI layers. Protocol suites are often referred to by the suite's Transport and Network protocols. In TCP/IP, for instance, TCP is a Transport Layer protocol and IP is a Network Layer protocol. (Note, however, that TCP/IP predates OSI and diverges from OSI in a number of ways.)

> **IPX/SPX is another protocol suite known by its Transport and Network Layer protocols, but the order of the protocols is backward from the way the protocols are listed in TCP/IP. IPX is the Network Layer protocol; SPX is the Transport Layer protocol.**

The lower Data Link and Physical Layers provide a hardware-specific foundation, addressing items such as the network adapter driver, the media access method, and the transmission medium. Transport and Network Layer protocols, such as TCP/IP and IPX/SPX, rest on that

Physical and Data Link Layer foundation. With the help of the NDIS and ODI standards, multiple protocol stacks can operate simultaneously through a single network adapter.

Upper-level protocols provide compatibility with a particular networking environment. For instance, *NetBIOS over TCP/IP* (sometimes called NBT) provides Microsoft clients with full connectivity over TCP/IP.

Table 2.3.2   Common Transport and Network Layer Protocols

TCP/IP	A standards-based networking protocol defined by the IETF in a series of RFCs. It is the protocol used on the Internet and the one that everything seems to be moving toward.
IPX/SPX	A protocol defined by Novell for use with its NetWare servers, but now used by other devices and companies. It is less popular than TCP/IP and is derived from Xerox's XNS.
NWLink	Microsoft's version of the IPX/SPX protocol essentially spans the Transport and Network Layers.
NetBEUI	Designed for Microsoft networks, NetBEUI includes functions at the Network and Transport Layers. NetBEUI isn't routable and therefore doesn't make full use of Network Layer capabilities.
AppleTalk Transaction Protocol (ATP) and Name Binding Protocol (NBP)	ATP and NBP are AppleTalk Transport Layer protocols.
Datagram Delivery Protocol (DDP)	DDP is the AppleTalk Network Layer protocol.

B.   Windows NT Networking

In the Windows NT networking structure, it is the NDIS interface, NDIS wrapper, and NDIS-compatible drivers that enable the TCP/IP, NWLink, NetBEUI, AppleTalk, and DLC protocols to interact simultaneously with the lower layers (see fig. 2.3.2).

The Transport Driver Interface (TDI) is an interface that enables the server, redirector, and file system drivers to remain independent of the transport protocol.

Windows NT (like other Microsoft operating systems such as Windows for Workgroups and Windows 95) services client requests by using the Server Message Block (SMB) protocol. *SMB* is an Application Layer protocol primarily used for file and print sharing.

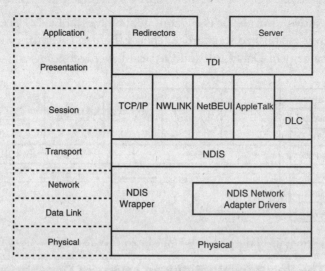

Figure 2.3.2 Microsoft Windows NT networking architecture.

Three stages must take place before a protocol is useful:

1. **A model describes the general function of the protocol.**

2. **The protocol is defined in complete detail.**

3. **The protocol must be realized by software and hardware designers in real products.**

Consider the process of designing a building. The architect first produces sketches that describe the general nature of the building. Then the architect, possibly working with a specialist in particular building trades, develops blueprints that describe every detail of the building. Finally, an actual building is constructed.

C. Internet Protocols (TCP/IP)

The Internet protocol suite (also commonly called the TCP/IP protocol suite) was originally developed by the United States Department of Defense to provide robust service on large internetworks that incorporate a variety of computer types.

In recent years, the Internet protocols have become increasingly popular and constitute the most popular network protocols. Two reasons for this popularity are:

- **No one vendor owns TCP/IP:** TCP/IP evolved in response to input from a wide variety of industry sources. Consequently, TCP/IP is the most open of the protocol suites and is supported by the widest variety of vendors. Virtually every brand of computing equipment now supports TCP/IP.

- **Early availability on Unix:** The protocols were built into the Berkeley Standard Distribution (BSD) Unix implementation. Since then, TCP/IP has achieved universal acceptance in the Unix community and is a standard feature on all versions of Unix.

TCP/IP doesn't include protocols for the Data Link or Physical Layers (see fig.2.3.3). It was designed to work over established standards such as Ethernet. Over time, TCP/IP has been interfaced to the majority of Data Link and Physical Layer technologies.

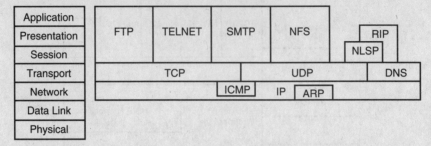

Figure 2.3.3   The relationship of the protocols in the Internet suite to the layers of the OSI reference model.

Table 2.3.3   The Relationship Between Layers of Department of Defense Model and OSI Model

Department of Defense	OSI	Significance
Network Access	Data Link, Physical	Enables the DoD protocols to coexist with existing Data Link and Physical Layer standards
Internet	Network	Moves data between devices on networks
Host-to-Host	Transport	Enables peer communication between hosts on the internetwork
Process/ Application	Session, Presentation, and Application	Provides network services

One huge advantage of TCP/IP is that TCP/IP is required for communication over the Internet. The biggest disadvantage is that it is usually considered harder to manage because the network administrator has to manage network addresses carefully and beware of the possibility of conflicts.

Table 2.3.4   Protocols Associated with TCP/IP Relevant to Microsoft's Networking Essentials Test

Protocol	Description
Internet Protocol (IP)	A connectionless protocol that provides datagram service at the OSI Network Layer. IP is primarily responsible for addressing.
Routing Information Protocol (RIP)	Not the same protocol as RIP in the NetWare suite, although the two serve similar functions and operate in basically the same way. IP RIP performs route discovery by using a distance-vector method, calculating the number of hops that must be crossed to route a packet by a particular path. Each router running RIP broadcasts all the routes it knows about and the hop count it uses for each one to all of its neighbors.

Protocol	Description
Open Shortest Path First (OSPF)	A link-state routing protocol that is designed to overcome the limitations of RIP. OSPF's primary advantages over RIP are that it learns about changes in the network much faster and that it consumes less bandwidth for overhead.
Transmission Control Protocol (TCP)	An internetwork protocol that corresponds to the OSI Transport Layer. TCP provides a reliable Transport Layer for connections. TCP and UDP operate at the same layer.
User Datagram Protocol (UDP)	A connectionless Transport (host-to-host) Layer protocol. UDP does not provide message acknowledgments or error correction; rather, it simply transports datagrams.
Address Resolution Protocol (ARP)	Given an IP address, the Address Resolution Protocol (ARP) can determine the data link address (MAC layer address) to use for packets destined to that station.
Domain Name System (DNS)	Provides name and address resolution as a service to client applications. DNS servers enable humans to use logical node names instead of IP addresses to access network resources.
File Transfer TCP/IP hosts	Enables users to transfer files between Protocol (FTP) by supporting a request/response structure that is independent of specific operating systems.
Simple Mail Transfer Protocol (SMTP)	Used for transferring electronic mail through TCP/IP internetworks. SMTP doesn't provide a mail interface for the user, just one between systems.
Telnet	A terminal emulation application and protocol. Telnet enables PCs and workstations to function as dumb terminals in sessions with host systems on internetworks.
Network File System (NFS)	A family of file-sharing protocols for TCP/IP developed by Sun Microsystems. These protocols enable an NFS client to access disk space on an NFS server as if the drives were directly attached. NFS is the traditional file-sharing protocol in Unix networks.

Table 2.3.5   Address Information Used on TCP/IP Internetworks

Type of Address	How it is Used
Physical addresses	Used by the Data Link Layer
IP addresses	Provide logical network numbers and host IDs. IP addresses consist of 32 bits typically expressed in dotted-decimal form. An example of an IP address is 134.135.100.13.
Logical node names	Identify specific hosts with alphanumeric identifiers, which are easier for users to recall than the numeric IP addresses. An example of a logical node name is MYHOST.MYCOMPANY.COM.

D. NetWare IPX/SPX

The NetWare protocols have been designed with a high degree of modularity, which makes them adaptable to different hardware and simplifies the task of incorporating other protocols into the suite. Windows NT uses a Microsoft implementation of the IPX/SPX suite, the *NWLink IPX/ SPX Compatible Transport,* to communicate with NetWare resources. NWLink IPX/SPX is generally smaller and faster than Microsoft's TCP/IP and, like TCP/IP, it is routable. Because of these advantages, NWLink IPX/SPX is the best choice for modern small networks that don't require Internet connectivity. The NetWare protocol architecture is shown in relation to the OSI model in figure 2.3.4, and its components are described in table 2.3.6.

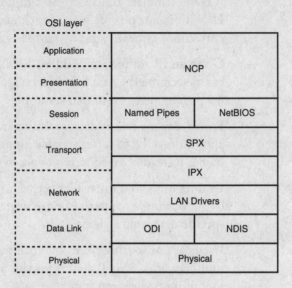

Figure 2.3.4 The NetWare protocol architecture.

Table 2.3.6   Components of NWLink IPX/SPX

Protocol	Description
Internetwork Packet Exchange Protocol (IPX)	A Network layer protocol that provides connectionless (datagram) service. Responsible for internetwork routing and maintaining network logical addresses. Relies on hardware physical addresses found at lower layers to provide network device addressing, which makes it much easier to manage than TCP/IP.
Sequenced Packet Exchange (SPX)	A Transport Layer protocol that provides connection-oriented services with reliable delivery. Reliable delivery is ensured by retransmitting packets in the event of an error. SPX is used in situations in which reliable transmission of data is needed.

Protocol	Description
NetWare Core Protocol (NCP)	Provides remote function calls that support network services, such as file sharing, printing, name management, file locking, and synchronization. NetWare client software uses NCP to access NetWare services. NCP covers aspects of the Session, Presentation, and Application Layers of the OSI reference model.

E. NetBEUI

NetBEUI is a transport protocol that serves as an extension to Microsoft's Network Basic Input/Output System (NetBIOS). Because NetBEUI was developed for an earlier generation of DOS-based PCs, it is small, easy to implement, and relatively fast. Because it was built for small isolated LANs, however, NetBEUI is non-routable, making it somewhat anachronistic in today's diverse and interconnected networking environment. In general, one shouldn't design new LAN's to use NetBEUI.

Fortunately, the NDIS standard enables NetBEUI to coexist with other, routable protocols. For instance, you could configure a network to use NetBEUI for communications on the LAN segment and to use TCP/IP for communications that require routing. Because NetBEUI cannot be routed, you have to use a switch, bridge, or brouter if you need to introduce some isolation on network segments that use it.

F. AppleTalk

AppleTalk is the network computing architecture developed by Apple Computer for the Macintosh family of personal computers (see fig. 2.3.5).

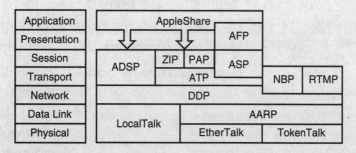

Figure 2.3.5 A layered perspective of the AppleTalk protocol suite.

Table 2.3.7 The AppleTalk Protocol Family

Protocol	Description
Datagram Delivery Protocol (DDP)	A Network Layer protocol that provides connectionless service between two AppleTalk systems.
AppleTalk Transaction Protocol (ATP)	A connectionless Transport Layer protocol that provides reliable service through a system of acknowledgments and retransmissions.

continues

Table 2.3.7   Continued

Protocol	Description
AppleTalk File Protocol (AFP)	Provides remote file services. Responsible for enforcing file system security. Verifies and encrypts logon names and passwords during connection setup.
AppleShare	A client/server system for Macintosh. Provides file and print sharing services.

G.   Data Link Control (DLC)

In a Windows networking environment, the Data Link Control (DLC) protocol is most commonly used to access Hewlett-Packard JetDirect network printers. DLC's more traditional use has been for connectivity to IBM mainframes via 802.2 LLC Type 2.

Summary of Protocol Characteristics

The Microsoft Networking Essentials Test is intended to ensure that you are able to select the appropriate network and transport protocols for various Ethernet and token ring networks. The table below provides you with a quick summary of the most important points of these protocols.

Protocol	Routable	Primary Use	Should Be Used
DLC	No	Communicate with mainframes and printers	Only when required
AppleTalk	Yes	Communicates with Apple Macintosh computers	For Apple Macintosh computers only
IPX	Yes	Novell NetWare networks	For small to moderate-sized networks
TCP/IP	Yes	Internet	For large networks, WAN communications, and Internet access
NetBEUI	No	Small LANs	Only when required for backward compatibility
NFS	Yes[1]	Unix file sharing	For Unix file sharing
SMB	Yes/No[2]	Windows file and print sharing	Windows file and print sharing

1. NFS uses TCP/IP

2. Depends on network layer protocol used

2.3 Exercise

Compare and contrast TCP/IP, IPX/SPX, and NetBEUI.

2.3 Exercise Explanation

NetBEUI is only well-suited for small networks because it is not routable. Because it is not routable, the entire network must be in a single broadcast domain. This does not scale well because excessive broadcasts cause network performance problems.

IPX/SPX is easy to configure because workstations always learn their addresses automatically. It is both fast and routable, and therefore is well-suited to use in large networks. Because networks that use IPX are not joined by a global IPX network, there are no restrictions on IPX network addressing other than network numbers must be unique within an area with IPX connectivity. IPX also must be used for any connections to NetWare servers.

TCP/IP is the language of the Internet and has always been the primary protocol on Unix-based computers. TCP/IP is routable and scales extremely well. It is the protocol of choice on both very large networks and networks that need to connect to the Internet. TCP/IP has historically been considered difficult to configure because network addresses had to be allocated by a central registry to ensure global uniqueness and host addresses had to be configured manually. Although the requirement for global network number uniqueness still exists so that the Internet can function, host configuration has largely been automated in recent years.

2

2.3   Practice Problems

1. Your network includes over 40,000 users at a total of 200 sites connected by WAN circuits. What protocol is most suitable for use with this environment?

   A. DLC

   B. AppleTalk

   C. NWLink IPX

   D. TCP/IP

2. What protocol should you configure if your network needs access to the Internet?

   A. DLC

   B. AppleTalk

   C. NWLink IPX

   D. TCP/IP

3. Your company's new CEO asks you to reconfigure the network file server so that he can access it from his Macintosh computer. What protocol do you need to configure on the server?

   A. DLC

   B. AppleTalk

   C. NWLink IPX

   D. TCP/IP

4. One of the advantages of TCP over UDP is:

   A. TCP uses very small packets.

   B. TCP uses link-state route discovery.

   C. TCP provides error correction.

   D. TCP is faster than any other protocol for small networks.

5. What native TCP/IP protocol would allow file sharing on a Unix system?

   A. TCP/IP

   B. NWLink IPX

   C. SMB

   D. NFS

6. What protocol is used for file sharing on a Windows NT Server?

   A. TCP/IP

   B. NWLink IPX

   C. SMB

   D. NFS

7. You have a Hewlett-Packard JetDirect-family printer to install for shared network use on the same LAN segment as the Windows NT Server. What is the easiest protocol to install for it?

   A. DLC

   B. AppleTalk

   C. NWLink IPX

   D. TCP/IP

8. You need to use the Simple Network Management Protocol (SNMP) to monitor the health of some Unix database servers at a remote site. What protocol does your network need to support?

   A. DLC

   B. AppleTalk

   C. NWLink IPX

   D. TCP/IP

9. ARP involves which two types of information?

   A. Network number and host ID

   B. Network address and data link address

   C. Logical node names and IP address

   D. Protocol type and frame number

10. NFS is functionally most similar to which of the following protocols?

   A. NWLink IPX

   B. TCP/IP

   C. SMB

   D. OSPF

11. Which of the following is true of the IPX/SPX protocol suite used by NetWare?

    A. It requires specialized hardware and configurations.

    B. It is incompatable with other protocols.

    C. Host number allocations must be carefully managed.

    D. It is routable.

12. A consultant is getting ready to configure a new Unix server on your network, and he asks you if it should support file sharing. If you say yes, which protocol will he probably add to the system configuration?

    A. TCP/IP

    B. NWLink IPX

    C. SMB

    D. NFS

13. You have 200 Windows 95 workstations configured with a mixture of TCP/IP and NetBEUI on your office network. The network performance is beginning to degrade because of frequent broadcast storms. What device can you install to reduce this problem while still retaining full connectivity for all the workstations?

    A. Repeater

    B. Bridge

    C. Brouter

    D. Router

14. You have 200 Windows 95 workstations all configured to use TCP/IP on your office network. You need to add another 100 workstations, but frequent broadcast storms are causing performance problems. What device should you add to reduce the broadcasts while still retaining full connectivity for all the workstations?

    A. Repeater

    B. Bridge

    C. Brouter

    D. Router

15. You have to design a large WAN. What protocol should that WAN use?

    A. TCP/IP

    B. NWLink IPX

    C. NetBEUI

    D. AppleTalk

16. You need to design a small network for a software company that is focused on Internet-related products. What protocol should you use?

    A. DLC

    B. TCP/IP

    C. AppleTalk

    D. NWLink IPX

17. What file and print sharing protocol do Windows networks use?

    A. TCP/IP

    B. NWLink IPX

    C. NFS

    D. SMB

18. You have been directed to configure some Windows NT Workstations to use LLC Type 2 connections to communicate with the company's mainframe through an IBM 3745 FEP. Which protocol do you need to install on the Windows NT Workstations?

    A. DLC

    B. TCP/IP

    C. AppleTalk

    D. NWLink IPX

19. You need to configure a Windows NT Server so that a Unix system can use one

of its printers. Which protocol will the Windows NT Server need to use?

- A. DLC
- B. TCP/IP
- C. AppleTalk
- D. NWLink IPX

20. You have to decide which protocol to use for your Windows networking. One requirement is that all workstations must be able to access NetWare servers. Which of the following protocols does this suggest that you should use?

- A. DLC
- B. TCP/IP
- C. AppleTalk
- D. NWLink IPX

21. Which of the following are standards that enable multiple network-layer protocols to coexist on the same computer without having to be aware of the datalink protocol in use?

- A. NDIS
- B. NDS
- C. ODI
- D. DLC

22. TCP uses port numbers:

- A. To identify which virtual circuit the data stream belongs to
- B. To identify the protocol in use
- C. To identify which data streams need to be passed to UDP
- D. For additional speed

23. Which of the following are generally parts of network data packets?

- A. Preamble
- B. Header

- C. Data
- D. Trailer

24. You need to subnet your TCP/IP network. Which of the following protocols might your routers use to communicate routes to each other?

- A. RIP
- B. SNMP
- C. ICMP
- D. OSPF

25. You have a large network with many redundant paths in it. When there is a problem in the network, it takes a long time before the routers all know how to direct the traffic around the problem. What is a reasonable way to alleviate this problem?

- A. Adjust the RIP timers so that route updates happen 10 times as often.
- B. Adjust the RIP timers so that route updates happen 10 times less often.
- C. Convert the routers to use only static routes.
- D. Convert the routers to OSPF.

26. Which part of the IPX family of protocols is most similar to Microsoft's SMB protocol?

- A. IPX
- B. SPX
- C. NCP
- D. ODI

27. Which IP-based protocol should an application use if it requires a reliable transport protocol with automatic error detection and recovery?

- A. TCP
- B. UDP
- C. SNMP
- D. SMTP

28. Which IP-based protocol should an application use if it cannot tolerate the overhead of a reliable transport protocol?

   A. TCP

   B. UDP

   C. SNMP

   D. SMTP

29. Which Novell protocol is most like TCP?

   A. IPX

   B. SPX

   C. NCP

   D. ODI

30. What protocol should you configure if you need to connect to Novell NetWare servers?

   A. NWLink IPX

   B. TCP/IP

   C. DLC

   D. AppleTalk

31. Which Novell protocol is most like UDP?

   A. IPX

   B. SPX

   C. NCP

   D. ODI

32. Which of the following is an advantage of distance vector routing protocols?

   A. They converge faster than link-state protocols.

   B. They use more bandwidth than link-state protocols.

   C. They use more reliable routing metrics than link-state protocols.

   D. They are easier to configure than link-state protocols.

33. Which of the following is a disadvantage of link-state routing protocols?

   A. They converge faster than distance vector protocols.

   B. They use more bandwidth than distance vector protocols.

   C. They are less likely to create loops.

   D. They are harder to configure than distance vector protocols.

34. Using a web browser to connect with www.microsoft.com uses which protocols?

   A. NWLink, NetBIOS, and NetBEUI

   B. TCP, OSPF, and DLC

   C. NWLink, RIP and SMB

   D. TCP, ARP, and DNS

35. It is taking your routers too long to respond to changes in the network. Which protocol change might help them?

   A. NetBIOS to NetBEUI

   B. RIP to OSPF

   C. AppleTalk to NWLink

   D. SMB to TCP/IP

36. Microsoft provides updates and patches to some of its programs on the Internet. Which protocol might you use to download the necessary files?

   A. FTP

   B. UDP

   C. IP

   D. DNS

37. On your network, you have PCs running Windows 95 that access both NetWare and NT Servers. The MIS department needs access to the Internet. Which of the following protocols do you not need at all?

   A. IPX/SPX

   B. TCP/IP

C. NCP

D. DLC

38. In order to check the configuration of your routers from off-site, you use which protocol?

   A. Telnet

   B. DLC

   C. RIP

   D. NFS

39. Which protocol should you configure on an NT Server if Mac computers need to access it for file sharing or printing?

   A. NWLink IPX

   B. TCP/IP

   C. DLC

   D. AppleTalk

40. You have to design a WAN to support 20,000 users and 200 NT Servers.

   Required Result:
   Efficient use of expensive WAN bandwidth

   Desired Results:
   Capbility to triple in size without changing protocol

   Good Internet connectivity

   Proposed solution:
   Use NetBEUI to minimize addressing problems

   Configure regional NT Servers as gateways to TCP/IP for Internet access

   A. This solution meets the required result and both the desired results.

   B. This solution meets the required result and one of the desired results.

C. This solution meets the required result but neither of the desired results.

D. This solution does not meet the required result.

2.3   Answers and Explanations: Practice Problems

1. **D**   TCP/IP makes the most efficient use of WAN circuits.

2. **D**   TCP/IP is the protocol used on the Internet.

3. **B**   Macintosh computers use AppleTalk.

4. **C**   TCP is a reliable protocol and, as such, provides error correction that unreliable protocols, such as UDP, do not.

5. **D**   NFS is the native way of file sharing on most Unix systems.

6. **C**   SMB is the protocol that Windows NT uses for file and print sharing. SMB can be transported inside of other protocols, including TCP/IP, NetBEUI, and NWLink IPX.

7. **A**   DLC is often considered the easiest protocol to configure because it has so few options.

8. **D**   Although SNMP *can* be carried inside of other protocols, it is almost always used with TCP/IP. The fact that the devices you are monitoring run Unix makes this an easy question because Unix devices almost exclusively support TCP/IP.

9. **B**   ARP finds the data link address by asking all stations whether they have the network layer address being looked for.

10. **C**   NFS is functionally most similar to SMB because they are both used for file sharing.

11. **D**   The IPX/SPX protocol suite popularized by NetWare is routable.

12. **D**   NFS is the traditional file-sharing protocol on Unix systems.

13. **C** You have to use a brouter to maintain full connectivity for both the routed TCP/IP and the bridged NetBEUI.

14. **D** Routers are used to contain broadcasts and to reduce broadcast storms.

15. **A** TCP/IP is considered the best protocol for a WAN.

16. **B** TCP/IP is the protocol used on the Internet, so it would be the best fit for this company.

17. **D** Windows networks use SMB as their file and print sharing protocol.

18. **A** DLC is used for LLC Type 2 connections, which are most commonly used to access mainframes and HP JetDirect printers.

19. **B** To interoperate with Unix systems, you'll need to configure TCP/IP.

20. **D** NWLink IPX is used to access NetWare servers.

21. **A, C** NDIS and ODI both define programmatic interfaces that enable upper-layer protocols to share the same network card seamlessly.

22. **A** TCP uses port numbers to identify which virtual circuit the data stream belongs to.

23. **B, C, D** Headers, data, and trailers are all generally parts of network data packets. Only Ethernet frames use a preamble.

24. **A, D** RIP and OSPF are both routing protocols that you might use.

25. **D** Converting the routers to OSPF enables them to learn about network changes faster.

26. **C** Novell's NCP protocol is similar in functionality to Microsoft's SMB protocol.

27. **A** TCP is a reliable transport protocol with automatic error detection and recovery.

28. **B** UDP is an IP-based protocol sometimes used to avoid the overhead of a reliable transport protocol.

29. **B** SPX is the Novell protocol most like TCP.

30. **A** NWLink IPX is used to connect to Novell NetWare servers.

31. **A** IPX is the Novell protocol most like UDP.

32. **D** Distance vector routing protocols are easier to configure than link-state protocols.

33. **D** Link-state routing protocols are harder to configure than distance vector protocols.

34. **D** TCP, ARP, & DNS are all used. DNS resolves the name into an address, ARP finds the hardware address of your default router, and TCP is used for the actual connection.

35. **B** Changing from RIP to OSPF can help routers learn about changes in the network faster.

36. **A** FTP is sometimes used to download files over the Internet.

37. **D** There was no connectivity requirement described for DLC.

38. **A** Telnet is a convenient way of providing a virtual terminal connection to devices like routers.

39. **D** Mac computers use AppleTalk for file sharing or printing.

40. **D** This solution does not meet the requirement because NetBEUI does not use WAN bandwidth efficiently.

2

2.3   Key Words

AppleTalk

ARP

Data

Datagram

DLC

DNS

FTP

Header

Internet Protocol (IP)

IP address

IPX

IPX/SPX

Logical node names

NetBEUI

NetBIOS

NFS

NWLink

OSI model

OSPF

Packet

RIP

SMB

SMTP

SNMP

SPX

TCP

TCP/IP

TELNET

Trailer

Transport protocol

UDP

2.4   Selecting the Appropriate Connectivity Devices for Various Token Ring and Ethernet Networks

> Connectivity devices include repeaters, bridges, switches, routers, brouters, and gateways.

An *internetwork* consists of multiple independent networks that are connected and can share remote resources. These networks can be dissimilar in type. The device that connects the independent networks might need to determine when packets stay on the local network and when they are forwarded to a remote network.

A.   Repeaters

Repeaters work at the Physical Layer of the OSI model. Each media type has a maximum distance that it can carry data reliably. The purpose of a *repeater* is to regenerate the data signal and thereby extend this maximum distance (see fig. 2.4.1).

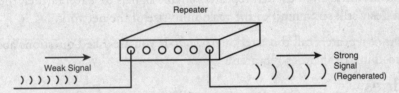

Figure 2.4.1   A repeater regenerates a weak signal.

Characteristics of Repeaters

The characteristics of repeaters are:

- Repeaters regenerate a signal that comes in on one port and transmit it out through the other repeater ports.

- They operate mostly in the OSI Physical Layer.

- They do not filter or interpret—merely repeat (regenerate) a signal, passing all network traffic (even errors) in all directions.

- Repeaters do not require any addressing information from the data frame because they merely repeat bits of data. This means that if data is corrupt, a repeater repeats it anyway. A repeater even repeats a broadcast storm caused by a malfunctioning adapter.

- They are inexpensive.

- They are simple.

- Although they cannot connect networks with dissimilar data frames (such as a token ring network and an Ethernet network), some repeaters can connect segments with similar frame types but dissimilar cabling.

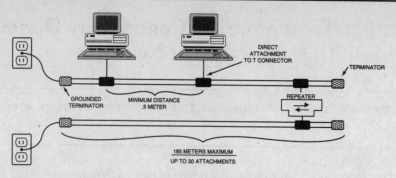

Figure 2.4.2 Using a repeater to extend an Ethernet LAN. Connecting two Ethernet cable segments results in doubling the potential length of the network.

All network designs limit the size of the network. The most important reason for this limitation is *signal propagation.* Networks must work within reasonable expectations about the maximum time a signal might be in transit. This is known as *propagation delay*—the time it takes for a signal to reach the farthest point on the network and return. If this maximum propagation delay interval expires and no signals are encountered, a network error condition is assumed. Given the maximum propagation delay allowed, it is possible to calculate the maximum permissible cable length for the network. Even though repeaters enable signals to travel farther, the maximum propagation delay still sets a limit to the maximum size of the network.

Most vendors of repeaters call those repeaters *hubs.* If you are asked questions about hubs, remember to think of them as repeaters.

B. Bridges

Bridges work at the Data Link Layer of the OSI model. Bridges can extend the maximum size of a network (see fig 2.4.3). Although the bridged network in figure 2.4.3 looks much like the earlier example of a network with a repeater, the bridge is a much more flexible device. Bridges operate at the MAC sublayer of the OSI Data Link Layer.

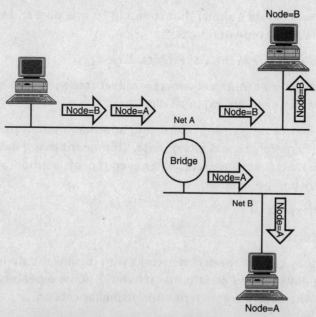

Figure 2.4.3 Extending a network with a bridge.

A repeater passes on all signals that it receives. A bridge is more selective and passes only those signals targeted for a computer on the other side. A bridge can make this determination because each device on the network is identified by a unique address. Each packet that is transmitted bears the address of the device to which it should be delivered. The process works as follows:

1. The bridge receives every packet on LAN A and LAN B.

2. The bridge learns from the packets which device addresses are located on LAN A and which are on LAN B. The bridge then builds a table with this information.

3. Packets on LAN A that are addressed to devices on LAN A are discarded, as are packets on LAN B that are addressed to devices on LAN B. These packets can be delivered without the help of the bridge.

4. Packets on LAN A addressed to devices on LAN B are retransmitted to LAN B for delivery. Similarly, the appropriate packets on LAN B are retransmitted to LAN A.

On truly ancient bridges, the network administrator had to manually configure the address tables. Modern bridges are called *learning bridges*. Learning bridges function as described in step 2, automatically updating their address tables as devices are added to or removed from the network.

Bridges accomplish two major things:

- **Divide busy networks into smaller segments:** If the network is designed so that most packets can be delivered without crossing a bridge, traffic on the individual network segments can be reduced. If the Accounting and Sales departments are overloading the LAN, for example, you might divide the network so that Accounting is on one segment and Sales on another. Only when Accounting and Sales must exchange packets does a packet need to cross the bridge between the segments.

- **Extend the physical size of a network:** Although the individual segments (made up of the cable and repeaters) still are restricted by the maximum size imposed by the network design limits, bridges enable network designers to stretch the distances between segments and extend the overall size of the network.

Bridges have certain limitations that become more significant in complex network situations:

- A network with bridges generally cannot make use of redundant paths.

- Bridges cannot analyze the network to determine the fastest route over which to forward a packet. When multiple routes exist, this is a desirable capability, particularly in wide area networks (WANs) where some routes are often considerably slower than others.

- Bridges do not filter broadcast packets, so they are of no help in avoiding broadcast storms.

- Bridges cannot join dissimilar types of LANs because bridges depend on the physical addresses of devices. Physical device addresses are functions of the Data Link Layer, and different Data Link Layer protocols are used for each type of network. A bridge, therefore, cannot be used to join an Ethernet segment to a token ring segment.

C.   Switches

A relatively recent addition to the networking scene has been the advent of *switches*. Switches operate at the Data Link Layer of the OSI model. A switch performs the same function as a learning bridge, but typically with many more ports and at higher throughput rates.

Switches do not block broadcast packets. The primary reason people use switches is to improve network performance by reducing network contention. A switch filters out traffic that isn't destined for a station on a given port, so that the station sees less network traffic and can perform better.

It has become common practice in the network industry to replace repeaters (often called *hubs*) with switches to increase the network's performance without requiring any changes to computers on the network.

D. Routers

Routers work at the Network Layer of the OSI model. Because each network in an internetwork is assigned an address, each network can be considered logically separate; that is, each network functions independently of other networks on the internetwork. Internetwork connectivity devices, such as routers, use network address information to assist in the efficient delivery of messages. Using network address information to deliver messages is called *routing*. The common feature that unites internetwork connectivity devices (routers and brouters) is that these devices can perform routing.

Routers organize the large network in terms of logical network segments (see fig. 2.4.4). Each network segment is assigned an address so that every packet has both a destination network address and a destination device address.

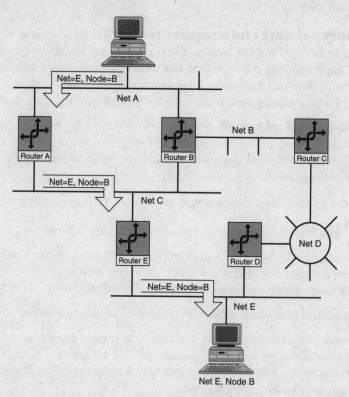

Figure 2.4.4   A complex network based on routers. Router A knows that the most efficient step is to send the packet to Router E, not Router B.

Routers are more intelligent than bridges. Not only do routers build tables of network locations, they also use algorithms to determine the most efficient path for sending a packet to any given network. Even if a particular network segment isn't directly attached to the router, the router knows the best way to send a packet to a device on that network.

Notice in figure 2.4.4 that Router B presents a redundant path to the path Router A provides. Routers can cope with this situation because they exchange routing information to ensure that packet loops don't persist. If Router A fails, Router B provides a backup message path.

You can use routers to divide large, busy LANs into smaller segments, much as you can use bridges. Routers, however, also can connect different network types. Notice that the network in figure 2.4.4 includes a token ring segment with the Ethernet segments. On such networks, a router is the device of choice.

Routers come in two types:

- **Static Routers:** These routers do not determine paths dynamically. Instead, you must configure the routing table, specifying potential routes for packets. If the network connections change, a router using statically configured routes must be manually reconfigured. These preprogrammed routers cannot adjust to changing network conditions.

- **Dynamic Routers:** These routers have the capability to determine routes dynamically (and to find the optimum path among redundant routes) based on information obtained from other routers via a routing protocol or routing algorithm.

After route costs are established, routers can select routes—either statically or dynamically—as follows:

- **Static route selection:** This selection method uses only routes that have been programmed by the network administrator. Static routers can use this method and no other.

- **Dynamic route selection:** Under this selection method, routing cost information is used to select the best route for a given packet. As network conditions change and are reflected in routing tables, the router selects different paths to continue using the lowest cost path.

Two common methods that dynamic routers use to discover routes are *distance vector routing* and *link-state routing*.

> Remember that routers are always used to connect different networks that run the same protocol. Also, if a question asks about subnetting (the process of subdividing a network into smaller pieces), it is implying that you must use either a router or a brouter.

Table 2.4.1   Generic Routing Protocol Comparison

	Distance Vector	Link State
How often routing information is sent	Repeated broadcasts	Only when a route changes
Which routes are transmitted	All routes, even those learned second-hand	Only routes for directly connected networks or subnets
How long until all routers know about route changes	At least several minutes, possibly many minutes	Seconds to tens of seconds
Ease of configuration	Simple and easy	More complex
Bandwidth overhead	Substantial in large networks	Small even in large networks (unless unstable)

Characteristics of Routers

The characteristics of routers are:

- Routers connect different types of LANs (different media types).

- They connect different networks (different network numbers).

- They isolate broadcasts to within their originating network, reducing and containing broadcast storms.

- Protocols used to send data through a router must be specifically designed to support routing functions. IP, IPX, and AppleTalk are routable protocols. NetBEUI and DLC are nonroutable protocols.

- Routers usually are employed to connect a LAN to a wide area network (WAN). WANs often are designed with multiple paths, and routers can ensure that the various paths are used most efficiently.

- There are two types: static and dynamic.

E. Brouters

A *brouter* is a router that also can act as a bridge. A brouter attempts to deliver packets based on network protocol information, but if a particular Network Layer protocol isn't supported, the brouter bridges the packet using device addresses.

If you need to connect networks that are using both a routable protocol such as TCP/IP and a non-routable protocol such as NetBEUI, you need to use a brouter. This gives you the subnetting advantages of a router, while maintaining the full connectivity of a bridge.

Almost all dedicated hardware routers (including those from 3Com, Cisco, and Bay Networks, for example) include an option to support bridging and can be considered brouters. *Brouter* is becoming an obsolete term in the networking industry, but it is still used on Microsoft's tests because it emphasizes the combination of bridging and routing functionality.

F. Gateways

Gateways function at the Application Layer of the OSI model. The term *gateway* originally was used in the Internet protocol suite to refer to a router. Today, the term *gateway* more commonly refers to a system functioning at the top levels of the OSI model that enables communication between dissimilar protocol systems. A gateway generally is dedicated to a specific conversion, and the exact functioning of the gateway depends on the protocol translations it must perform. Gateways commonly function at the OSI Application Layer.

Gateways connect dissimilar environments by removing the layered protocol information of incoming packets and replacing it with the packet information necessary for the dissimilar environment (see fig. 2.4.5).

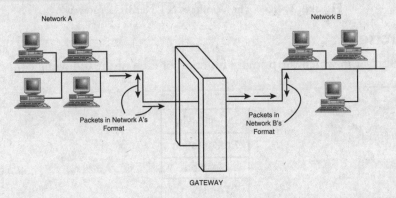

Figure 2.4.5 Gateways convert packet protocol information to connect dissimilar environments.

Gateways can be implemented as software, hardware, or a combination of both.

The NetBIOS Gateway

Windows NT 4.0 RAS can act as an IP or an IPX router, but RAS's NetBIOS gateway is an even more powerful feature. Not only does the NetBIOS gateway forward remote packets to the LAN, it also acts as a gateway, providing NetBEUI clients with access to the LAN even if the LAN uses only TCP/IP or IPX/SPX (see fig. 2.4.6).

The NetBIOS gateway is very much like the gateways described in this section. The NetBIOS gateway accepts a packet from the remote computer using one protocol (NetBEUI) and converts the packet, stripping incompatible protocol headers and replacing them with the headers the packet needs to circulate under a different protocol.

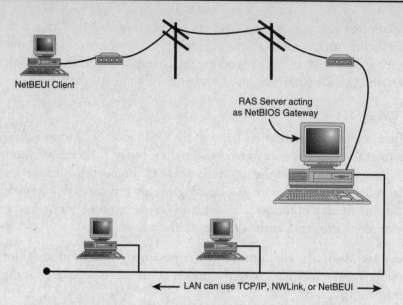

Figure 2.4.6 The Windows NT NetBIOS gateway.

2.4 Exercise

Name the OSI layer in which the primary function of each of the following connectivity devices occurs.

| Application |
| Presentation |
| Session |
| Transport |
| Network |
| Data Link |
| Physical |

1. Router

2. Concentrator

3. Bridge

4. Gateway

5. Hub

6. Switch

7. Repeater

8. Brouter

2.4   Exercise Explanation

1. Router: Network

2. Concentrator: Physical

3. Bridge: Data Link

4. Gateway: Application

5. Hub: Physical

6. Switch: Data Link

7. Repeater: Repeater

8. Brouter: Data Link and Network

2

2.4   Practice Problems

1. You need to connect an Ethernet network with a token ring network. Which device should you use?

    A. Repeater

    B. Bridge

    C. Router

    D. Gateway

2. You need to use 10Base-T to connect two computers that are 180 meters apart. What is the least expensive device you could use?

    A. Repeater

    B. Bridge

    C. Router

    D. Gateway

3. A multiport repeater:

    A. Is used to monitor network traffic

    B. Is a more technical name for a hub

    C. Must filter network traffic

    D. Provides ports for different networks such as token ring and Ethernet to connect

4. One simple, inexpensive way to connect or to extend two sections of the same network without any packet filtering is to install:

    A. A gateway

    B. A router

    C. A repeater

    D. A switch

5. A network is encountering a large number of Ethernet errors after installing yet another repeater. This problem is likely due to:

    A. Exceeding the network size limitations

    B. A need for a transceiver

    C. Using the wrong network number

    D. An incorrectly configured repeater

6. Due to the size of your network, you can't add any more repeaters to extend it. You should instead consider:

    A. A gateway

    B. A multiport repeater

    C. Rewiring with Category 5

    D. A bridge

7. What device is used to connect different networks?

    A. A gateway

    B. A bridge

    C. A repeater

    D. A router

8. In order to connect your token ring segment to your Ethernet segment you need a:

    A. Repeater

    B. Router

    C. Bridge

    D. Gateway

9. Network reliability is crucial for your company, and you have included redundancy in many components of your network design. In order to make efficient use of your network's redundant paths, you need to use:

    A. Bridges

    B. Repeaters

    C. Gateways

    D. Routers

10. Which connectivity device chooses to use the most efficient path between two networks?

    A. A repeater

    B. A bridge

C. A router

D. A gateway

11. The least expensive device that can connect two segments of coaxial cable is:

   A. A repeater

   B. A bridge

   C. A router

   D. All of the above

12. The retiming function of a repeater is necessary to:

   A. Allow data to cross time zones without corruption

   B. Keep network devices synchronized

   C. Prevent time outs

   D. Remove electrical noise from the signal

13. You need to use 10Base-T to connect two computers that are 180 meters apart. What is the fastest device you could use?

   A. Repeater

   B. Bridge

   C. Router

   D. Gateway

14. Your network has 150 stations all running NetBEUI, and traffic levels are becoming a problem. What device can help alleviate the problem without reconfiguring any workstations?

   A. Repeater

   B. Bridge

   C. Router

   D. Gateway

15. In token ring, subnets are connected via which of the following?

   A. Repeaters

   B. Bridges

C. Routers

D. Gateways

16. According to the OSI model, bridges work at the _____ and _____ layers of the network, connecting segments using the same LLC protocols.

   A. Data Link and Physical

   B. Data Link and Network

   C. Network and Transport

   D. Physical and Transport

17. Which device do you need for a station that uses only TCP/IP to communicate with another station on the network that uses only NetBEUI?

   A. Switch

   B. Router

   C. RPC

   D. Gateway

18. You need to connect many 10Base-T network segments. Which network device gives you the highest overall performance?

   A. Repeater

   B. Switch

   C. Router

   D. Gateway

19. You have PCs running only NWLink IPX. They need to communicate with a mainframe that expects LLC Type 2 connections. What device do you need to install?

   A. Repeater

   B. Switch

   C. Router

   D. Gateway

2

20. Your network has grown to 200 PCs and is beginning to experience severe broadcast storms. Which device is used to contain broadcasts?

    A. Repeater

    B. Switch

    C. Router

    D. Gateway

21. You need to configure a device to do protocol translation. What device fits this description?

    A. Repeater

    B. Switch

    C. Router

    D. Gateway

22. You need to extend a network farther than repeater limits will allow. Which device should you use?

    A. Repeater

    B. Bridge

    C. Router

    D. Gateway

23. You have a WAN. Which device uses the bandwidth most efficiently?

    A. Repeater

    B. Switch

    C. Router

    D. Bridge

24. You have redundant paths in your network. Which device uses the paths most efficiently?

    A. Repeater

    B. Switch

    C. Router

    D. Gateway

25. You have two networks that use different protocols. Which device must you use to connect them?

    A. Repeater

    B. Switch

    C. Router

    D. Gateway

26. Which network device removes electrical noise from a signal, but otherwise passes it without modification?

    A. Repeater

    B. Switch

    C. Router

    D. Gateway

27. **Scenario:**
    You have a 200- PC network running a mixture of NWLink IPX and NetBEUI. Broadcast storms are already a frequent problem, and you need to add 100 more PCs.

    Required:
    You need to implement a strategy to minimize broadcasts while allowing for continued growth.

    Desirable:
    1. Minimal reconfiguration
    2. Minimum expense

    Proposed solution:
    Replace the cabling with Category 5 and implement 100Base-TX switching to the desktop.

    A. Meets the requirement and both desirable goals

    B. Meets the requirement and one of the desirable goals

    C. Meets the requirement but neither of the desirable goals

    D. Does not meet the requirement

28. **Scenario:**
You have a 200-PC network running a mixture of NWLink IPX and NetBEUI. Broadcast storms are already a frequent problem, and you need to add 100 more PCs.

Required:
You need to implement a strategy to minimize broadcasts while allowing for continued growth.

Desirable:
1. Minimal reconfiguration
2. Minimum expense

Proposed solution:
Configure the stations running NetBEUI to use NWLink IPX instead and install an IPX router.

   A. Meets the requirement and both desirable goals

   B. Meets the requirement and one of the desirable goals

   C. Meets the requirement but neither of the desirable goals

   D. Does not meet the requirement

29. What is the least expensive device that connects different Ethernet media types?

   A. Repeater

   B. Bridge

   C. Router

   D. Gateway

30. You have a network that includes Ethernet, token ring, and FDDI. What device can join all of these?

   A. Repeater

   B. Bridge

   C. Router

   D. Gateway

31. Which device decides whether to forward a data frame based on the hardware address in the frame?

   A. Repeater

   B. Bridge

   C. Router

   D. Gateway

32. Which device decides whether to forward a data frame based on the logical address in the frame?

   A. Repeater

   B. Bridge

   C. Router

   D. Gateway

33. You have decided to subnet your network to reduce the broadcast levels. Which device do you use?

   A. Repeater

   B. Bridge

   C. Router

   D. Gateway

34. You have to connect to the Internet. Which device do you use?

   A. Repeater

   B. Bridge

   C. Router

   D. Gateway

35. The Windows NT servers your predecessor had configured for routing don't reroute traffic when a LAN segment goes down. What could be the problem?

   A. They are configured for Open Shortest Path First, and they always try to use the first path they learned.

   B. They are configured for RIP, which is a distance vector protocol.

C. They are configured for static routing.

D. They are using a link-state protocol.

36. The function of a traditional switch is:

    A. To switch between network types such as Ethernet and token ring

    B. To switch between network protocols such as NetBEUI and TCP

    C. To bridge network segments

    D. To block out broadcast packets for improved network efficiency

37. As a security measure, your Internet firewall isn't allowed to learn routes dynamically. This is a good reason for using:

    A. Network address translation (NAT)

    B. Proxies

    C. Firewalls

    D. Static routes

38. Which routing algorithm generates more traffic in a stable network?

    A. Distance vector

    B. Link state

    C. TPC/IP

    D. DNS

39. Gateways require

    A. Specialized configurable hardware

    B. An intelligent hub

    C. Identical protocol environments

    D. Different protocols

40. Your network utilization is high because of too much broadcast traffic. One way of improving this situation isto install:

    A. A network filter

    B. A router

    C. A switch

    D. A gateway

2.4 Answers and Explanations: Practice Problems

1. **C** Routers are the networking device that can connect different types of data links.

2. **A** A repeater is the least expensive device listed, and it would allow each 10Base-T cable to be up to 100 meters.

3. **B** A multiport repeater is a more technical name for an hub.

4. **C** Using a repeater is a simple, inexpensive way to connect or to extend two sections of the same network without any packet filtering.

5. **A** Exceeding the network size limitations generates a lot of Ethernet errors in the form of late collisions.

6. **D** Using a bridge starts the network size limits over at each port.

7. **D** A router is used to connect different networks or subnets.

8. **B** You need a router to connect a token ring segment to an Ethernet segment.

9. **D** Routers are able to take advantage of multiple redundant paths.

10. **C** A router can be configured to choose to use the most efficient path between two networks.

11. **A** A repeater is the least expensive device listed that can connect two segments of coaxial cable.

12. **D** The retiming function of a repeater is necessary to remove electrical noise from the signal.

13. **A** This distance is within the limits supported by a repeater, and because repeaters operate at the lowest layers of the OSI model, they have the least overhead.

14. **B** Because NetBEUI is not routable, you have to use a bridge or switch to filter this traffic.

15. **C** Routers are always used to connect subnets.

16. **A**   Bridges work at the Data Link and Physical Layers of the network. All devices that work at one layer must also include components of the lower layers.

17. **D**   Gateways must be used any time there is a translation from one protocol to another.

18. **B**   A switch is the highest performance device listed because it has lower latency than a router and it hides network traffic from ports that don't need to see that traffic.

19. **D**   You have to use a gateway any time there is a translation from one protocol to another.

20. **C**   Routers are used to contain broadcasts.

21. **D**   Gateways are the only devices that do protocol translation.

22. **B**   Bridges allow you to extend the same network farther than repeater limits allow. You can't use a routers because they divide networks.

23. **C**   Routers use the bandwidth on a WAN most efficiently.

24. **C**   Routers can calculate how to use redundant paths most efficiently.

25. **D**   Gateways must be used between networks that use different protocols.

26. **A**   Repeaters remove electrical noise from a signal but otherwise pass it without modification.

27. **D**   Replacing the cabling with Category 5 and implementing 100Base-TX switching to the desktop does not meet the requirement because it does nothing to change the broadcast levels.

28. **A**   Configuring the stations running NetBEUI to use NWLink IPX instead and installing an IPX router reduces broadcasts while requiring minimal reconfiguration and expense. You might even be able to use an existing NT Server or NetWare server for the IPX router if you really have no budget.

29. **A**   A repeater is the least expensive device listed that connects different Ethernet media types.

30. **C**   Routers must be used to join networks with different data links.

31. **B**   A bridge decides whether to forward a data frame based on the hardware address in the frame.

32. **C**   A router decides whether to forward a data frame based on the logical address in the frame.

33. **C**   Routers are the only type of device that can divide a network into subnets.

34. **C**   Routers are used to connect to the Internet.

35. **C**   It is still common to configure Windows NT servers for static routing, in which an administrator has to reconfigure the routing table to reflect network changes.

36. **C**   A classical switch is just an high-performance bridge with a lot of ports.

37. **D**   If the firewall can't learn routes dynamically, the only alternative is to use static routes.

38. **A**   Distance vector routing protocols produce much more traffic than link-state protocols in a stable environment because they have to rebroadcast their entire routing table periodically.

39. **D**   Gateways are only used to convert between different protocols.

40. **B**   Routers are used, among other things, to filter broadcasts.

2.4   Key Words

Bridge

Brouter

Gateway

Hub

Internetwork

Repeater

Router

2.5 Learning the Characteristics, Requirements, and Appropriate Situations for WAN Connection Services

---

WAN connection services include: T1, X.25, ISDN, Frame Relay, and ATM.

A. Digital and Analog Signaling

Signaling amounts to communicating information. The information being communicated can take one of two forms:

Analog	Changes continuously and can take on many different values. Music is a good example.
	Analog signals constantly vary in one or more values, and these changes in values can be used to represent data (see fig. 2.5.1). Analog waveforms frequently take the form of sine waves that have these characteristics: frequency, amplitude, and phase. These characteristics can be used either in combination or individually to encode data.
Digital	Characterized by discrete states, typically "on" and "off" or "one" and "zero." Computer data is a good example.
	Because computer data is inherently digital, most WANs use some form of digital signaling.

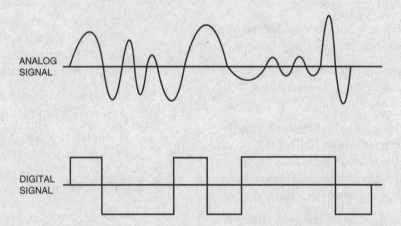

Figure 2.5.1   Analog signals constantly change and take on values throughout the range of possible values. Digital signals take on only two (or a few) specific states.

Frequently, information existing as one form must be converted to the other. This conversion involves the use of an encoding scheme that enables the original information to be recovered from a signal after the signal has been received. When an analog or a digital signal is altered so that it contains information, the process is called *modulation* or *encoding*.

A *modem* is the most common computer connectivity device that transmits an analog signal. Modems transmit digital computer signals over telephone lines by converting them to analog form. Modems are wonderfully handy for PC-to-PC communications or for accessing a LAN from a remote location, but modems are generally too slow and too unreliable for linking LAN segments into a WAN.

B. The Public Switched Telephone Network (PSTN)

Public telephone networks offer two general types of service:

- **Dial-up services:** The customer pays on a per-use basis. Subscribers don't have exclusive access to a particular data path.

- **Leased dedicated services:** The customer is granted exclusive access to some amount of bandwidth.

Table 2.5.1   Types of Leased Dedicated Services

Type	Description
T1	A very popular digital line, *T1,* provides point-to-point connections and transmits a total of 24 channels across two wire pairs—one pair for sending and one for receiving—for a transmission rate of 1.544 Mbps in each direction. *DS-1* service is a full T1 line.[1]
T3	T3 is similar to T1, but T3 has an even higher capacity. In fact, a T3 line can transmit data at up to 45 Mbps.
Fractional and multiple T1 or T3	Subdivided channels of a T1 or T3 line or combined channels of a T1 or T3 line, respectively. Each channel of a T1's 24-channel bandwidth can transmit at 64 Kbps. This single-channel service is called *DS-0,* and it is one of the most popular service types.
Digital data service (DDS)	Usually implies a relatively low-speed digital service used for SNA connectivity. DDS circuits usually transmit data point-to-point at 2.4, 4.8, 9.6, or 56 Kbps.
Switched 56	A full-duplex, wide area, digital data line offering 56-kbits/s service on a dial-up basis.

1. DS-2 is four T1 lines. This is uncommon. You typically have to order as a fractional T3.

C.   Packet Services

Many organizations must communicate between several points. Leasing a line between each pair of points can prove too costly. Many telecommunications services are now available to route packets between different sites. Packet-routing services include:

X.25

Frame Relay

ISDN

ATM

These services are available on a leased basis from service providers. An organization that must communicate between many sites simply pays to connect each site to the service, and the service assumes the responsibility of routing packets. The expense of operating the network is then shared among all network subscribers. Because the exact switching process is concealed from the subscriber, these networks frequently are depicted as a communication cloud. This sort of WAN architecture can be vastly more cost effective than leasing enough lines to provide equivalent connectivity.

1. Virtual Circuits

Packet-switching networks use virtual circuits to route data from the source to the destination. A *virtual circuit* is a specific path through the network—a chain of communication links leading from the source to the destination (as opposed to a scheme in which each packet finds its own path). Virtual circuits enable the network to provide better error checking and flow control.

Types of Virtual Circuits	Description
Switched Virtual Circuit (SVC)	Is created for a specific communication session and then disappears after the session. The next time the computers communicate, a different virtual circuit might be used.
Permanent Virtual Circuit (PVC)	A permanent route through the network that is always available to the customer. With a PVC, charges may or may not be billed on a per-use basis.

2. X.25

X.25 is a packet-switching network standard, referred to as *Recommendation X.25*, implemented most commonly in old or international WANs.

X.25 is one level of a three-level stack that spans the Network, Data Link, and Physical Layers (see fig. 2.5.2). The middle layer, *Link Access Procedures-Balanced (LAPB),* is a bit-oriented, full-duplex, synchronous Data Link Layer LLC protocol. Physical Layer connectivity is provided by a variety of standards, including X.21, X.21bis, and V.32.

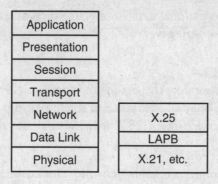

Figure 2.5.2 The relationship of X.25 to the OSI reference model.

X.25 packet-switching networks provide the options of permanent or switched virtual circuits. X.25 is required to provide reliable service and end-to-end flow control. Because each device on a network can operate more than one virtual circuit, X.25 must provide error and flow control for each virtual circuit.

The error checking and flow control slow down X.25. Generally, X.25 networks are implemented with line speeds up to 64 Kbps. These speeds are suitable for the mainframe terminal activity that comprised the bulk of network traffic when X.25 was defined. Such speeds, however, are inadequate to provide LAN-speed services, which typically require speeds of 1 Mbps or better. X.25 networks, therefore, are poor choices for providing LAN application services in a WAN environment.

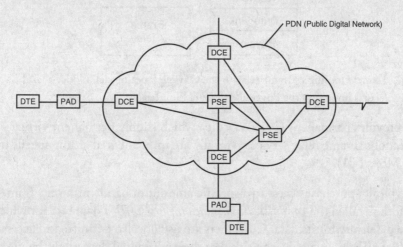

Figure 2.5.3 A typical X.25 network.

In X.25 parlance, a computer or terminal is called *data terminal equipment (DTE)*. A DTE could also be a gateway providing access to a local network. *Data communications equipment (DCE)* provides access to the *public switched telephone network (PSTN)*. A PSE is a packet-switching exchange, also called a *switch* or *switching node*.

The X.25 protocol defines the communication between the DTE and the DCE. A device called a *packet assembler/disassembler (PAD)* translates asynchronous input from the DTE into packets suitable for the PDN.

X.25 should be used for international data circuits in which other, higher-speed technologies are either not available or not cost-effective.

3. Frame Relay

Frame relay was designed to support the *Broadband Integrated Services Digital Network (B-ISDN)*. The specifications for frame relay address some of the limitations of X.25. Frame relay is a packet-switching network service like X.25, but frame relay was designed around newer, faster fiber-optic networks.

Unlike X.25, frame relay assumes a reliable network. This enables frame relay to eliminate much of the X.25 overhead required to provide reliable service on less reliable networks. Frame relay networks rely on higher-level protocol layers to provide error control.

Frame relay typically is implemented as a public data network and, therefore, is regarded as a WAN protocol.

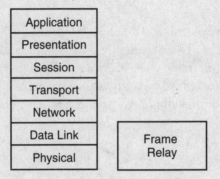

Figure 2.5.4   The relationship of frame relay to the OSI reference model. Notice that the scope of frame relay is limited to the Physical and Data Link Layers.

Frame relay provides permanent virtual circuits, which supply permanent virtual pathways for WAN connections. Frame relay services typically are implemented at line speeds from 56 Kbps up to 1.544 Mbps (T1).

Customers typically purchase access to a specific amount of bandwidth on a frame-relay service. This bandwidth is called the *committed information rate (CIR)*, a data rate for which the customer has guaranteed delivery for its data. Customers are usually also permitted to access data rates faster than their CIR by incurring the risk that their additional data might be discarded by the network if it becomes congested. Many people feel that this is an acceptable risk because most applications can tolerate some amount of packet loss.

Frame relay circuits generally should be used when they are less expensive than equivalent point-to-point circuits, and the data being transported can tolerate the additional delay that packet switching introduces.

Frame relay has less overhead than other packet- or cell-switching technologies such as ATM and X.25.

4. ISDN and B-ISDN

Integrated Services Digital Network (ISDN) is a term used for a group of ITU (CCITT) standards designed to provide full-featured, next-generation services via digital telephone networks.

The original idea behind ISDN was to enable existing phone lines to carry digital communications. Thus, ISDN is more like traditional telephone service than some of the other WAN services discussed in this chapter. ISDN is intended as a dial-up service and not as a permanent, 24-hour connection. Like other dial-up services, it often includes a per-use fee.

ISDN Types	Description
Basic Rate ISDN (BRI)	The most common type, originally intended to replace standard analog telephone lines. Uses three channels. Two channels (called *B channels*) carry the digital data at 64 Kbps. A third channel (called the *D channel*) provides link and signaling information at 16 Kbps. Commonly described as *2B+D*. A single PC transmitting through ISDN can sometimes use both B channels simultaneously, providing a maximum data rate of 128 Kbps (or higher with compression).
Primary Rate ISDN (PRI)	Larger scale, supports 23 B channels at 64 Kbps and one 64-Kbps D channel. Sometimes used in place of a T1.
Broadband ISDN (B-ISDN)	A refinement of ISDN that is defined to support higher-bandwidth applications. Physical Layer support for B-ISDN is provided by *Asynchronous Transfer Mode (ATM)* and the *Synchronous Optical Network (SONET)*. Some typical B-ISDN data rates are 51 Mbps, 155 Mbps, and 622 Mbps.

ISDN BRI circuits should be used for places that don't need full-time connectivity or high speeds. If you have many dial-in connections using BRIs, it is most cost effective to have them dial in to different channels on a PRI.

5. Asynchronous Transfer Mode (ATM)

Asynchronous Transfer Mode (ATM) is considered the best choice for mixing voice, video, and data. It is a high-bandwidth switching technology developed by the ITU Telecommunications Standards Sector (ITU-TSS). An organization called the ATM Forum is responsible for defining ATM implementation characteristics. ATM can be layered on other Physical Layer technologies, such as SONET or SDH (see fig. 2.5.5).

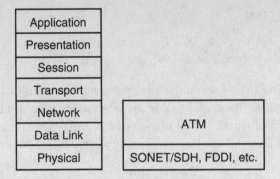

Figure 2.5.5   The relationship of ATM to the OSI reference model.

ATM is based on fixed-length, 53-byte cells (with 5 bytes of header and 48 bytes of data), whereas other technologies employ frames that can vary in length to accommodate different amounts of data. Because ATM cells are uniform in length, switching mechanisms can be easily implemented in hardware to operate with a high level of efficiency. This high efficiency results in very high data-transfer rates. Some ATM systems can operate at several gigabits per second, but the most common two speeds for ATM are 155 Mbps and 622 Mbps.

Asynchronous delivery refers to the characteristic of ATM in which transmission time slots don't occur periodically (as in the traditional telecommunications TDM environment) but are granted at irregular intervals as needed. Traffic that is time-critical, such as voice or video, can be given priority over data traffic that can be delayed slightly with no ill effect. A high-priority transmission need not be held until its next time slot allocation. Instead, it might be required to wait only until the current 53-byte cell has been transmitted.

As in other switched WAN services, devices communicate on ATM networks by establishing a virtual circuit.

ATM is relatively new technology, and only a few suppliers provide the equipment necessary to support it. (ATM networks must use ATM-compatible switches, routers, and other connectivity devices.)

An interesting advantage of ATM is that ATM makes it possible to use the same technology for both LANs and WANs. Some disadvantages, however, include the cost, the limited availability of the equipment, and the present lack of expertise regarding ATM due to its recent arrival.

The most compelling reason to use ATM is that you require WAN speeds of over 100 Mbps. Relatively few networks have this very expensive requirement.

2.5 Exercise

Given that a single channel of a T1 is a DS-0 that provides you with 64 kbps, and that a T1 is made up of 24 DS-0 circuits, calculate the speed of a T1. Next, given that a T3 is made up of 28 T1s (672 DS-0 channels), calculate the speed of a T3. Compare these speeds to typical LAN speeds.

2.5   Exercise Explanation

Sample T1 calculation:

```
  64000
  ×24
  ─────
 256000
1280000
  ─────
```

1536000 bits per second*

* The actual speed of a T1 is 1.544 Mbps, but 8000 bps of that is used for line overhead and cannot be used for other purposes.

A T1 transmits data at about 15 percent of the speed a standard Ethernet does. T1s, however, always operate in full-duplex mode, whereas Ethernet is usually in half-duplex. T1s are much slower than regular LANs.

Sample T3 calculation:

```
 1536000
   ×28
 ───────
12288000
30720000
 ───────
```

43008000 bits per second*

* The actual speed of a T3 is 44.736 Mbps, but 1.728 Mbps of that is used for line overhead and cannot be used for other purposes.

A T3 is fast compared to a standard Ethernet, running at almost 4.5 times the standard LAN speed and in full-duplex. It would be a huge waste of money and resources to hook a single Ethernet to a T3 because the Ethernet wouldn't be able to keep up. A T3 runs at close to half the theoretical speed of a full-duplex 100Base-T or FDDI LAN.

2.5 Practice Problems

1. *Analog* signals:

    A. Can take on many values

    B. Can take on only two values

    C. Cannot be transmitted over long distances

    D. Are primarily used with asynchronous services like ATM

2. *Digital* signals:

    A. Can take on many values

    B. Can take on only two values

    C. Cannot be transmitted over long distances

    D. Are primarily used by dial-up modems

3. You require LAN connectivity between two sites at 1 Mbps or faster. What type of leased line most cost-effectively meets this requirement?

    A. DS-0

    B. T1

    C. T2

    D. T3

4. Your company already uses several T1 lines to provide Internet access and is considering ordering a faster line. What is the next commonly available standard leased line speed?

    A. 56 kbps

    B. 1.544 Mbps

    C. 10 Mbps

    D. 45 Mbps

5. How many T1s are in a T3?

    A. None—a T1 is faster than a T3.

    B. One—they are different names for the same speed.

    C. 3 T1s are in a T3.

    D. 28 T1s are in a T3.

6. Which of the following is fastest?

    A. DS-0

    B. DS-1

    C. DS-2

    D. DS-3

7. You need high-speed (minimum of 1.5 Mbps guaranteed) connectivity between two LANs in distant cities. Which type of WAN connection is probably most cost effective?

    A. Leased T1

    B. X.25

    C. ATM

    D. SMDS

8. You need to build an international WAN that supports mostly terminal emulation traffic. What WAN type should you use?

    A. Leased T1

    B. X.25

    C. ATM

    D. Frame relay

9. You require several LANs to have any-to-any communication at 1 Mbps or greater, but you want to minimize cost. What WAN type should you use?

    A. Leased T1

    B. X.25

    C. ATM

    D. Frame relay

10. A switched virtual circuit:

    A. is always active

    B. becomes active only where there is data to transfer

C. is another name for a PVC

D. is typically used with point-to-point leased lines

11. Which WAN connection service can use a PAD to packetize asynchronous data?

A. Leased T1

B. X.25

C. ATM

D. Frame relay

12. Which WAN connection service has the most overhead?

A. Leased T1

B. X.25

C. ATM

D. Frame relay

13. Which WAN connection service has the least overhead?

A. Leased T1

B. X.25

C. ATM

D. Frame relay

14. You require a WAN connection with throughput of at least 100 Mbps. Which WAN connection service meets this requirement?

A. Leased T1

B. X.25

C. ATM

D. Frame relay

15. You require a reliable, error-correcting WAN protocol. Which WAN connection service meets this requirement?

A. Leased T1

B. X.25

C. ATM

D. Frame relay

16. You need to configure a dial-backup for use when there is a problem with your leased T1 to headquarters. Which WAN connection service is well-suited for dial-up?

A. Leased T1

B. X.25

C. ISDN BRI

D. Frame relay

17. Which of the following technologies are usually limited to 64 kbps and below?

A. Leased T1

B. X.25

C. ATM

D. Frame relay

18. Which of the following WAN connection services is sometimes described as 2B+D?

A. Leased T1

B. X.25

C. ISDN BRI

D. Frame relay

19. You determine that you need a low-overhead packet-switching WAN connection service. Which one of the following best fits this description?

A. Leased T1

B. X.25

C. ATM

D. Frame relay

20. You have some remote offices that only need occasional connectivity to the main office. Which WAN connection service is best suited to on-demand connections?

A. Leased T1

B. X.25

C. ISDN BRI

D. Frame relay

21. Which of the following is NOT a disadvantage of ATM?

    A. There are relatively few suppliers.

    B. It is expensive.

    C. It supports very high speeds.

    D. It is difficult to work with.

22. You need to build a WAN that connects offices in China, France, and Australia. What WAN connection type is best suited for this type of requirement?

    A. Leased T1

    B. X.25

    C. ISDN BRI

    D. Frame relay

23. Your new CEO decides that the company must use the same technology on both the LAN and on the WAN. What WAN connection type enables him to do this?

    A. Leased T1

    B. X.25

    C. ATM

    D. Frame relay

24. Which WAN connection type is typically the most expensive?

    A. Leased T1

    B. X.25

    C. ATM

    D. Frame relay

25. Which WAN connection type is typically the least expensive?

    A. Leased T1

    B. X.25

    C. ISDN BRI

    D. Frame relay

26. You need a WAN connection that can simultaneously carry voice, video, and data traffic to allow your company to realize a cost savings from consolidating these existing WAN circuits. Which WAN connection service meets this requirement?

    A. Leased T1

    B. X.25

    C. ATM

    D. Frame relay

27. You want to take advantage of a WAN cloud for communications between your offices. Which type of WAN cloud commonly provides speeds of around 1 Mbps?

    A. Leased T1

    B. X.25

    C. ATM

    D. Frame relay

28. Which of the following uses a cell-based architecture?

    A. Leased T1

    B. X.25

    C. ATM

    D. Frame relay

29. Which of the following uses data frames that can vary in size?

    A. Leased T1

    B. X.25

    C. ATM

    D. Frame relay

30. Select all of the following technologies that can be used with a router:

    A. Leased T1

    B. X.25

C. ATM

D. Frame relay

31. You determine that your WAN traffic is very bursty. What WAN connection service has a feature that can let you send data above the speed at which delivery is guaranteed?

    A. Leased T1

    B. X.25

    C. ATM

    D. Frame relay

32. What WAN connection service is sold with a Committed Information Rate (CIR) guaranteeing a certain throughput?

    A. Leased T1

    B. X.25

    C. ATM

    D. Frame relay

33. If your headquarters needs to accept up to 20 ISDN dial-up calls on individual B channels, what would be the best way to deliver those calls?

    A. On B-ISDN

    B. ATM

    C. SONET

    D. PRI

34. What assumption does frame relay make that X.25 didn't?

    A. That the speed of light will be the limiting factor in data transmission

    B. That the underlying network media may be error prone

    C. That larger packets are always better packets

    D. That there will be very few errors introduced

35. How do devices on ATM networks communicate?

    A. They establish a session with the router, which forwards all their traffic to the correct ATM host.

    B. They use broadcasts for most ATM-related communications.

    C. They establish virtual circuits between the devices that need to communicate.

    D. They use IP addresses for all communications.

36. One of the advantages of ATM's using such small cells is that:

    A. It means there is less overhead than larger cells would have.

    B. Each cell can contain complete, end-to-end addressing.

    C. Time-sensitive data can be safely multiplexed with non-time-sensitive data.

    D. Software-based cell switching is much faster.

37. Which WAN connection services can run at high enough speeds to require delivery on fiber optic cables?

    A. ATM

    B. Frame Relay

    C. T3

    D. X.25

38. You need to transport high-quality video across a WAN that normally carries only data traffic. Which WAN connection service should you choose?

    A. X.25

    B. Frame relay

    C. ISDN

    D. ATM

2

39. You have to design a WAN that connects three offices. One is in Boston, another is in Minneapolis, and another is in San Diego.

    Required outcome:
    Each site must be able to communicate with the other sites.

    Desired outcome:
    Connection speed must be 1 Mbps or greater.

    Communications between all sites must continue even if one WAN line fails.

    Your solution:

    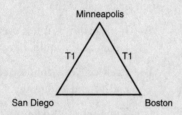

    A. This solution meets the required outcome and both of the desired outcomes.

    B. This solution meets the required outcome and one of the desired outcomes.

    C. This solution meets the required outcome but neither of the desired outcomes.

    D. This solution does not meet the required outcome.

40. You have to design a WAN that connects three offices. One is in Boston, another in is Minneapolis, and another is in San Diego.

    Required outcome:
    Each site must be able to communicate with the other sites.

    Desired outcome:
    Connection speed must be 1 Mbps or greater.

    Communications between all sites must continue even if one WAN line fails.

Your solution:

A. This solution meets the required outcome and both of the desired outcomes.

B. This solution meets the required outcome and one of the desired outcomes.

C. This solution meets the required outcome but neither of the desired outcomes.

D. This solution does not meet the required outcome.

2.5   Answers and Explanations: Practice Problems

1. **A**   Analog signals can take on many values.

2. **B**   Digital signals can take on only two values, one or zero.

3. **B**   A T1 transmits data at 1.544 Mbps, the closest choice to 1 Mbps presented.

4. **D**   A T3 is the next commonly available leased line speed, and it runs at 45 Mbps.

5. **D**   There are 28 T1s in a T3.

6. **D**   A DS-3, which runs at 45 Mbps, is the fastest choice presented.

7. **A**   Leased T1s are usually most cost effective of the choices presented when there is a point-to-point full-time connectivity requirement.

8. **B**   X.25 is best suited for international use because of its wide availability.

9. **D**   Frame relay is the most cost-effective way to provide any-to-any connectivity for LANs because it runs at over 1 Mbps and only requires one line at each site.

10. **B** A switched virtual circuit becomes active only when there is data to transfer.

11. **B** An X.25 service can use a PAD to packetize asynchronous data.

12. **B** X.25 has the most overhead of the choices presented.

13. **A** A leased T1 network has the least overhead because it is point-to-point and therefore doesn't require the additional header information that packet switching networks do.

14. **C** ATM is the only WAN connection service that runs at speeds of at least 100 Mbps.

15. **B** X.25 is the only reliable, error-correcting WAN protocol listed.

16. **C** ISDN BRI circuits were originally envisioned as replacing analog dial-up lines, and they remain well-suited for dial-up applications.

17. **B** X.25 is usually limited to 64 kbps and below because of its high overhead.

18. **C** ISDN BRI circuits are sometimes described as 2B+D because they have two B channels and one D channel.

19. **D** Frame relay is a low-overhead packet-switching WAN connection service.

20. **C** ISDN BRI circuits are best suited to on-demand connections.

21. **C** Being able to go very fast is not a disadvantage.

22. **B** X.25 is best suited to international WANs.

23. **C** ATM has the potential of being used both on the WAN and on the LAN.

24. **C** ATM is typically the most expensive because it usually is only used for very high speeds.

25. **C** ISDN BRIs are typically the least expensive WAN connection service because they are used for dial-on-demand applications in which full-time connectivity isn't required.

26. **C** ATM was designed to carry voice, video, and data traffic simultaneously.

27. **D** A frame relay WAN cloud commonly provides speeds of around 1 Mbps.

28. **C** ATM uses a cell-based architecture.

29. **A, B, D** Leased T1, X.25, and frame relay all use data frames that can vary in size.

30. **A, B, C, D** Leased T1, X.25, ATM, and frame relay can all be used with a router.

31. **D** Frame relay has a feature that can let you send data above the speed at which delivery is guaranteed.

32. **D** Frame relay is sold with a Committed Information Rate (CIR) guaranteeing a certain throughput.

33. **D** A PRI circuit delivers 23 ISDN B channels.

34. **D** Frame relay assumes there will be very few errors introduced, so it doesn't do any error recovery, unlike X.25 which assumes that it will need to correct errors.

35. **C** Devices on ATM networks have to establish at least one virtual circuit between the devices that need to communicate.

36. **C** Because ATM cells are so small, time-sensitive data can be safely multiplexed with non-time-sensitive data.

37. **A** ATM can run at high enough speeds to require delivery on fiber-optic cable.

38. **D** ATM can support the efficient mixing of data and video.

39. **B** This solution meets the required outcome and one of the desired outcomes. The connectivity requirement is met, and the speed goal is met. There is, however, no redundancy.

40. **A** This solution meets the required outcome and both of the desired outcomes.

2.5   Key Words

Amplitude

Analog

ATM

Digital

Frame relay

ISDN

T1

T3

X.25

Practice Exam: Planning

1. You need to design a 100-Mbps backbone network connecting five heavily used LANs. You should use:

   A. Fiber

   B. Coaxial cable

   C. 10Base-T

   D. Token ring

2. You need to design a LAN to run at 100 Mbps. What kind of cabling should you use?

   A. Category 3 UTP

   B. Category 5 UTP

   C. Fiber

   D. Coaxial

3. A device used to penetrate the cable in a thicknet connection is:

   A. An AUI connector

   B. A T-connector

   C. A vampire tap

   D. An N-connector

4. The best network cable in terms of transmission characteristics is which of the following?

   A. STP

   B. Cat 5 UTP

   C. Fiber

   D. Thinnet

5. Cable length limitations of 100 meters are fairly standard for which type of cable

   A. Fiber

   B. Thicknet

   C. Thinnet

   D. Twisted pair

6. You are getting ready to move to a new building that already has network cables installed. You require 100 Mbps support, and the building is already wired. You have the cabling tested and find that it passes all Category 3 tests. The best course of action is to:

   A. Replace all the cable with Category 5

   B. Use the cable as it is

   C. Install fiber cable

   D. Explore wireless options

7. In which topology is a single cable failure a serious problem?

   A. Star

   B. Bus

   C. Ring

   D. Mesh

8. To increase bandwidth in an existing network, you need to _____.

   A. Segment the network

   B. Re-cable the network

   C. Add RAM to the server

   D. Upgrade the Network Interface Cards

9. Which type of network topology requires a connection from every device to every other device?

   A. Bus

   B. Star

   C. Ring

   D. Mesh

10. In an Ethernet network, collisions:

    A. Indicate network overload

    B. Are caused by synchronization problems with the server

    C. Are normal events

    D. Are errors

2

11. According to the OSI model, what is responsible for making sure data is delivered reliably?

    A. The Physical Layer

    B. The Data Link Layer

    C. The Network Layer

    D. The Transport Layer

12. In an Ethernet network, a network interface card accepts a frame if:

    A. The destination Data Link address matches the NIC

    B. The destination Network Layer address matches the NIC

    C. The source Data Link address matches the NIC

    D. The source Network Layer address matches the NIC

13. Token rings are similar to Ethernet LANs in that they both:

    A. Can support multiple protocols

    B. Use source route bridging

    C. Rely on a token

    D. Can experience collisions

14. You determine that there are too many collisions on your network. The best solution is to:

    A. Change to a token ring network

    B. Add an Ethernet switch

    C. Install a NetBEUI to TCP/IP gateway

    D. Upgrade the network cable to Category 5

15. You determine that there are too many broadcasts on your network. The best solution is:

    A. To install a router to subnet the network

    B. To install a repeater to block the broadcasts

    C. To install a bridge to divide the network in two

    D. To install an Ethernet switch because it will reduce the broadcasts by filtering them at ports that don't need to see them

16. You are using a mixture of NetBEUI and TCP/IP, and the network performance is poor because of the broadcast levels. What device can be installed to minimize the problem while maintaining full connectivity?

    A. A repeater

    B. A bridge

    C. A router

    D. A brouter

Answers and Explanations: Practice Exam

1. **A**　Fiber is the best choice for backbone networks that may have to run under high loads or be upgraded to higher speeds.

2. **B**　Category 5 UTP is the best choice for most 100 Mbps LANs.

3. **C**　A vampire tap is used to penetrate the cable in a thicknet environment.

4. **C**　Fiber network cables have the best transmission characteristics.

5. **D**　Twisted-pair cables are commonly limited to 100 meters.

6. **A**　If you need 100 Mbps support, you should replace all the cable with Category 5.

7. **B**　In a bus topology, a single cable failure can cripple the entire network.

8. **A**　Segmenting the network is a common way to increase bandwidth.

9. **D**　A mesh network topology requires a connection from every device to every other device.

10. **C**   In an Ethernet network, collisions are normal events.

11. **D**   The Transport Layer is responsible for making sure data is delivered reliably.

12. **A**   In an Ethernet network, a network interface card accepts a frame if the destination data link address matches the NIC's address.

13. **A**   Token rings are similar to Ethernet LANs in that they both can support multiple protocols.

14. **B**   Ethernet switches are the most effective way to reduce collisions on a network without making other changes.

15. **A**   A router is the only device listed that can block broadcast traffic.

16. **D**   You have to use a brouter because one of the protocols is routable and the other one is not routable.

2

CHAPTER 3

Implementation

3.1 Choose an Administrative Plan to Meet Specified Needs, Including Performance Management, Account Management, and Security

The Networking Essentials test focuses heavily on elements of Microsoft networking. Other network architectures, such as Novell NetWare and AppleTalk, are not as important.

In order to choose an administrative plan, it is important that you understand the scope of what you are managing.

We list users last, because the core of the network is actually the *network resources*, made available via the concept of *sharing*, which in turn is modified through *permissions*. Only then are users, as defined by your user administrative plan, able to access network resources.

The core elements of your management plan will incorporate the following:

- **Resources:** These are typically disk drives or printers. However, a mail or mainframe gateway, a shared modem or fax device, or a shared tape drive can all be resources.

  A disk drive or printer is not a network resource simply by virtue of being part of a networked PC, though. It must be *shared* (as defined next) or otherwise accessible from the network. If the disk or printer in question is accessible only from the one computer to which it is attached, it is not a network resource.

  As network technology advances, more and more device types can be shared across a network. Because of this, the list of possible resources is constantly changing. Simply remember this: If it can be accessed from another computer on the network, it is a network resource. Any computer sharing a resource can be called a "server." This includes Windows for Workgroups and Windows NT workstation.

- **Sharing:** This is how a particular device becomes a network resource. Your hard drive or printer must be given a *share name*. This share name is how the resource is accessed by other computers on the network. For example, I might share my printer using the name \\workstation\inkjet. (This format is often referred to as *servername**sharename*. "Servername" does not refer to the domain controller or network name, but the name of the computer sharing the resource.)

- **Permissions:** *Permissions* refers specifically to the security access a user or group has to a resource. Permissions can be managed in two ways: with share-level security or user-level security.

    ### Share-Level Security

    Share-level security is a simple security implementation. The share can be made either read-only or full access, either or both of which can be protected with a password. The user supplies the appropriate password to access the share for read- only or full access.

    Owing to the minimal security offered by share level, this security scheme is typically not recommended. However, share-level security is the only level of security available if you do not have an NT server, NT workstation, Novell server, or other OS/2 LAN server. If you have a network of only Windows for Workgroups and Windows 95 workstations, you cannot implement user-level security.

    The administrative burden with share-level security is considerably less than with user-level security. For this reason, Microsoft will recommend it in cases where some security is required but the administrative burden must be reduced.

    ### User-Level Security

    User-level security is far more secure than share-level security. To implement user-level security, the network must contain a database of users, typically on a Windows NT or Novell NetWare server. If a user management tool such as *User Manager for Domains* is used, access permissions can be granted to individual users or groups of users. An access control list is maintained for each network resource.

    When a user attempts to connect to or "use" a server share, the server first checks to see if the user's name exists in the user accounts database. If so, the user's password is checked. If both of these security checks pass, the server completes the connection, and the user is allowed access to the shared resource according to the permissions in the resource's Access Control List.

- **Users:** A *user* is any entity that requests network resources. Some user accounts, such as *Administrator* or *guest*, are built-in, but most users are added. You assign a unique username and password to each individual on your network. Users can be created on a number of operating systems, including Windows NT, NetWare, and UNIX.

- **Groups:** Users can be placed into *groups* to simplify user management. Resources can then be made available to groups. A system administrator might create a group called "marketing," which could be given access to the marketing files and printers. Because users can be added or removed, this is far easier than modifying the rights of each user.

- **Rights:** *Rights* refer to specific abilities a user or group might possess. Unlike permissions, rights focus on the user or group instead of the resource. Typical rights include the ability to perform the following actions:

    Create accounts

    Log on to a particular computer

    Log on as a service

Take ownership of files or other objects

Back up and restore files

Basically, rights modify the abilities of a particular user or group, enabling that person or group to carry out administrative functions.

A. Managing User Accounts and Groups

One of the most important items in user management is the interaction of user accounts and group membership. Windows NT includes Global groups and Local groups.

Most user accounts are typically created for a single user. Exceptions to this are special accounts created for a network service. User accounts contain:

- **Username:** This must be unique. No two users can have the same username.
- **Password:** This secures the account and prohibits one user from logging on as another user. Individual passwords should be kept private to avoid unauthorized access.
- **Group membership:** If resource permissions have been appropriately granted to groups, group membership determines the user's rights and permissions on the network.

A number of other optional components exist, such as a home directory (a place where a user can store personal files on the network) or specific information about the user (such as his full name or description).

The simplest way to manage user accounts is through groups. The Microsoft definition of *groups* is a tool for simplifying user management. Windows networks contain two types of groups:

- **Global groups:** Domain-level groups that can contain only users. These groups may be exported to other domains via trust relationships.
- **Local groups:** Groups that can contain users and global groups. Local groups are given certain rights to network resources.

Using groups simplifies user management. Remember this phrase:

Users go into global groups; global groups go into local groups; local groups get the resources.

Windows NT comes ready-made with a set of groups that are adequate for most security needs. Here is a list of those groups and a brief description of each:

Domain Users: A group that contains all users in the domain. User rights and resources granted to this group are usually severely limited. For example, the Domain Users group does not have the right to access parts of the control panel on a Windows NT workstation.

Domain Admins: A very powerful *global* group. This group is able to create and delete users, take control of files and other resources, and act as part of the operating system. Only authorized persons should be in this group.

Administrators: A *local* group. The global group Domain Admins typically is placed in this local group on each server in the domain.

Power users: A group that is given greater rights over their own workstations than domain users are given.

Everyone: A special group that contains all users in local or trusted domains, as well as unrecognized users. It is impossible to add or delete users to this special group.

Other groups are defined with the rights necessary to perform particular tasks. These built-in groups are adequate for most network needs.

A system administrator must balance the concerns of security, user-access, and administrative ease when defining security. If the network requires little security or requires a minimum of administration, use an easy password policy and perhaps only share-level security.

B. Implementing Security on Windows NT

After you assign an account to a user in a group, you can assign that group access to resources. This follows the use pattern explained above: Place users into global groups, place global groups into local groups, grant resources to local groups. You must set permissions on each resource. Setting permissions is a time-consuming process that should be undertaken with care. If not, the process can become confusing.

Basically, network security can take three forms:

- **Access permissions applied to a shared resource**

  Access permissions refer to the simple password-protection schemes applied to network shares. A resource is shared with two passwords, one for full access and one for read-only access. The user supplies the correct password for access.

- **User-level security applied to a shared resource**

  This is more robust than simply applying access-level protection using a password. In this method, the network administrator shares a certain resource and adds user groups from the user database to have access. This type of access is the most common.

- **File-level security applied to a shared resource**

  This is the highest level of network security, and it requires the shared drive to be formatted NTFS (the native file system of Windows NT). In addition to the share-level security, the network administrator can grant (or deny) individual users and groups the ability to read specific files or directories individually.

C. Creating and Assigning Permissions to a Shared Folder on Windows NT

In exercise 3.1.2, you create and share a directory called Public. You will:

- Grant the group Everyone Read access.
- Grant the group Local Training Full Control.

All security in this example is assuming no NTFS file-level security, so security is granted at the share level.

You can also give rights and permissions directly to user accounts themselves, but such security is cumbersome and difficult to administer. For ease of use and administration, remember: Place users into global groups, place global groups into local groups, and grant resources to local groups.

D. Assigning File-Level Permissions on an NTFS Partition

Exercise 3.1.3 assumes that your network partition is formatted with NTFS. NTFS is superior because it allows the administrator to implement a very sophisticated security policy. Also, NTFS provides local security. Local users are unaffected by share-level security options but are stymied by NTFS file-level security.

In the Public folder shared in exercise 3.1.2, you see that two share-level permissions exist for this directory:

Everyone: Read

Administrators: Full Control

In exercise 3.1.3, you assign a new permission to the directory, this time through NTFS security. The permission to be assigned will be:

Everyone: Change

Use a dedicated server such as Windows NT or NetWare to provide resource access on your network. In some situations, though, you might need to implement a workgroup sharing model or use a Windows 95 machine as a server. This is more common in situations where the sensitivity of data is relatively low, or where the administrative cost of managing a large user database is high.

E. Implementing Access-Level Security

Windows 95 also can act as a server, but it does not support user-level security unless there is a server on your network. Under Windows 95's security model, passwords are assigned to permit access to each directory or printer share. To access the share, a user must supply the correct password. When creating a shared directory using share-level security, you can grant one of three types of access:

- **Read-only access:** Users can access files and subdirectories in a directory but cannot delete or save files to that share.

- **Full access:** Users can read, write, and delete files in the directory.

- **Depends on password:** Two different passwords can be created, one that allows read-only access and one that allows full access. The type of access granted to a user depends on the password that user supplies.

If no password is entered, all users have full or read-only access to the directory, depending on which option was specified when the shared directory was created.

Table 3.1.1 outlines both the advantages and disadvantages of using Windows 95's model of access-level security.

Table 3.1.1   Advantages and Disadvantages of Access-Level Security

Disadvantages	Advantages
To access different shares, a network user must know numerous passwords.	Very simple to administer.
Passwords can easily be forgotten.	Flexible, as a user can be granted new permission with a new password.
Nothing prevents a user from disclosing the password to unauthorized users.	

F.   User-Level Security on Windows 95

Windows 95 cannot manage user accounts by itself. Instead, it requires a Windows NT or NetWare server to authenticate the user trying to access the resource.

When a directory is shared with user-level security, the users or groups to be granted access to the share are assigned privileges. You can grant each user or group one of the following privileges:

- **Read-only:** Users can access files and subdirectories in a directory but cannot delete or save files to that share.

- **Full access:** Users can read, write, and delete files in the directory.

- **Custom:** Any number of the following privileges can be granted: Read Files, Write to Files, Create Files, List Files, Delete Files, Change File Attributes, Change Permissions.

G.   Security for Printer Resources

To connect to a network printer, you first must install and configure the printer on a server. Both Windows NT and NetWare support printing directly to print devices, such as HP JetDirect cards.

To use either a Windows NT or Windows 95 printer as a network print server, you simply share a printer directly connected to the computer. The printer must then be shared to allow other users to access it. To share a printer in Windows 95 installation, the File and Print Sharing component must be enabled. This feature is on by default in Windows NT.

When the printer has been configured and shared on the network print server, users from Windows 95, Windows for Workgroups, Windows NT, or Novell's DOS requester can be configured to connect to the print server and print to the printer over the network.

H. Monitoring the Security Policy

The typical systems administrator has the following security responsibilities:

- **Auditing:** The Windows NT Event Viewer can be used to view system events that affect security. In *User Manager for Domains*, the system security policy can be set to audit security events.

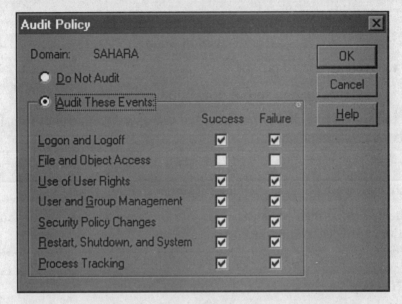

Figure 3.1.1 This window is used to create a security audit. System Administrators can view events that could become security threats.

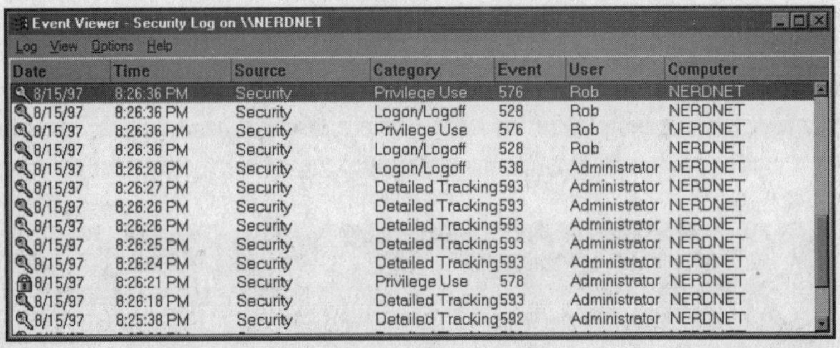

Figure 3.1.2 Here is a sample audit trail created using the auditing functions selected in Figure 3.1.1. Events in this window can easily be viewed and analyzed as potential security threats. Note the logon, access, and logoff functions.

- **Virus protection:** Computers are susceptible to virus programs. A new type of virus can spread through word-processing macros. Networked computers are particularly susceptible to viruses due to the extraordinary rate of interaction.

  In order to detect viruses, your antivirus software must search for every specific virus that exists. Most antivirus programs maintain these definitions in a data file. You *must* periodically update this definition file. Most antivirus manufacturers have mailing lists or Web sites that list their latest virus definition files.

- **Physical security:** If your data is sensitive, you will need to consider physical security of your network servers. If your server is not secure, no amount of backups, RAID, share security, and NTFS permissions will protect your data from prying eyes.

  As with all security issues, you need to weight the needs of security against the costs of administration and ease of use.

Section Goals

Be able to create users and groups.

Be able to configure sharing and security for Microsoft resources.

Be able to connect to either Windows NT or Windows 95 machines to gain access to their shared files and printers.

Have knowledge of optional security measures available for sensitive data.

Know how to create network resources through sharing.

Experiment with permissions and user rights and have a clear understanding of the relationship between groups and users.

3.1   Exercises

1. Creating a User Account in Windows NT

Objective: Create a new Windows NT user account.

Estimated time: 10 minutes

1. Click Start, Programs, Administrative Tools. Choose either User Manager (Windows NT Workstation) or User Manager for Domains (Windows NT Server). User Manager opens. The Guest account is disabled by default and should remain that way unless your security policy dictates otherwise.

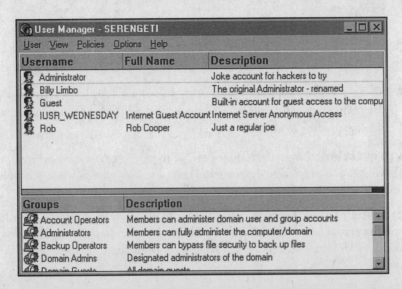

Figure 3.1.3   Account administration is done through the Windows NT User Manager for Domains program.

2. Click File, New User. The New User dialog box appears.

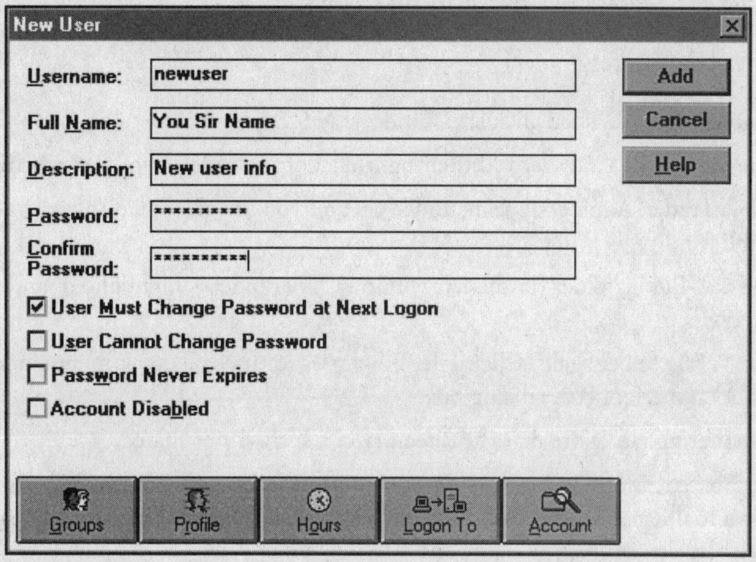

Figure 3.1.4   The Windows NT New User dialog box enables you to record information about a new user.

3. In the top field, type a unique username (in this case, **newuser**) for the new account. This name can be between 1 and 20 characters and cannot include spaces or any of the following characters:

   " / \ [ ] : ; | = , + * ? < >

4. Fill in the two text fields in order to identify the user for whom the account is being created.

5. In the password field, enter any combination of 1 to 14 characters of your choice, with the same exceptions that apply to the creation of usernames. The password will not be displayed. All passwords are case-sensitive.

6. Examine the check boxes below the Confirm Password field. By default, the User Must Change Password at Next Logon field should be checked. The first time that new user logs on, he is asked to provide a new password.

7. The User Cannot Change Password option generally is used only for guest or multi-user accounts to prevent one guest from changing the password and locking all other guest users out. Leave this box unchecked.

8. The Account Disabled field enables you to disable an account temporarily while a user is on vacation or when he is no longer allowed network access. Leave this box unchecked.

9. Click the Add button.

10. Click Close to return to User Manager. Your new user will appear with the others. You can delete the new user if you want.

2. Sharing a Directory and Implementing Share-Level Security

Objective: Share a Windows NT directory and assign share-level security to it.

Estimated time: 15 minutes

1. Click Start, Programs. Then click the Windows NT Explorer icon to bring up the Explorer window.

2. Select the root of the C: drive, and then right-click it to display a context-sensitive menu.

3. Select New, Folder. A folder appears under C:, and you are prompted to enter a name for the folder. Type **Public** and press Enter.

4. Click the new Public folder (in the left window). The folder is highlighted, and the right window is now empty.

5. Select the Public folder again. Click File, Properties (or use the quick menu and select Sharing from there) to open the Properties dialog box.

6. Click the Sharing tab. Note that the directory currently is not shared.

7. Click the Shared As option button. "Public" appears in the Share Name box. You can change or leave this initial name. In this case, change the share. Replace Public with **My Share** to illustrate the difference between a directory name and a share name.

8. Observe the Maximum Connections option. Leave the default setting, which enables unlimited concurrent connections to the share.

9. Click the Permissions button to call the Access Through Share Permissions dialog box. Observe that, by default, Everyone has Full Control over the new share.

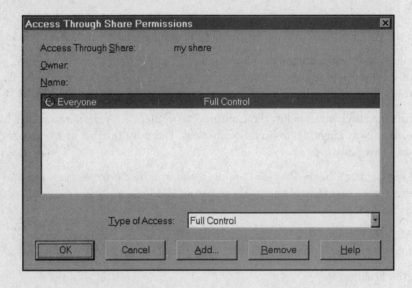

Figure 3.1.5   The Access Through Share Permissions dialog box enables you to determine the type of access for a particular group.

10. Select the Everyone group and click the Type of Access drop-down arrow. The following four selections appear:

> **No Access:** A member of any group with this permission is banned from the shared resource.

> **Read:** Members can list, read, and execute files but cannot modify or delete them.

Change: Members can read, list, execute, and delete files but are not able to change file permissions or assume ownership of the files.

Full Control: Members have complete control of the resources, assuming that they have sufficient rights to match their permissions.

3. Setting NTFS Permissions on a Shared Folder

Objective: Add NTFS security to the Public share.

Estimated time: 15 minutes

1. Click Start, Programs. Select Windows NT Explorer to open the Explorer window. Choose a directory on an NTFS partition. If you do not have an NTFS partition, you cannot complete this lab.

2. Create a directory called TestNTFS, and then right-click it. Select the Properties option from the menu to open the TestNTFS Properties window.

3. In the TestNTFS Properties window, click the Security tab, and then click the Permissions button to open the Directory Permissions dialog box.

4. Observe that the directory has only one permission set: Everyone: Full Control.

5. Select Everyone. Click the Type of Access drop-down arrow and choose Read.

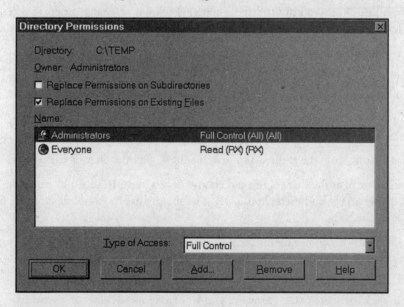

Figure 3.1.6 The Directory Permissions dialog box enables you to update or replace permissions for a group.

6. Take note of the check boxes near the top of the window. The Replace Permissions on Files option is checked, while the Replace Permissions on Subdirectories option is not checked. Because no subdirectories exist in this instance, leave the defaults as they are.

7. If you need to enter additional groups into the list, you can do so by using the Add button. Click this button, and then observe the Add Users and Groups window. Give Administrators Full Control permissions.

8. Click OK to return to the Directory Permissions window. Then click OK to set the new permissions and return to Explorer.

9. Click File, Exit to close Explorer.

10. Share the TestNTFS directory with Everyone—Full Control permissions and log on to the share from a remote machine. You should be able to modify, create, and delete files across the share if you are logged on as an Administrator, but you should only be able to read and execute while logged on as a TestUser.

4. Sharing a Directory Using Share-Level Security

Objective: Share a Windows 95 directory using share-level security.

Estimated time: 10 minutes

1. From the Start menu, choose Settings, Control Panel to display the Control Panel.

2. Double-click the Network icon to display the Network dialog box.

3. Choose the Access Control tab, and then choose share-level access control.

4. Select the Configuration tab and choose File, Print Sharing to display the File and Print Sharing dialog box.

5. Select both the I Want to be Able to Give Others Access to My Files check box and the I Want to be Able to Allow Others to Print to My Printer(s) check box to enable others to access your printers and files. Then choose OK to automatically install File and Printer Sharing for Microsoft Networks.

6. Choose OK and restart the computer.

7. After Windows 95 restarts, click Start, Windows Explorer and make a new folder on your C: drive named Password. Then choose the Password directory and make a text file within it called Password Test.

8. Right-click the Password directory to display the context-sensitive menu.

9. Choose Sharing from the context-sensitive menu to open the Sharing dialog box.

10. Accept Password as the share name and choose Access Type: Read-Only. Enter the password **read** for read-only access, and then choose OK. The sharing hand symbol replaces the folder symbol for the shared directory.

11. If you have another computer on the network, browse the first computer in Network Neighborhood to display the share name. The share name Password is displayed under the appropriate computer name.

12. Double-click the share name Password, and you are prompted for the password.

13. Enter **read** at the password prompt and choose OK to display the directory contents.

14. Copy the Password Test file from the share to your local hard drive. The file read will be successful.

15. Modify the file and try to copy it back. Then try to delete the original from the shared directory. Neither the file write nor the file delete will be allowed.

5. Creating a Local Printer with Windows NT

Objective: Create a locally installed printer on Windows NT

Estimated time: 20 minutes

1. Click Start, Settings. Then choose Printers to open the Printers window.

2. Click Add Printer to display the Add Printer Wizard. As with many other administrative tasks, the process of creating and sharing a printer has been streamlined and simplified by the use of a *wizard*, a small program that leads you through a particular task. Choose My Computer and click Next.

3. The wizard asks you to specify the port or ports to which the new printer should print. Choose LPT1: and click Next.

4. The wizard now asks you to specify the type of physical device to which you are printing or the device type that your printer emulates. Click HP in the left pane, and then find and select Color LaserJet. Then click Next.

5. Now you are asked to name your new printer. Remember that each printer on your machine must have a unique name and that the name should be descriptive of its type or function. Type **Color Printer** and click Next.

6. Now you are asked whether the printer will be shared and, if so, what other operating systems will access it. Click Shared, call the new share **MyLaser,** and select Windows 95 from the list of additional operating systems. Note that each supported Windows NT platform requires a different driver. Click Next.

7. The wizard now has all the information it needs. Leave the Print Test Page option on and click Finish. You will need the source files for both your Windows NT Server or Workstation and for Windows 95. You are prompted for the location of the source files, and the necessary drivers are loaded.

8. The Printer icon for Color Printer is created in the Printers window. Select it, and the queue appears. Print a document to the new printer and check the queue again. The document should be waiting to print.

3

3.1　Practice Problems

1. An overall administrative plan must consider:

   A. Users, resources, sharing, and permissions.

   B. Security, resources, permissions, and files.

   C. Files, printers, and network adapters.

   D. Users, files, documents, and resources.

2. Which of the following can be a *network resource*?

   A. Disk drives

   B. Printers

   C. A modem

   D. All of the above

3. In order to restrict access to a network resource, you modify:

   A. User rights.

   B. File locations.

   C. Permissions.

   D. Passwords.

4. True or False: Only a limited number of items can be *network resources*.

   A. True

   B. False

5. A *networked printer* is:

   A. Any printer attached to a networked computer.

   B. A printer shared using network server software.

   C. A printer attached to a shared networked PC.

   D. A printer attached or connected to a dedicated network server.

6. *Sharing* refers to:

   A. Users in a workgroup accessing common documents.

   B. Software-enabling access across the network.

   C. Passwords used by multiple users.

   D. None of the above.

7. A share name:

   A. Is used to access the resource and should indicate its characteristics.

   B. Must include department or workgroup information about the device.

   C. Is required by the UNC naming convention to include the two-slash "\\" server name.

   D. Must be mapped to a drive letter before it can be used.

8. The UNC naming system uses the following syntax:

   A. \\username\servername

   B. net use d: \\vol1\sys

   C. \\servername\sharename

   D. \\sharename\username

The next five questions use the following scenario.

Network type:

Windows NT server with Windows 3.11 workstations

Protocols used:

TCP/IP, NetBEUI

Network size:

1 server, 10 workstations

You are the administrator of a small network, in addition to your primary job of law clerk. Most of the users know each other very well, yet there is some data on the network that is not appropriate for all users. In addition, most of the users are computer literate and can be considered "power users." Your department has been awarded a large grant, so cost is no object for your network.

You want to implement a security plan.

Required goals:

- The plan must protect the sensitive data.
- The plan cannot adversely impact the current business practices.

Desired goals:

- You want the plan to be exceedingly simple and easy to administer.
- You would like to track user access to the sensitive data.

9. You decide to implement Windows NT workstation and convert to NTFS on the workstations with auditing enabled. This plan will:

    A. Perform both of the required goals and both of the desired goals.

    B. Perform both of the required goals and one of the desired goals.

    C. Perform both of the required goals and none of the desired goals.

    D. Not perform the required goals.

10. You implement Windows NT workstation, and you use user-level access permissions on the sensitive network resources to protect them. This plan will:

    A. Perform both of the required goals and both of the desired goals.

    B. Perform both of the required goals and one of the desired goals.

    C. Perform both of the required goals and none of the desired goals.

    D. Not perform the required goals.

11. You leave the workstations at Windows 3.11 and create user accounts for each user. You then assign them into groups and control access to network resources. This plan will:

    A. Perform both of the required goals and both of the desired goals.

    B. Perform both of the required goals and one of the desired goals.

    C. Perform both of the required goals and none of the desired goals.

    D. Not perform the required goals.

12. You leave the workstations at Windows 3.11 and convert the Windows NT server's disk to NTFS. You enable auditing for the shared resources, and you use a shared password to protect the sensitive data. This plan will:

    A. Perform both of the required goals and both of the desired goals.

    B. Perform both of the required goals and one of the desired goals.

    C. Perform both of the required goals and none of the desired goals.

    D. Not perform the required goals.

13. You leave the workstations at Windows 3.11 and create user accounts for each user. You convert the Windows NT server's disk to NTFS and enable file-level auditing. You enable user-level access to control access to network resources. This plan will:

    A. Perform both of the required goals and both of the desired goals.

    B. Perform both of the required goals and one of the desired goals.

    C. Perform both of the required goals and none of the desired goals.

    D. Not perform the required goals.

3

14. Which of the following groups of operating systems natively support user-level share access?

   A. Windows for Workgroups 3.11, Windows 95, Windows NT Workstation, Windows NT Server

   B. Windows 95, Windows NT Workstation, Windows NT Server

   C. Windows NT Server, Windows NT Workstation

   D. Windows 95, Windows NT Workstation

15. When using a network share,

   A. The password in the user account is checked against the password in the network resource. If they match, the user is authenticated.

   B. The network resource is checked in the Access Control List (ACL) to see if that user is granted access. If the resource is listed, the user is granted access.

   C. The username is checked against the user accounts database. If the user exists, the user's password is checked. Then the user is granted access.

   D. Because the user is authenticated by the domain controller during login, there is no need to check the user database. The server checks the user's password. Then the user is granted access.

16. A user is:

   A. Placed into groups to be given access to resources.

   B. Granted *permissions* to use resources.

   C. An entity that requests access network resources.

   D. All of the above.

17. Windows 95 security

   A. Uses the same 32-bit engine as Windows NT and is, therefore, secure.

   B. Uses only passwords to enforce security and is, therefore, easier to administer.

   C. Can use Windows NT Workstation database to control access to resources.

   D. Cannot access NTFS partitions over a network.

18. Global groups

   A. Add a layer of complexity on user management and are, therefore, difficult to administer.

   B. Are available across platforms to Windows NT, Novell NetWare, and UNIX.

   C. Must contain users before they can be given access.

   D. Can contain users, local groups, or global groups.

19. User rights include:

   A. The ability to access printers and files.

   B. The ability to create printers and files.

   C. The ability to create users or other accounts.

   D. Focus on network resources.

20. Windows NT user accounts are:

   A. Created as part of the installation process and can be created later.

   B. Created with a tool such as *User Manager for Domains* and can be created during the installation process.

C. Transferable to a Windows 95 workstation.

D. Used via the Access Control List to manage resources.

21. Share-level security:

A. Uses passwords to restrict access to Full Access or Read-Only.

B. Cannot be used with NTFS file-level security.

C. Is not adequate security for protecting data.

D. Cannot be used to restrict a *network user*.

22. On Windows NT, the Administrator account

A. Cannot be renamed but can be deleted.

B. Is very powerful but can be protected with NTFS file-level security.

C. Cannot be deleted but can be renamed.

D. Is created during installation, but like *guest*, it is disabled.

23. User accounts:

A. Are typically shared among people on small networks.

B. Can be placed into groups to ease administrative burdens.

C. Are saved in the Access Control List (ACL).

D. Are managed using the Administrative Tools program in Windows NT Server.

24. Usernames on a network server:

A. Can appear to use the same name because the SID (Security ID) is different for each user.

B. Must be unique.

C. Must contain information about that user.

D. Are saved in the global ACL.

25. Passwords should be:

A. Case sensitive (to avoid being compromised by hackers).

B. Written down and stored in a very safe place to keep them private.

C. Used to restrict access to user accounts.

D. Generated by the system administrator to ensure that hard-to-guess passwords are used.

26. A *user profile*

A. Contains security information about a user to ensure sensitive data is not shared.

B. Can contain optional user information, such as a home directory or desktop settings.

C. Is a database of access rights for each user.

D. Can be copied from one user to another, creating duplicates.

27. When permissions are granted to groups:

A. Permissions cannot be granted to users.

B. Users should be added to groups.

C. Users should be granted group permissions.

D. Groups are added to the Access Control List (ACL).

28. Which of the following is an example of a special user account?

A. A system account to log in as a service

B. A user account to log in as a service

C. The Administrator and Guest accounts created during installation

D. All of the above

29. Which of the following is a tool used to simplify user management?

A. Groups

B. *User Manager for Domains*

C. *Syscon*

D. The ACL (Access Control List)

30. True or False: In order to manage your user database properly, you will most likely need to modify or add to the default groups provided in *User Manager for Domains.*

A. True

B. False

31. Which of the following is true about Windows NT groups?

A. Local groups can be added together and exported into global groups.

B. Global groups can be added to other global groups.

C. Global groups can be added to local groups.

D. Local groups can be exported into other trusted domains.

32. A system administrator:

A. Must consider security above all else when determining network configuration.

B. Must balance ease-of-use, user convenience, and security when determining network configuration.

C. Must affix a dollar value to each resource to determine if security is appropriate for that resource.

D. Must never let mere economics be a driving force in determining network configuration.

33. Which of the following is not true? Passwords should:

A. Be set to expire frequently to expose stolen or misused passwords.

B. Use upper- and lowercase letters to stymie password-cracking programs.

C. Be set in *User Manager for Domains* to require a mixture of characters and numbers to stymie password-cracking programs.

D. Be set in *User Manager for Domains* to ensure that they meet minimum length requirements.

34. In order for the *Backup* group to back up files, it must:

A. Have the appropriate user right.

B. Be a member of the local Administrators group.

C. Be in the global ACL (Access Control List) for that resource.

D. Be modified from the default group created during installation.

35. The *Everyone* group:

A. Like the *guest* account, should be disabled to avoid unauthorized access.

B. Is a global group.

C. Is a special group that cannot be modified.

D. Is a special group that contains the global ACL (Access Control List).

36. Most network operating systems:

A. Manage groups through a dedicated tool such as *Group Manager for Domains.*

B. Do not use groups the way an advanced operating system such as Microsoft Windows NT Server does.

C. Use groups and users interchange-
    ably.

D. Manage groups through the user
    management tool.

37. Which is the phrase you should have
    memorized to simplify user and resource
    management?

    A. Users go into local groups, local
        groups go into global groups, global
        groups are shared across domains.

    B. Users are grouped together into a
        local group, local groups are
        grouped together into a domain
        group, global groups are grouped
        together into a domain group.

    C. Users go into global groups, global
        groups go into local groups, local
        groups get resources.

    D. Local groups are placed into
        workgroups, workgroups are placed
        into domain groups, domain groups
        are placed into global groups, global
        groups go into the group *Everyone*,
        which cannot be modified.

38. To set user permissions,

    A. You must first select a group for
        that user to be placed in.

    B. You must create a user account and
        should place the user in a group.

    C. You must first place the user in a
        local group.

    D. You must add the user to the ACL
        (Access Control List).

39. Setting permissions:

    A. Can be a time-consuming process
        that should be undertaken with
        care.

    B. Is necessary for users to have access
        to files and printers.

C. Is a simple process eased by the use
    of user accounts and groups.

D. Cannot be performed on a Win-
    dows 95 machine.

40. Access permissions applied to a shared
    resource

    A. Describes sharing an item with two
        passwords, one for read-only and
        one for full access.

    B. Must be enabled to grant access to
        the network resource.

    C. Is the act of adding users to a shared
        resource.

    D. Requires a Windows NT or Novell
        NetWare server.

41. Access permissions applied to a shared
    resource

    A. Is the easiest method of network
        security to administer.

    B. Requires that a user be added to a
        group before he or she can be
        authenticated.

    C. Enables workgroups to share data.

    D. Happens automatically when you
        connect a PC to the network.

42. User-level security applied to a shared
    resource:

    A. Cannot be performed on a Win-
        dows 95 workstation.

    B. Requires a Windows NT Server.

    C. Uses the ACL (Access Control List)
        to authenticate users.

    D. Requires that a user be placed in a
        local or global group.

43. A shared resource using user-level security
    on a Windows 95 workstation

    A. Requires a Windows NT computer
        for the user database.

    B. Can use a Novell NetWare server
        for user authentication.

C. Is the easiest secure way to manage access control.

D. Can use NTFS-level security if a Windows NT server is used for authentication.

44. File-level security

    A. Is easy and fast to administer.

    B. Requires NTFS on the partition to be secured.

    C. Cannot be used with users belonging to the *Everyone* user group.

    D. Should only be used for C-2 level security.

45. Rights and permissions can be granted to users directly to:

    A. Make things easier in the long run instead of dealing with users and groups.

    B. Streamline system performance.

    C. Avoid security breaches by separating users and not keeping them in the same group.

    D. Implement a quick-fix, but it will be more cumbersome in the long run.

46. NTFS file-level security

    A. Allows the administrator to implement a very sophisticated security policy.

    B. Is self-configuring, using the built-in groups and permissions created during the Windows NT installation process.

    C. Can be used on a FAT volume.

    D. Does not use the ACL (Access Control List).

47. NTFS file-level security

    A. Does not work over the network because all network shares are equal.

    B. Works over the network but can be overridden by an administrator with physical access to the server.

    C. Allows for advanced auditing functions and will lock out a user logging in at the server as well as over the network.

    D. Removes the need for physical security of your server.

48. If your NTFS-level security volume can be accessed by the *Everyone* group,

    A. Your file system is secure because *Everyone* is a special built-in group creating during the Windows NT installation process.

    B. You can remove users from the *Everyone* group to secure the volume.

    C. You cannot secure this volume because the *Everyone* group cannot be modified.

    D. You can remove the *Everyone* group's access.

49. A relatively weak password policy

    A. Is a bad idea.

    B. Might be appropriate if security needs are light.

    C. Can be overridden by effective NTFS file-level security.

    D. Would use numbers and letters as part of the password.

50. Which of the following is not contained in a Windows NT profile?

    A. Password

    B. Home directory

    C. Login script

    D. None of the above: All of these are contained in the profile

51. Windows 95's level of security gives the sharing PC these choices:

   A. Login, print, read-only, full access

   B. Full access, read-only, execute

   C. Full, read-only, depends on password

   D. User, group, domain user

52. If no password is used on Windows 95's access control,

   A. All users have read-only access.

   B. All users have full access.

   C. The administrator can still choose read-only or full access.

   D. Windows 95 requires a password.

53. Which of the following is a disadvantage of Windows 95's access control implementation?

   A. It is a relatively insecure security implementation.

   B. It becomes difficult to administer because you have to remember so many passwords.

   C. The system administrator must change the access control when the passwords expire.

   D. They will not work over a network connection.

54. Which of the following is an advantages of Windows 95's access control implementation?

   A. It uses a smaller ACL (Access Control List).

   B. It works with NTFS partitions.

   C. It is very easy to grant full access to a new user (by giving him or her the new password).

   D. Passwords can be made case-sensitive to improve security.

3.1   Answers and Explanations: Practice Problems

1. **A**   Files, network adapters, and documents are not core aspects of an administrative plan.

2. **D**   If an item can be accessed using the network, it is a network resource.

3. **C**   Permissions are used to modify access to resources.

4. **A**   The scope of network resources is limited only by the skill and imagination of programmers and engineers.

5. **B**   The printer must be shared in order to be used across the network. The software enabling this does not have to be on a dedicated server, as any software creating a network resource is called server software.

6. **C**   A network resource is made available by sharing.

7. **A**   The UNC name can be used instead of a drive letter. In addition, there is no requirement that it be a meaningful name, although network administrators should use meaningful names when possible. In addition, the share only refers to the resource name, not the full UNC in \\servername\sharename construction.

8. **D**   \\servername\sharename

9. **D**   This result will not track any activity on the server, nor will it protect sensitive data.

10. **D**   Windows NT workstation would involved a major network overhaul that could upset the business flow. This plan is not easy to administer, nor will it track sensitive data.

11. **C**   This plan will not be easy to administer, as you must create and manage user accounts. In addition, it will not track access to files.

12. **D** This plan will not function. Windows NT Server does not support a shared password to protect resources. In this scenario, item 11 is the best alternative, even though it does not meet all the required and desired goals.

13. **B** This plan, though not perfect, is the best available option for this network. Because it involves the management of user accounts, it will involve some administrative burden.

14. **C** Windows 95 does not natively support user-level security. It must use the database in Windows NT or Novell NetWare.

15. **C** This level of redundancy may seem unnecessary, but it is the core of Windows NT security.

16. **C** Users can be given access directly; groups are merely used to make administration easier. Permissions are applied to resources, not users.

17. **B** A partition that is NTFS is viewed the same as any partition when shared over a network. Windows 95 uses passwords only to handle security; it must authenticate users to a Windows NT Server (not workstation) to enforce security.

18. **D** Global groups are a Windows NT group that make administration easier and can be exported to other Windows NT domains.

19. **C** User rights focus on abilities, not resources. Therefore, the ability to create files and printers is associated with permissions.

20. **A** Two user accounts, Administrator and Guest, are always created during the installation process.

21. **A** Share-level access works great with NTFS file security. Also, it is perfectly acceptable to restrict access to data, depending on your specific security needs.

Also, if any network user does not have the correct password, that network user will not have access.

22. **C** You should rename your Administrator account to protect it from intrusion.

23. **B** User accounts should never be shared by people. If they are, security is at risk.

24. **B** Usernames must always be unique.

25. **C** Never write down passwords. Only the user should know his or her password.

26. **B** A user profile can contain a home directory and desktop settings, and it can be mandatory or user-generated. It can be copied, but not to create duplicates.

27. **B** Groups are not added to the ACL; the users in the groups are added to the ACL. Add users to groups to grant them permissions.

28. **D** All of the above. A user account or a system account can log in as a service.

29. **A** Groups are used to simplify user management.

30. **B** False. Microsoft has provided a large number of groups, most of which are adequate for user and resource management.

31. **C** Remember this for user management: Place users into global groups, place global groups into local groups, grant resources to local groups.

32. **B** All of the business needs, including economics and user satisfaction, must be considered when determining network security configuration.

33. **C** Setting the minimum length for a password is reasonable and is supported in User Manager for Domains.

34. **A** The group should have the appropriate user right. Adding the Backup Operators group to the Administrators group defeats the purpose of having a group that is capable of backing up and restoring files.

35. **C** The Everyone group contains all defined and undefined users and cannot be modified. No users can be added to or removed from this group.

36. **D** There is no tool called Group Manager for Domains.

37. **C** Remember this phrase: Users go into global groups, global groups go into local groups, local groups get resources.

38. **B** You may assign resources directly to a user, but you will save yourself many administrative headaches by placing users in groups and assigning rights on a group basis.

39. **A** It is not necessary to set permissions to give users access.

40. **A** This method of access is called Access Permissions applied to a shared resource.

41. **A** Although it's not very secure, it is the easiest to administer.

42. **C** The ACL is the list of users that have access to the resource.

43. **B** A Novell NetWare server will authenticate users, and although access-control is not as secure as user-level control, it is secure enough for some networks.

44. **B** File-level security requires that your server be formatted NTFS on the drive to be secured.

45. **D** If you eschew placing users into groups for management, it will come back to haunt you at a later date. A good administrator always uses groups.

46. **A** Setting up permissions on an NTFS volume can be time-consuming, but it's very secure. It will not function on a FAT volume.

47. **C** Although NTFS can keep a user with physical access from logging in, there is never a substitute for physical security.

48. **D** Simply remove the Everyone group's access, as shown in exercise 3.1.3.

49. **B** Even the most stringent security in the world can be broken if passwords are not secure. However, some organizations do not require a high degree of security.

50. **A** The password is the user account. The profile contains only additional information.

51. **C** Windows 95 only allows share-level security set by a password. You may set a password for read-only, full access, or both.

52. **C** If no password is used, the "depends on password" box is grayed out and the administrator has to choose between read-only and full-access.

53 **A** This level of access is the least secure of all Microsoft implementations. Windows 95 passwords do not expire.

54. **C** It's very quick and easy to administer.

3.1 Key Words

Server

User

Resource

Authenticate

Groups

Print Server

User-level security

Share-level security

Read-only

Depends on password

3.2   Choose a Disaster Recovery Plan for Various Situations

One of the major issues that a network administrator must address is the possibility of system failure and associated downtime. The administrator must handle two major issues to guard against the danger of a failed server:

Protecting data

Reducing downtime

A.   Protecting Data

Natural disasters, equipment failures, power surges, and deliberate vandalism can all damage your network. Microsoft focuses on these strategies for preventing data loss:

Backup (technical, procedural)

Uninterruptible Power Supply (UPS)

1. Backup

A backup schedule is an essential part of any data-protection strategy. You should design a backup system that is right for your situation and the data on your network. A comprehensive backup policy will fall into one of the following categories:

Single backup server

Individual tape units on each server

Independent, redundant backup network

The old method of simply copying data from one drive to another is not effective for a network. Many companies choose to rotate multiple copies of tape and store the additional copies off-site. Storing the backups off-site is a critical part of any backup policy, as it guards against physical calamity.

- **Single backup server:** This strategy uses a centralized backup server with a very large tape drive or an array of multiple tape drives. Each server is connected to the backup server over the network. If you have a large amount of data to back up, you may need a large array of multigigabyte tape drives to store all the data. This can get very expensive.

    If your servers are spread out over multiple floors, you can administer and monitor all the backup activity from a central location.

- **Individual tape units:** This system involves a smaller tape unit installed on each server. Individual units may cost less than the larger array required to back up an entire network. However, this can be more difficult to administer, and you must manage a larger number of individual tapes. For a network spread across several buildings, this may present an attractive alternative if management of the units can be delegated to on-site personnel.

- **Independent, redundant backup network:** If you have chosen a centralized backup server, you should be aware that huge amounts of data are transferred during a backup. This enormous amount of data can seriously degrade system performance. For that reason, you may want to connect your servers to the central backup server using a second network card in each data server.

Any backup plan should include a combination of full and incremental backups. A *full* backup is used to create a complete backup, whereas an *incremental* backup is used to backup all files modified since the last full backup.

If your network is capable, you should attempt to perform full backups nightly. Most likely, this is an option for only the smallest servers. Because full backups can be so lengthy, most administrators perform full backups weekly and perform incremental backups each night during the week.

A log of backups can be important. Also, a strategy that uses tape names and dates create a self-organizing log that can assist in managing tapes. Don't rely on your server as the tape log!! If it crashes and you need to restore from tape, you won't be able to get to the log. Microsoft recommends that you make two copies of the backup log: Store one with the backup tapes, and keep one at the computer site.

You should simulate a disaster recovery plan before you rely on your system. Never experiment with crucial data. Only test with items you can afford to lose.

2. Uninterruptible Power Supply

An Uninterruptible Power Supply (UPS) is a special device that continues to supply electricity after a power failure. UPSs commonly are used with network servers to prevent a disorderly shutdown that could damage data on the server.

The UPS can communicate with the server via software. In the event of a power failure, you can configure the server to:

- Shut down the server gracefully to avoid data loss.
- Send a broadcast message to all users about the power failure and notify them that the server will shut down.
- Send an administrative alert to the system administrator about power loss.
- Page the administrator using a regular phone pager (not all systems support this).

Most UPSs provide roughly fifteen minutes within which the server will be shut down gracefully.

Backups mainly provide a quick method for system recovery. They require a long and tedious restore process that can cost your company dearly in lost revenue and productivity.

B.   Recovering from System Failure

In order for a network to be secure, it must perform as expected. If the network is not kept up and running on a daily basis, the users will be unable to rely on it. Therefore, procedures for preventing downtime from a hardware failure should be implemented.

1. Implementing a Fault-Tolerant Design

Any fault-tolerant design needs to balance the concerns of cost versus the loss to be avoided. If your network absolutely must function 24 hours a day, 7 days a week, 365 days a year (as in a medical environment, for example), a more-expensive design that provides advanced levels of redundancy is more appropriate. The severity of a projected loss must be balanced against the likelihood of the disaster occurring.

2. Using RAID

A vital tool for protecting a network's data is the use of a Redundant Array of Inexpensive Disks (RAID). A RAID system combines two or more disks to create a virtual disk structure that can continue functioning even if one of the disks fails.

RAID 1 and RAID 5 are the only fault-tolerant RAID levels currently in use. RAID 2 through 4 were attempts to perfect what later became RAID 5. RAID 1 refers to *disk mirroring*, in which a complete duplicate of the mirrored disk is created. If one disk fails, the array continues to function. If you split your RAID 1 array across multiple disk controllers, this is called *duplexing* instead of *mirroring*. RAID 5 uses three or more disks to create a *stripe set with parity*. RAID 0 is used, but is not fault-tolerant.

Disk mirroring is defined as two hard drives—one primary, one secondary—that use the same disk channel (controller cards and cable). Disk mirroring is most commonly configured by using disk drives contained in the server. Duplexing is a form of mirroring that enables you to configure a more robust hardware environment.

Both RAID 1 and RAID 5 require that you have disks of approximately the same size. Both Windows NT and Novell NetWare will build RAID arrays using software only. A number of different vendors also offer hardware RAID systems, which tend to be faster and more expensive. Hardware RAID will operate with any operating system, including Windows 95.

Most network administrators prefer the RAID 5 solution. However, mirroring tends to be the favorite on smaller, non-dedicated servers.

> **A fault-tolerant disk scheme is used only to speed recovery time from a hardware fault. None of these RAID levels is intended to be a replacement for regular tape backups. If you damage your data, the RAID array will faithfully duplicate your mistake.**

Table 3.2.1 provides a comparison of the two types of RAID.

Table 3.2.1   RAID 1 versus RAID 5

RAID 1	RAID 5
Costs less initially, as it requires only two disks.	Costs more initially because it requires at least three disks.
Costs more per megabyte because the array gives you only 50% of the usable space. The other 50% is used as the mirror.	Costs less per megabyte. This advantage grows as you add additional disks. The usable space is drivesize * n−1.
Is the only software RAID type available for the Windows NT system partition.	A software RAID 5 array cannot be used for the Windows NT system volume.

RAID 1	RAID 5
Drives are paired or mirrored, with each byte of information being written to each identical drive. You can duplex these devices by adding a separate drive controller for each drive.	A Windows NT server using software RAID can combine a maximum of 32 disks. Assuming a 20G disk, this would be a 640G array. As the saying goes, 640G should be more space than anyone should ever need.
	Uses striping with parity information written across multiple drives to enable fault-tolerance with a minimum of wasted disk space. This level also offers the advantage of enabling relatively efficient performance on writes to the drives, as well as excellent read performance.
	RAID 5 requires at least three drives because it writes data across two of them and then calculates parity block on the third disk.

3.2 Exercise: Exploring Windows NT's Disk Administrator

Remember that changes made to your disk configuration can have a serious effect on the system. Do not make any changes in Disk Administrator unless you have carefully planned them previously!

Objective: Explore the options available through Disk Administrator, such as establishing and breaking mirrored drives and creating or regenerating stripe sets with parity.

To complete this exercise, log on to a Windows NT 4.0 server or workstation with an account that has administrative authority. The server or workstation used can be a production machine; no changes will actually be made to the computer's configuration during this exercise.

1. Click Start, Programs, Administrative Tools. Then choose Disk Administrator.

2. Observe the Disk Administrator window and maximize it if it is not already in this state. The configuration of the disk or disks on your machine appears.

3. Click one of the partitions on your screen. A dark black line appears around the partition, indicating that the partition is selected. Right-click the partition to open the context-sensitive menu. Note that you can format the partition, change its logical drive letter, or examine its properties. If the disk is removable, the Eject option is also available.

4. Click Partition in the menu bar and examine the choices. Most of the choices are unavailable, but they include Create Volume Set and Create Stripe Set. You also can change your active partition in this menu.

5. Click Fault Tolerance on the menu bar (Windows NT Server only) and observe that this menu enables you to establish and break mirrored drives, as well as to create or regenerate stripe sets with parity.

6. Feel free to explore further. When you are finished examining the menus and options, close the Disk Administrator by clicking Partition, Exit.

3.2　Practice Problems

1. The possibility of catastrophic system failure:

    A. Is reduced through the robust architecture of Windows NT Server.

    B. Is a very real possibility that must be planned for to minimize its negative impact.

    C. Can be prevented through the use of tape backups.

    D. Requires that you use a rotating schedule of tape backups.

2. Disaster recovery should include

    A. Antivirus software and a tape backup.

    B. A backup system or, if necessary, a fully redundant backup network.

    C. A copy of the user database and user passwords.

    D. A plan for protecting crucial data and reducing downtime.

3. A UPS is crucial for a backup plan because

    A. It can deliver new equipment faster than the US post office.

    B. A UPS can allow your system to shut down gracefully in a power outage.

    C. A UPS allows your tape units to restore the software even while the power is out.

    D. A UPS will act as a central tape library.

The following four questions use this situation as a scenario.

Network type:

Windows NT servers, NetWare servers

Protocols:

NetBEUI, IPX

Workstations:

30 Windows NT workstations

Servers:

7 servers, NetWare and Windows NT

Your network contains some mission-critical data. If a disaster caused the data to be permanently lost, the company would have no choice but to go out of business. However, it is acceptable to roll back to the previous day's work. Traffic and network performance are operating within normal baseline parameters. The office has three locations, connected via a WAN.

You want to implement a backup plan.

Required objectives:

- The network must have no more than eight hours of downtime.

- If one site goes down, the others must be able to function.

Desired objectives:

- Network performance should not be adversely impacted by the strategy.

- Cost should be kept to reasonable levels.

4. You decide to implement a fully redundant backup network. You use an isolated network segment and a centralized tape backup server. You also keep a spare server in reserve. This plan will:

    A. Perform both of the required objectives and both of the desired objectives.

    B. Perform both of the required objectives and one of the desired objectives.

C. Perform both of the required objectives and none of the desired objectives.

D. Not perform the required objectives.

5. You decide to use single tape units on each server. You maintain a spare server just in case. In addition, you do daily full backups and move the tapes to each of the other locations. This plan will:

A. Perform both of the required objectives and both of the desired objectives.

B. Perform both of the required objectives and one of the desired objectives.

C. Perform both of the required objectives and none of the desired objectives.

D. Not perform the required objectives.

6. You decide to implement a redundant-heartbeat server for each server so that if a catastrophe occurs, the new server will simply take over for the failed unit. You augment this with tape units on each server. This plan will:

A. Perform both of the required objectives and both of the desired objectives.

B. Perform both of the required objectives and one of the desired objectives.

C. Perform both of the required objectives and none of the desired objectives.

D. Not perform the required objectives.

7. You implement full RAID 1 mirroring for each disk drive on your servers. In this way, you determine that you can recover

from a failure quickly, and you no longer have to rely on tapes. This plan will:

A. Perform both of the required objectives and both of the desired objectives.

B. Perform both of the required objectives and one of the desired objectives.

C. Perform both of the required objectives and none of the desired objectives.

D. Not perform the required objectives.

8. A single centralized backup server can:

A. Reduce network traffic.

B. Back up all servers at once.

C. Remove tapes to remote sites.

D. Help in the event of network cable failure.

9. With a central backup server, the tape unit

A. Can be more expensive, because it tends to have more capacity than a standalone unit.

B. Is always cost-effective because it can do more work per tape unit.

C. Is more useful in larger networks.

D. Is faster than a directly connected unit.

10. Which of the following is an advantage of using centralized tape servers?

A. Larger tape drives

B. Shorter access times

C. Self-rotating tapes

D. Centralized administration

11. If your network is spread across multiple buildings, your backup strategy could include:

    A. A separate, redundant backup network.

    B. Single tape units on each server.

    C. Both A and B.

    D. Neither A nor B.

12. An *incremental backup*:

    A. Is a backup of only the important data.

    B. Always uses the DOS *archive* attribute to mark files.

    C. Is a backup of the data that has changed since the last full backup.

    D. Is always much smaller than a full backup.

13. A satisfactory backup plan should use

    A. A combination of full, incremental, and differential backups.

    B. A full backup every night if possible and incremental nightly backups if the capacity for daily full backups is unavailable.

    C. Your existing supply of tapes over and over again.

    D. A combination of tape and disks to back up all crucial files.

14. *Differential* backups are used to

    A. Back up more data than an incremental backup.

    B. Reset the DOS *archive* attribute.

    C. Measure the difference in tape speed between a full and incremental backup.

    D. Create backups between full backups.

15. Your network tapes should be

    A. Kept in a central, safe location.

    B. Kept in separate locations. That way, if a physical disaster strikes, the data will survive.

    C. Secured with passwords to prevent infiltration from hackers.

    D. Kept near the server in case they are needed during an emergency.

16. A written log of your tape backups

    A. Is a security risk.

    B. Will be very helpful if you need to piece your network back together from tapes.

    C. Is redundant; that data is all on the server and is backed up on the tapes.

    D. Might be destroyed in a fire.

17. Disaster recovery planning should:

    A. Be taken very seriously. Don't joke around by having a simulated disaster. No one likes a comedian!

    B. Be practiced by having a complete simulated disaster drill. This will uncover holes in your recovery plan.

    C. Use your actual server for testing purposes. What good is a test unless it's on your real server?

    D. Be done without the rest of your department or company's knowledge. After all, how could it be a legitimate test?

18. An independent, redundant backup network

    A. Uses separate protocols over your existing network to minimize traffic and provide a secure path for data to travel.

    B. Uses routers and bridges to create a separate path to your backup server.

C. Uses an additional NIC and cabling to provide a redundant isolated network segment for backups.

D. Uses separate global groups and local groups and keeps a backup copy of the domain controller database.

19. Full backups

A. Should be reserved only for the times when you need to perform a complete backup.

B. Should be performed weekly or, if you can manage it, daily.

C. Should contain all the data that has *fully* changed since the last backup.

D. Are created by combining all the *incremental* backups.

20. When managing tapes, you should

A. Overwrite your tapes nightly (there's no reason to keep old data around anyway).

B. Lock them in a safe in the server room so they're available during an emergency.

C. Have a regular plan that moves tapes off-site, so if a disaster strikes the building, your data will be safe.

D. Password protect them to keep them safe from hackers.

21. If you decide to keep a log of your tape backups,

A. A date-oriented log would be nearly self-organizing (and ease-of-use helps in an emergency).

B. You should use a secret code to organize the tapes so hackers cannot uncover your organizational plan.

C. Simply save it on the server; no reason to duplicate data.

D. You must use a rigid plan that balances cost, secrecy, and economic impact.

22. Which of the following statements is Microsoft's recommendation for a tape backup log?

A. Create duplicates so you can keep one with the off-site backups and one on-site near the server.

B. Keep it safely secured in a safe place.

C. Keep it off-site with the off-site backup tapes. After all, you won't need it on-site if the server is still functioning.

D. Keep the log on a Microsoft Windows NT NTFS file-level secured partition.

23. A UPS can do which of the following?

A. Shut the server down gracefully.

B. Send a broadcast message to the users.

C. Send a telephone pager message to the system administrator.

D. All of the above.

24. An *uninterruptible power supply* is used to

A. Provide uninterrupted power during a power outage.

B. Move your server from one building to the next without unplugging it.

C. Shut the server down gracefully, providing roughly fifteen minutes of power during an outage.

D. Replace the standard fuse box in a server room.

25. Which of the following is the most common type of hardware failure?

A. Power failure

B. Drive failure

C. Server failure

D. User failure

26. A system that is able to function despite a hardware failure is:

   A. Using a UPS to provide power.

   B. Called *fault-tolerant*.

   C. Called *hardware-resistant*.

   D. Not yet a possibility; however, advanced operating systems like Microsoft Windows NT Server help a system continue to function.

27. A fault-tolerant design must

   A. Not be concerned with price and performance. Fault-tolerance defines only its ability to function.

   B. Use a *redundant array* of servers and disks.

   C. Use an advanced operating system, such as Microsoft Windows NT or Novell NetWare.

   D. Balance the concerns of downtime versus cost and performance. No one solution is best for all users.

28. A good plan for balancing the needs of a fault-tolerant system would

   A. Consider the cost of the operating system, the time needed to reinstall, and the likelihood of disaster.

   B. Balance price of the fault-tolerant array with the performance of no array.

   C. Balance the severity of a projected loss with the likelihood of the loss occurring.

   D. Use meetings to talk to each department in your company.

29. A fully redundant network array with duplicate hubs, wiring, routers, and switches would

   A. Not be justified because you need to weigh the cost against the severity of a projected loss.

   B. Be justified if the severity of the projected loss were high enough.

   C. Not be required if you back up your data with tapes and move the tapes to off-site locations.

   D. Keep the primary network from being overburdened during back-ups.

30. Hardware RAID

   A. Kills software bugs dead.

   B. Is slower than software RAID.

   C. Groups disks into a fault-tolerant design.

   D. Can be used in place of tape backups.

31. Which is true of RAID?

   A. RAID 2 should always be used instead of RAID 1.

   B. RAID 1 is disk mirroring; RAID 2 is duplexing with two controllers.

   C. RAID 1 and RAID 5 are the only fault-tolerant RAID designs being used.

   D. The RAID number refers to the number of disks in your array, so the higher the number, the more fault-tolerant your array. That's why RAID 0 is not fault-tolerant.

32. RAID 1 is called

   A. Disk mirroring or disk duplexing.

   B. Disk mirroring or disk striping.

   C. Disk mirroring with parity.

   D. Disk parity with striping.

33. Which is not true of RAID 1?

   A. You can split your disk mirror across multiple controllers.

   B. You can split your disk stripe across multiple controllers.

C. RAID 1 is preferred over RAID 2.

D. You can rebuild a disk array if one disk completely fails and crashes.

34. RAID mirroring:

A. Creates a complete duplicate of the primary drive.

B. Uses parity information stored on the mirrored disk to rebuild lost information.

C. Can be used instead of a tape backup.

D. Can be used with three or more disks.

35. RAID 5

A. Can be used with 2 to 32 disks.

B. Duplexes data across multiple controllers.

C. Includes disks, tapes, and a UPS.

D. Requires at least three disks.

36. All fault-tolerant RAID arrays

A. Can use disks of different sizes if RAID is implemented in software.

B. Should use disks of approximately the same size.

C. Can continue running during a power failure if properly configured.

D. Require special *software drivers* to function.

37. RAID can be

A. Implemented in hardware only.

B. Implemented in hardware and software.

C. Implemented in software only.

D. Replaced by a redundant backup network.

38. Software RAID

A. Must be used if you use Windows 95, because Windows 95 does not support hardware RAID.

B. Requires an advanced operating system such as Windows NT or Novell NetWare.

C. Is faster than hardware RAID.

D. Uses the HMA (High Memory Area) to store buffers and data.

39. Which of the following statements about the cost of a RAID array is true?

A. RAID 1 cost more in larger arrays.

B. RAID 1 costs the same as RAID 5; the difference is software.

C. RAID 1 costs less in larger arrays.

D. RAID 5 costs more in larger arrays.

40. Which is NOT true of RAID 1?

A. It is the only software RAID level available for Windows NT Work-station.

B. It is the only software RAID level available for the Windows NT system partition.

C. It stores a parity checksum on a duplicate drive.

D. It is available in Novell NetWare.

41. RAID 5

A. Can use an infinite number of disks to create large arrays.

B. Uses half of the space to store parity checksum data.

C. Can use up to 32 disks in a Windows NT array.

D. Costs less than RAID 1 to start.

42. A hardware RAID 5 array

    A. Is slower than a more advanced Windows NT software array.

    B. Is faster than a Windows NT or Novell NetWare software array.

    C. Does not support "hot swapping" of disks.

    D. Creates a duplicate disk for each disk in the array.

43. A truly fault-tolerant disk array and plan

    A. Does not replace your tape drive; the RAID array will faithfully recreate all your mistakes in disk management.

    B. Allows you to move away from slow, cumbersome tape drives.

    C. Includes a log of each disk, kept off-site to guard against physical calamity.

    D. Will page the administrator and send a broadcast alert to users.

44. Which is true of RAID arrays?

    A. Disk mirroring is a form of disk duplexing.

    B. Disk duplexing is a form of disk striping.

    C. Disk duplexing is a form of disk mirroring.

    D. Disk striping is a form of disk duplexing.

45. The purpose of a fault-tolerant RAID array is to

    A. Speed recovery in the event of a hardware failure.

    B. Replace cumbersome tape devices and procedures.

    C. Duplicate data across servers and WAN networks.

    D. Keep the server functioning in the event of a power failure.

46. The term *fault tolerance* actually refers to

    A. Only RAID levels 1 through 5.

    B. The ability of a system to continue functioning despite a hardware failure.

    C. A RAID array or a UPS device.

    D. The prevention of downtime.

3.2   Answers and Explanations: Practice Problems

1. **B**   Count on it. If you plan for it, it won't hurt as bad.

2. **D**   The core components of a disaster recovery are safeguarding data and getting the network back up and running quickly.

3. **B**   An uninterruptible power supply is crucial for server integrity.

4. **D**   If the centralized tape server fails, the entire network is without a backup.

5. **A**   Network performance will not suffer because the tape units are directly connected to each server.

6. **C**   This is not a cost-effective solution.

7. **D**   A RAID unit will not save you in the event of data loss. It will faithfully replicate your mistake across all drives in the array.

8. **B**   A centralized server can increase network traffic.

9. **A**   The costs can vary, but centralized tape servers tend to be more expensive per tape unit. Because of this, they tend to be more effective in small to mid-sized networks.

10. **D** A large tape unit could be used in a standalone tape unit. The key benefit is centralized administration.

11. **C** Both of these plans would work in a multibuilding WAN.

12. **C** Some incremental backups can be huge, and some file systems do not use the DOS *archive* attribute.

13. **B** Smaller networks can use a full backup daily. If you use a large number of tapes, you can still restore data that dates back a week, a month, or as long as you have tapes for.

14. **A** An *incremental* backup can be used instead, but it will take longer to restore.

15. **B** If you kept the tapes in a separate location, you would be able to rebuild the entire network with all new equipment.

16. **B** A written log is not an appreciable risk, but it can save volumes of time during an emergency.

17. **B** You should have a drill, but don't keep it a secret. And don't use your company's production network either. Sensitive data is at stake.

18. **C** The backup network is completely separate from the primary network.

19. **B** If you can manage, do a full backup daily.

20. **C** Keep the tapes off-site.

21. **A** A log can be very useful. If it's based on date and time, it's practically self-organizing!

22. **A** Microsoft recommends duplicating the tape log and keeping one on-site and one with the off-site backups.

23. **D** UPSs can typically do all of these things.

24. **C** A UPS is designed to bring the server down gracefully.

25. **B** Hard disk drive failure is the most common type of hardware failure.

26. **B** This system would be called *fault tolerant.*

27. **D** All system plans should be concerned the cost of downtime versus the cost of a fault-tolerant system.

28. **C** You should balance the severity against the likelihood of a projected loss.

29. **B** If the severity of the projected loss is high enough, an expensive solution might be justified.

30. **C** RAID is the acronym for redundant disk arrays.

31. **C** RAID 1 and RAID 5 are the only fault-tolerant RAID types currently in use. RAID 0 is not fault-tolerant, and RAID 2 through RAID 4 were precursors to RAID 5.

32. **A** Disk mirroring uses one controller; disk duplexing is just like mirroring, but it uses two controllers.

33. **B** RAID 1 does not use disk striping.

34. **A** RAID 1 uses only two disks; parity information is how RAID 5 stores data.

35. **D** RAID 5 cannot be used with fewer than three disks.

36. **B** All fault-tolerant RAID arrays should use disks of approximately the same size.

37. **B** RAID can be implemented in hardware and software.

38. **B** NetWare and Windows NT support software RAID.

39. **A** RAID 1 costs more in larger arrays because you must double the disk size to be mirrored.

40. **C** RAID 1 stores a copy of the data, not a checksum. RAID 5 stores a checksum.

41. **C** Windows NT can create an array with up to 32 disks.

3

42. **B** Hardware RAID is faster than software RAID.

43. **A** RAID does not replace tape. RAID guards against hardware failure.

44. **C** Duplexing and mirroring both create drive duplicates, but duplexing simply uses an additional disk controller.

45. **A** The primary purpose of RAID is to get the system back up quickly or to continue running if a drive fails.

46. **B** Fault tolerance means the system will tolerate a fault or hardware failure.

3.2 Key Words

Disk mirroring

Disk duplexing

RAID 1

RAID 0

Fault tolerant

RAID 5

UPS

Antivirus software

3.3   Given the Manufacturer's Documentation for the Network Adapter, Install, Configure, and Resolve Hardware Conflicts for Multiple Network Adapters in a Token-Ring or Ethernet Network

A *network adapter card* is required for network communications. Ethernet and token-ring are two types of network adapter cards. You should be able to install and configure your network adapter cards, and you should be able to troubleshoot problems associated with them.

A Network Interface Card (NIC) links a PC with the network cabling system. The card has one or more user-accessible ports to which the network cabling medium is connected. Typical connections include RJ-45 and BNC. It is the job of the NIC to prepare the data for transmission over the network.

All NICs require a *driver*, (software that manages the device). The driver activates the NIC and *binds* it to the network protocols being used. If you were to view the OSI 7-layer model, you'd see the NIC near the Data Link Layer at the bottom. The Data Link Layer is right above the physical layer and has been split into two sublayers: the Media Access Control and the Logical Link Control. The driver is found in the Media Access Control sublayer, from which we derive the MAC address, the unique burned-in address of the NIC.

Functions of the NIC include:

- **Preparing data for the transmission medium**

  This role is where the data from higher layers is placed into an Ethernet frame or token-ring frame. On the receiving card, the data packet is removed from the frame and passed to higher layers.

- **Sending data**

  This refers to the physical communications of the network. For example, on a 10-Base 2 network, this refers to the card creating the pulses of electricity and sending them over the coaxial cable. On a token-ring network, this would refer to the card inserting into the ring and generating a token, if necessary.

- **Controlling the flow of data from the PC to the transmission medium**

  On an Ethernet network, the card is responsible for collision-detection and avoidance. If the card detects a collision, it will wait a random interval before retransmitting. On a token-ring network, the card will generate a token or receive a token before communicating.

A.   Installing Network Adapter Cards

The details of how to install a network adapter card depend on the card. You should check the manufacturer's documentation. On the *Networking Essentials* test, some questions will state that you have followed the manufacturer's instructions; some will not. Also, the installation steps will vary depending on the operating system. Common steps will be something like this:

1. Physically plug the card into the expansion slot, configuring jumpers and DIP switches as required, or configure the card using the manufacturer's software utility.

2. Install the network adapter card driver.

3. Configure the card so that the network adapter card won't conflict with other devices.

4. Add the appropriate network protocols for your network.

5. Add the appropriate client software for your network.

6. Attach the network cable to the card.

Depending on the hardware and operating system, some of these steps might happen automatically when you plug a card into the slot and start your system.

If the NIC will not physically fit in your system, you have probably purchased the incorrect *data bus* type. PCs currently support four data bus types:

- **ISA:** This is the standard data bus architecture, originally developed for the IBM AT.

- **VESA Local Bus:** This is one enhancement to the ISA bus. An additional slot continues after the ISA slot for VESA Local Bus devices. VESA Local Bus cards *can* be installed in ISA slots, but they will then function only in ISA mode.

- **EISA:** These slots will accept either EISA cards or ISA cards. However, EISA cards cannot be placed into an ISA slot.

- **MicroChannel:** This standard was proposed by IBM to replace the ISA bus. It was not widely accepted and has fallen into disuse.

- **PCI:** This is the most popular bus today. Most Pentium and above systems include both ISA and PCI slots. PCI slots are shorter and more offset than ISA slots.

If you can't physically install your card into the slot, you have probably purchased the incorrect data bus type for your computer.

In addition, certain network cards support only some types of cabling. In general, three types of cabling connections are used:

- **RJ-45** is used to connect to Category 5 or Category 3 twisted-pair cable.

- **RG-56** is used to connect to coaxial cable used for 10-Base 2 networks.

- **AUI connectors** are used to connect to Category 5 or Category 3 twisted-pair cables through a *media filter*, which converts the 9-pin AUI interface to the RJ-45 style interface.

If you cannot physically connect your NIC to the network cable, you have probably purchased a NIC with the wrong connector type for your network.

B. Configuring Network Adapter Cards

You must configure your card to communicate with the operating system. In many cases, you must manually configure the adapter card (through jumper or DIP switch settings) so that it can communicate with the operating system. In other cases, you may use a software utility provided by the manufacturer to configure the card.

There are several settings that must be properly set in order to prevent conflict with other devices on your system. These are some of the resource settings for a network adapter that you have to be concerned with:

IRQ

Base I/O port address

Base memory address

Table 3.3.1 contains a list of IRQs, including those that should *not* be used for a NIC and those that *might* be used for a NIC.

Table 3.3.1

IRQ	Reserved By	Might Be Used By
1	Keyboard	
2	IRQ9	
3		COM2 (modem, mouse)
4		COM1
5		LPT2
6	Floppy controller	
7	LPT1	
8	System Clock	
9		
10		
11		
12		PS/2 Mouse
13	Math processor	
14	Hard drive controller	
15	Additional IDE controller	

Those items reserved by a device cannot be used by the NIC. The possible exception is IRQ 2, which is linked to IRQ9. Other IRQs might be used by some devices but might not be used for others. For example, IRQ 3 is a popular choice for NIC cards, but it will not function on a computer that has a modem or mouse operating on COM2.

The base I/O port address defines a memory address through which data flows to and from the adapter. The base I/O port address functions more like a port, defining a channel to the adapter.

The *base memory address* is a place in the computer's memory that marks the beginning of a buffer area reserved for the network adapter. Not all network adapter cards use the computer's RAM, and therefore, not all adapters require a base memory address setting. Typical regions are C800 through CFFF or D800 through DFFF. If you are using a DOS memory manager such as EMM386.exe, you must exclude this region from use by EMM386.exe.

C.   Resolving Hardware Conflicts

Hardware conflicts occur when the devices on the system compete for the same system resources, such as interrupt request lines, base I/O port addresses, and base memory addresses.

In Windows NT, a hardware conflict might invoke a warning message from the system or an entry in the Event Log. If you experience a hardware conflict, use Windows NT Diagnostics to check resource settings for system devices. Then change the resource settings of any conflicting devices.

In Windows 95, use Device Manager (see the following note) to spot hardware conflicts and track resource settings.

If the NIC won't initialize correctly, the problem is one of three things:

- IRQ conflict with another device
- I/O base address conflict with another device
- The NIC has a physical problem and should be replaced

An adapter RAM conflict will typically not show as a physical problem. The symptoms associated with a RAM conflict are more subtle. The adapter will appear to initialize correctly, but it will not be able to view any resources on the network. In some cases, the configuration lights on the back of the NIC will fail to light.

D.   Resolving Software Conflicts

Many questions on the *Networking Essentials* exam will assume your NIC is functioning properly. When this is the case, you may rule out IRQ conflicts, base address conflicts, and adapter RAM conflicts. You must then turn your attention to software issues.

There are several problems associated with software problems and their common symptoms. Memorize this list:

- **Protocol mismatch:** Many networks will use multiple protocols. This is because different server types traditionally use different protocols. For example, Novell NetWare servers typically use IPX to communicate. UNIX servers might use TCP/IP, whereas older Microsoft servers might use NetBEUI.

  If your client can connect to only some network resources but not others, and all other workstations can connect to all network resources, your workstation probably is suffering from a protocol mismatch. You must load the correct protocol to connect to the appropriate resource.

- **Client misconfiguration:** In addition to protocols, each server type requires that client PCs are using the correct client software. For example, both Windows NT and Novell NetWare can use the IPX protocol, but they use different client software. Windows 95 and Windows NT have a specific client for NetWare networks that must be loaded before the client PC can connect to a NetWare server.

For a DOS workstation, the NetWare requester must be loaded before that workstation can connect to a NetWare server. The Microsoft MS-DOS networking client must also be loaded before the workstation can connect to a Windows NT server.

If all your servers and workstations run the IPX protocol only, but your workstations can only see some of the servers, you likely have a client misconfiguration issue.

- **Protocol misconfiguration:** Finally, you may suffer from a protocol misconfiguration issue. The IPX protocol may use different frame types. Most modern implementations use the more advanced 802.2 frame type, while older implementations use 802.3.

A Microsoft workstation will attempt to auto-detect the appropriate frame type. If it is unable to correctly detect the frame type, it will default to 802.2. If this is not correct, you will not be able to communicate with the server. If this occurs, you must manually set the frame type to 802.3.

This section examined the network adapter card—an essential component in Ethernet and token-ring networks. The network adapter card performs several functions, including preparing, sending, and controlling the flow of data to the network transmission medium. This chapter also discussed how to install and configure network adapters. Configuration tasks for a network adapter card include setting jumpers or DIP switches on the card itself, as well as configuring resource settings (such as IRQ, Base I/O port address, and base memory address) that the operating system must use to communicate with the card.

3.3   Exercises

1. Network Adapter Resource Settings

Objective: Become familiar with the process of configuring network adapter resource settings in Windows NT

Estimated time: 10 minutes

Earlier in this chapter, you learned how to install a network adapter card driver by using Windows NT's Network application. You also can use the Network application to check or change the resource settings for an adapter that is already installed.

1.   Click the Start button and choose Settings/Control Panel. Double-click the Windows NT Control Panel Network application.

2.   In the Network application, click the Adapters tab.

3.   Select the network adapter that is currently installed on your system.

4.   Click the Properties button, and the Network Card Setup dialog box appears on your screen.

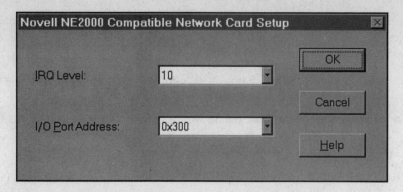

Figure 3.3.1 A Network Card Setup dialog box.

5. In the Network Card Setup dialog box, you can change the resource settings as required. Don't change the settings unless you're experiencing problems, though, because you could introduce a hardware conflict with another device.

6. Click Cancel to leave the Network Card Setup dialog box, and then click Cancel again to leave the Network application.

2. Windows NT Diagnostics

Objective: Learn to check resource settings through Windows NT Diagnostics

Estimated time: 10 minutes

Windows NT Diagnostics tabulates a number of important system parameters. You can use Windows NT Diagnostics to help resolve resource conflicts for network adapters.

1. Click the Start button and choose Programs/Administrative Tools. Choose Windows NT Diagnostics from the Administrative Tools menu.

2. Windows NT Diagnostics provides several tabs with information on different aspects of the system. Choose the Resources tab.

3. Figure 3.3.2 displays the IRQ settings for system devices. (Note that the network adapter card for which the resource settings were displayed in Figure 3.3.2 is listed here beside IRQ10.) The buttons at the bottom of the screen invoke views of other resource settings. Click a button to see the associated list, such as the I/O ports. Don't be alarmed if the list looks complex.

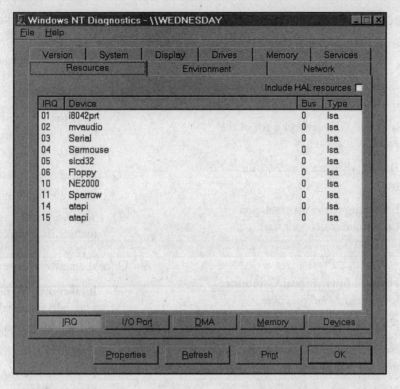

Figure 3.3.2   The Windows NT Diagnostics Resources tab showing IRQ settings.

3.3 Practice Problems

1. The Network Card *driver* is responsible for

    A. Enabling the hardware and binding the software.

    B. Managing the network path of the protocol software.

    C. Pushing the data across the network.

    D. Beaconing to the other adapter cards to limit network traffic.

2. NIC is shorthand for:

    A. Network International Committee for standards and practices.

    B. Network Interface Card.

    C. Networking Intelligent Card management software.

    D. New International Conference for networking.

3. If your network card cannot be physically connected to the cable,

    A. You don't have enough cable.

    B. Your network adapter uses the wrong connector type.

    C. You need a converter to connect the cable.

    D. You must re-read the manufacturer's instructions.

4. Once the network driver is loaded,

    A. You can communicate to all devices on your network.

    B. You can communicate to all devices that use a compatible protocol.

    C. You can communicate using the selected protocols.

    D. You can communicate to all devices that use a compatible client.

5. The network driver is located where in the 7-layer OSI model?

    A. Near the bottom, to interface between the physical layer and the protocol stack.

    B. Near the top, so it can direct and control action further down in the protocol stack.

    C. Near the session and transport layers in the protocol stack.

    D. The 7-layer OSI model does not include the network driver.

6. Once the network driver is loaded:

    A. It takes over all functions of the OSI 7-layer model.

    B. The OSI 7-layer load sequence is complete.

    C. Frames can be transmitted across the network.

    D. Protocols and higher levels of the OSI 7-layer model can be loaded.

7. The Network Interface Card is responsible for which actions?

    A. Only a small part of communications; preparing data for the transmission medium, sending data, and controlling the flow of data from the PC to the transmission medium

    B. Binding protocols and clients to lower-level processes

    C. Inserting the ring-token into the Ethernet

    D. Managing communications between each level of the OSI 7–layer network model

8. When installing a Windows NT-compatible NIC,

    A. The process is the same for all Windows NT-compliant cards.

B. You can use Plug-n-Play to configure the card.

C. You should consult the manufacturer's installation instructions.

D. You always need to use NetBEUI to communicate to Windows NT.

9. When configuring your NIC,

A. You must decide between the available protocols and load the one you need for your network.

B. You can decide to load all protocols to your NIC and use as many of them as you want.

C. You must explicitly bind each protocol to the network card after loading that protocol.

D. You can decide to load all network drivers to your NIC and use as many of them as you want.

10. The manufacturer's instructions for a NIC should be

A. Stored in a safe place away from the server in case a physical disaster occurs.

B. Usd during the installation of the card.

C. Used during the installation of the protocol.

D. Checked only as a last resort; advanced operating systems such as Microsoft Windows NT Server and Novell NetWare are too complicated for them.

11. When configuring the NIC, it is most important to

A. Avoid conflicts with other devices.

B. Avoid conflicts with other protocols.

C. Configure the NIC to use the correct protocol type.

D. Configure the 10-Base 2 NIC to use an RJ-45 connector.

12. Once the NIC is installed and is not conflicting with other devices, it is important to:

A. Load the token and insert it into the frame.

B. Load the frame type into the protocol stack.

C. Create a unique token based on the MAC address.

D. Load the driver, protocols, and clients and attach the network cable.

13. If you suspect that your NIC is not compatible with Windows NT,

A. Check the H.A.L.

B. Check the H.C.L.

C. Check the A.C.L.

D. Check the manufacturer's instructions.

14. Some network adapters will not fit in all systems. If yours doesn't fit:

A. Push really hard; new computer slots are often very tight.

B. Make sure you have the correct data bus architecture.

C. Make sure you have the correct CPU processor type.

D. Check the H.C.L.

15. Which of the following is not true?

A. MCA cards can be used in a VESA LB slot.

B. VESA LB cards can be used in an ISA slot.

C. EISA cards cannot be used in a PCI slot.

D. ISA cards can be used in an EISA slot.

16. Which of the following describes the PCI bus slot?

A. It was invented by IBM to work on their MicroChannel™ PCs.

B. It was invented by Intel for the Pentium™ line of computers.

C. It was an industry reaction against the MicroChannel™ architecture, and it can accommodate ISA cards.

D. It was invented for the original AT™ line of computers.

17. If your NIC supports 10-Base 2 networks:

A. You can connect it to twisted-pair wire using RJ-45.

B. You can connect it using BNC connectors.

C. You must insert it into your token-ring before enabling communications.

D. It will support token-ring but not Ethernet.

18. To configure your NIC,

A. You must set DIP switches and jumpers.

B. You must consult the manufacturer's documentation.

C. You can configure it using software.

D. You must insert it into the computer.

19. Plug and Play

A. Works with Windows NT to configure network adapters.

B. Works with Windows 95 to configure network protocols.

C. Works with Windows 95 to configure hardware devices.

D. Works with Windows 95 or Windows NT to configure hardware devices.

20. When configuring your network adapter, typical settings you must configure are:

A. IRQ, I/O port, and RAM address.

B. IRQ, I/O port, and interrupt.

C. Slot number, protocol, and IRQ.

D. I/O port, DMA channel, and adapter ROM.

21. Which of the following is a good IRQ to use for your NIC?

A. 7

B. 4

C. 3

D. 14

22. Which of the following typically uses IRQ 7?

A. COM1

B. LPT1

C. A Sound Blaster™

D. IRQ 9

23. Which of the following typically shares with IRQ 2?

A. IRQ 9

B. A Sound Blaster™

C. LPT2

D. COM1

24. If your computer uses a serial mouse and an external modem, which of these should you configure the NIC to use?

A. IRQ 4

B. IRQ 3

C. IRQ 10

D. IRQ 1

25. What tool would you use in Windows NT to see if resources are available?

   A. System Administrator

   B. NT Diagnostics

   C. Resource Administrator

   D. Right-click Resources and double-click Availability.

26. If you configure your NIC and the software fails to load properly,

   A. You probably have a conflict with the shared RAM address.

   B. You are using the incorrect protocol stack.

   C. You probably have a conflict with the I/O port or IRQ.

   D. Your I/O port and IRQ are conflicting with one another.

27. If you configure your NIC and the software loads properly but the NIC is not functioning at all,

   A. You have loaded the incorrect network driver.

   B. Your protocol stack is incompatible with the network driver.

   C. Your adapter is not connected to the network.

   D. Your memory manager may be conflicting with your RAM address.

28. Hardware conflicts occur:

   A. When you have the incorrect data bus architecture.

   B. When two components compete for the same resource.

C. When two protocols compete for the same network card.

D. With incompatible software.

29. In Windows NT, where should you check if you suspect a hardware conflict?

   A. The Event Viewer

   B. The Hardware Manager

   C. The Resource Viewer

   D. The Windows NT System Manager

30. In Windows 95, where should you check if you suspect a hardware conflict?

   A. The Event Viewer

   B. The Device Manager

   C. The Resource Viewer

   D. The Windows 95 System Manager

31. Base Memory Address:

   A. Is the central area used by all applications for memory.

   B. Is the area of a network card shared with the PC's main memory.

   C. Is the memory area the network uses in 10-Base T and 10-Base 2 baseband communication.

   D. Is the hardware location of the NIC's resources.

32. A hardware conflict is usually apparent because

   A. The adapter fails to initialize or the software does not load.

   B. The yellow exclamation point in Windows 95's Device Manager shows up.

   C. The Hardware Conflict Wizard (in the Control Panel) shows the conflict.

   D. The adapter's software loads fine but the card fails to function.

3

33. The lights on the back of the network
    card

    A. Are used only during the boot-up
       phase to isolate hardware conflicts.

    B. Always flash regularly when the
       adapter is functioning properly.

    C. Indicate the adapter status.

    D. Are used to illuminate the PC when
       you are working under a dark desk
       or cabinet.

The following four questions use this
situation as a scenario.

Network type:

Windows NT servers, NetWare servers,
UNIX servers

Protocols:

NetBEUI, IPX, TCP/IP

Workstations:

Windows NT workstations, Unix
workstations, Windows 95 workstations

NIC cards:

Ethernet 10-base T using twisted pair

34. You recently installed several new Win-
    dows 95 workstations on your network.
    Although you installed all the default
    software, you cannot see all of the servers.
    Others on your segment can see all of the
    servers, and you can see all the computers
    on your segment and some of the
    computers on other segments.

    Your network software appears to have
    loaded properly. The most likely reason
    you cannot see the servers is:

    A. A hardware conflict with other PCs
       on your segment.

    B. An inappropriate TCP/IP address
       or subnet mask.

C. A protocol mismatch between your
   workstations and the servers.

D. You are using 10-base 2 NICs on
   your 10-base T network.

35. One user cannot access the file and print
    servers, but he can access all the Internet
    applications. What is the most likely
    source of the problem?

    A. Your client software is
       misconfigured.

    B. You are using the incorrect frame
       type for your NetBEUI servers.

    C. The networking software has not
       been loaded, and the Internet
       software has been loaded in its
       place.

    D. The user has not installed any file
       or printer drivers.

36. One client cannot access the NetWare
    servers, but he can access the Windows
    NT and Unix servers just fine. Your
    troubleshooting has determined that the
    correct client software and protocols are
    loaded. The most likely problem is:

    A. An incorrect Ethernet link.

    B. An incorrect BNC to 9-pin media
       filter.

    C. An incorrect token-ring link.

    D. An incorrect frame type.

37. You decide that you need to access only
    the Novell NetWare servers. For your
    Windows 95 workstation, you install and
    configure all the protocols correctly. You
    recall that you were able to connect to the
    Windows NT servers before removing the
    other protocols.

    A. You need to load the Microsoft
       Client for Windows 95.

    B. You need to load the Novell
       NetWare client.

C. You need to load the Novell Client for Windows NT servers.

D. You need to configure the IPX protocol.

38. DOS workstations

    A. Must load a redirector or requester before attaching to a network.

    B. Must load special memory-management software before attaching to a network.

    C. Must redirect memory to the requester before attaching to the network.

    D. Are not capable of attaching to the network.

39. If your network contains NT servers,

    A. MS-DOS workstations must "break the 640K" barrier before attaching to the server.

    B. MS-DOS workstations cannot participate in domain networking.

    C. MS-DOS workstations must request their network traffic through a NetWare redirector before attaching to the servers.

    D. MS-DOS workstations must load the Microsoft MS-DOS network client before attaching to the servers.

40. Suppose your network contains Novell NetWare servers and you add Windows NT or Windows 95 clients to your network. If the clients you added can view one another but not the servers, you should

    A. Let Windows 95 autodetect the frame type.

    B. Manually choose 802.3 because it is more advanced.

    C. Manually choose 802.2 because it is more advanced.

D. Calculate the 802.2 and 802.3 to 802.5 *parity checksum*.

41. Which is not true about frame types?

    A. 802.3 can connect to 802.2, but not vice-versa.

    B. 802.2 can connect to 802.3 because it is more advanced.

    C. Windows 95 workstations can request the appropriate frame type from a DCHP server.

    D. All of the above.

The following four questions use this situation as a scenario.

Network type:

Windows NT servers using NetBEUI, NetWare servers using IPX, Unix servers using TCP/IP

Workstations:

Windows NT workstations, Unix workstations, Windows 95 workstations

NIC cards:

Ethernet 10-base T using twisted pair

42. You have a large network with multiple routers. You limit access to certain servers by loading only those protocols necessary for communication. You find that you cannot connect to your Windows NT servers across your router. The most likely problem is:

    A. Your routers are using frame type 802.2, but the Windows NT servers have defaulted to 802.3.

    B. You have a protocol misconfiguration issue.

    C. Your TCP/IP address is invalid.

    D. NetBEUI is not a routable protocol.

43. You trace the trouble to the NetBEUI protocol. The most likely trouble you are having with it is:

   A. NetBEUI has defaulted to frame type 802.3.

   B. You must configure NetBEUI to use the router broadcast address.

   C. NetBEUI is not a routable protocol.

   D. NetBEUI is causing a software conflict with IPX.

44. You decide to abandon your plans to use protocols to secure the network. However, for Microsoft networking you will need to use NetBIOS. Because of this, you *must* use which protocol:

   A. IPX

   B. TCP/IP

   C. NetBEUI

   D. You may use any of the above protocols.

45. Which is true about NetBIOS and NetBEUI?

   A. NetBIOS (basic-input-output-system) is an interface, while NetBEUI (basic-enhanced-user-interface) is a protocol.

   B. NetBIOS (basic-input-output-system) is a protocol, while NetBEUI (basic-enhanced-user-interface) is an interface.

   C. NetBEUI can be used with any protocol, even TCP/IP.

   D. NetBEUI is required to connect to a Windows NT server.

46. When installing network components:

   A. Always install the software and drivers before you install the network adapter, in order to enable Plug and Play.

   B. Always install the network adapter before you install the software and drivers.

   C. Never install the adapter software while the PC is on.

   D. Always connect to a network location to install the software and drivers for the network adapter.

47. If you are unsure about a certain network adapter:

   A. Install all the network driver software, because one of them will work.

   B. Consult the manufacturer's documentation.

   C. Install the generic IBM-compatible networking software.

   D. Use the Windows NT Plug and Play utility.

48. If you are unsure which protocols your network uses:

   A. Install all the protocols, because one of them will work.

   B. Consult the manufacturer's documentation.

   C. Install the generic Ethernet-compatible networking software.

   D. Use the Windows NT Plug and Play utility.

49. Networking protocols

   A. Must be loaded separately to avoid causing a conflict.

   B. Do not conflict and can be loaded one after the other.

   C. Can conflict if they are not on the Windows NT HCL list.

   D. Require a unique IRQ address.

50. Multiple networking client software in Windows NT and Windows 95:

    A. Usually conflict if they are from different network cards.

    B. Can be run simultaneously.

    C. Are not necessary; they're built-in to the operating system.

    D. Use the Windows 95 Plug and Play model.

51. Network adapter drivers

    A. Can only be used one at a time. You cannot load two adapter drivers for one card.

    B. Do not conflict and can be loaded one after the other.

    C. Must be on the HCL to be used by Windows NT.

    D. Use the protocol stack to communicate with the network card.

52. A Microsoft Windows NT or 95 workstation will do what with the frame type?

    A. Set it to 802.2

    B. Set it to 802.3

    C. Attempt to detect it

    D. Insert the frame type into the token-ring

53. The purpose of the NDIS standard is:

    A. To replace the older and more cumbersome ODI standard.

    B. Like the MLID standard, to provide an API for developers.

    C. Like the ODI standard, to provide an API for developers.

    D. To create a meaningful transition to the OSI 7-layer model.

54. If the network adapter loads the software but nothing happens,

    A. There is probably a hardware conflict preventing the software from functioning.

    B. The software is empty and must have protocols installed in it.

    C. There is probably a protocol or client misconfiguration issue.

    D. There is probably a software error preventing the hardware from functioning.

55. In Windows NT, hardware errors usually show up in which of the following?

    A. Hardware Manager

    B. Conflict Viewer

    C. Device Manager

    D. Event Viewer

56. Typical devices that may conflict with your network adapter include

    A. Video adapters, sound cards, and game ports.

    B. Mice, modems, and other network adapters.

    C. Joysticks, video accelerators, and game ports.

    D. Sound cards, video accelerators, and game software.

57. Software that tends to conflict with DOS networking software includes:

    A. TSRs and mouse drivers.

    B. DOS games and sound programs.

    C. Memory-management software.

    D. Modem and mouse software.

58. If your network adapter is not functioning and you suspect a hardware conflict, you should

   A. Remove all cards except the video card and see if the problem persists.

   B. Unload all software and reboot the system from scratch.

   C. Re-read the manufacturer's instructions.

   D. Use the manufacturer's configuration utility.

59. The IRQs can be:

   A. Shared among several devices because they can "interrupt" one another.

   B. A major source of conflict.

   C. Moved from any device to another using Windows NT diagnostics or the Windows 95 device manager.

   D. Hidden system files.

60. A *reserved* IRQ means:

   A. It is available for use because it is "reserved" by the operating system.

   B. Proceed cautiously before using.

   C. It does not conform to the OSI 7-layer networking model, nor is it on the HCL.

   D. It is used by a built-in component, such as the hard drive controller.

61. An I/O port

   A. Is used by a device to communicate to the computer.

   B. Is used by a communication device to connect to the Internet via a modem.

   C. Uses an IRQ to connect to a hardware device.

   D. Uses an *expanded memory manager* to manage resources.

3.3   Answers and Explanations: Practice Problems

1. **A**   Without a *driver*, or software, the NIC will fail to function. In addition to enabling the NIC, the driver also binds the protocols to the adapter.

2. **B**   NIC is short for Network Interface Card.

3. **B**   NICs can use a variety of connectors and cable types. If your card doesn't match your cable, you won't be able to connect the two.

4. **C**   The NIC binds the protocols to the adapter. At that point, the protocols are available for use.

5. **A**   The driver is located in layer 2, the Data Link Layer.

6. **D**   Protocols cannot be loaded until the NIC driver has enabled the card. Without the NIC driver, the card will not function.

7. **A**   The card itself actually plays a relatively small role in network communications. It is, however, a crucial role.

8. **B**   NT installation can be more difficult. The manufacturer's instructions may indicate whether or not the card is compatible with Windows NT and where software updates can be obtained.

9. **B**   You cannot load multiple drivers per card, but there is often no limit to how many protocols you can bind to a card.

10. **B**   Instructions are seldom used after installation and often needed during installation.

11. **A**   Hardware conflicts can cause the NIC (or the rest of your system) to stop functioning.

12. **D**   Installation of the NIC is only a small step.

13. **B**   The HCL is the Hardware Compatibility List.

14. **B** Varying bus types are common. As bus types advance, this problem will continue.

15. **A** The EISA slot will accept both EISA and ISA slots. Technically, you can fit a VESA LB card into an ISA slot, but the VESA connector will not be connected, and the card will not function in VESA LB mode.

16. **B** The PCI standard was developed to work with the Pentium.

17. **B** 10 Base-2 is defined as using BNC connectors and coaxial cable. RJ-45, by contrast, uses Category 5 twisted-pair.

18. **C** Not all cards use jumpers, and you cannot use the instructions if you want. If your card does use jumpers, you can even configure it outside the PC. The only correct answer is that you can configure it using software.

19. **C** Plug and Play is not supported by the current versions of Windows NT.

20. **A** B is incorrect: The IRQ and interrupt are the same thing. C is incorrect: The slot number is not required. D is incorrect: NICs don't use a DMA channel. A is correct.

21. **C** IRQ 7 is used by LPT1, the printer. IRQ 14 is used by the hard disk controller. IRQ 4 might work, but almost all PCs have COM1.

22. **B** Even though a Sound Blaster™ can be configured to use IRQ 7, as it uses by default, LPT1 is the most typical device using LPT1.

23. **A** IRQ 2 and IRQ 9 are the links between the two IRQ controllers. For this reason, Windows 95 lists IRQ 2 as "programmable interrupt controller." Because of this, you cannot use both IRQ 2 and IRQ 9.

24. **C** IRQ 1 is reserved, and IRQ 3 and 4 are used by COM2 and COM1, respectively. If you have a serial mouse and

external modem, you are most likely using both COM ports. This leaves IRQ 10.

25. **B** NT Diagnostics is the only choice that exists. All the others are not NT components.

26. **C** If the software fails to load, it is because it cannot allocate one or more of the resources, such as IRQ or I/O port.

27. **D** A and B are not possible options. Once the software loads, the card will function unless overwritten. This can happen with memory managers that allocate memory after the network drivers have loaded.

28. **B** This is the dictionary definition of a hardware conflict.

29. **A** There are no such items as the Hardware Manager, the Resource Viewer, or the Windows NT System Manager.

30. **B** Windows 95 does not have an event viewer. You must use the Device Manager found in the SYSTEM applet of the control panel.

31. **B** This is different than the I/O port. This is an area of memory the NIC can use to store card information or other items needed. It executes much faster than ROM memory.

32. **A** It is true the yellow exclamation point will show up in Windows 95's Device Manager, but this doesn't work in other operating systems, and you must open several windows before viewing the Device Manager. It is better to rely on the behavior of the device—in this case, the software not loading.

33. **C** The behavior of the light varies from adapter to adapter. The only common behavior is that the lights are used to indicate the status of the adapter (another name for NIC).

34. **C** If some servers use TCP/IP and you have loaded only NetBEUI or IPX/SPX,

3

you will not be able to connect to the TCP/IP-enabled servers. This is a *protocol mismatch.*

35. **A** This is akin to a protocol mismatch. However, even if different server types use the same protocols, they may still require different client software, such as the Client for Microsoft Networks.

36. **D** IPX can use more than one frame type. The frame types cannot be used with one another.

37. **B** Because the protocols have been installed and configured correctly, no configuration of IPX is necessary. This is a client misconfiguration issue. You need to load the client for NetWare networks.

38. **A** All operating systems must load a redirector or requester before attaching to a network, or they must have one built into the operating system.

39. **D** The MS-DOS network client is the DOS-mode redirector for Microsoft networks.

40. **C** 802.2 is more advanced. Unfortunately, Windows 95's autodetect function works like this: It checks for 802.3; if it finds another PC using 802.3, it uses it. If it doesn't, it checks for 802.2 the same way. Occasionally Windows 95 machines checking for 802.3 will find one another and default to that frame type.

41. **D** None of the answers are true. The frame types cannot read one another, and DHCP is not for IPX, but only TCP/IP.

42. **D** In the situation described, the resources that can't be seen are running NetBEUI from the other side of a router. If they were running a routable protocol, the workstations could connect to the servers.

43. **C** Once again, NetBEUI cannot be routed. All the other answers in this question are gibberish.

44. **D** NetBIOS is an interface, not a protocol. It can be bound to any protocol.

45. **A** Unfortunately, NetBIOS is the interface, and NetBEUI is the protocol. This is confusing because NetBEUI stands for Network Basic Enhanced User Interface. The important point is that Microsoft Networking, which requires NetBIOS, can use any protocol, including TCP/IP only.

46. **B** A is incorrect because Plug and Play will load the software and drivers. C is incorrect because it is impossible to install software of any kind while the PC is off. D is incorrect because you will be unable to load anything from the network until you have connected to the network. With no software or drivers, it would be difficult to connect to the network.

47. **B** Network adapters are not easy to configure without the manufacturer's documentation.

48. **A** Although this seems like an inelegant solution, it will allow you to connect to the network resources. Multiple protocols can be used simultaneously. This might cause additional network traffic if all PCs were configured this way, but it is an excellent troubleshooting tool.

49. **B** Protocols do not use an IRQ, nor would they appear on the Windows NT hardware-compatibility list. You can load as many protocols as you want.

50. **B** Like protocols, you can run multiple network clients.

51. **A** Only one driver can be loaded for a particular NIC. D is incorrect because the protocol stack uses the driver to communicate with the card, not the other way around.

52. **C** Windows workstations attempt to detect the frame type currently in use on the network.

53. **C** The NDIS standard for networking was developed differently from Novell's

ODI standard, but both were designed to allow a more flexible interface for networking programmers and device driver manufacturers. They both segment the networking layers, but not as cleanly as the OSI theoretical model did.

54. **C** If the NIC is functioning properly but the user cannot access anything, it usually means the network resources and the networking client on the user's workstation are using different protocols.

55. **D** The only valid choice here is the Event Viewer. None of the other items exist.

56. **B** Typically, IRQ conflicts are the most frequent conflicts in network adapters, with COM2 and COM1 using IRQ3 and 4, respectively. Next, additional network cards typically take the last remaining bit of resources.

57. **C** Memory management software has a special problem with networking software. During installation, memory management software, such as QEMM or EMM386.EXE will scan the upper memory area for available areas. While sound cards, serial cards, and other devices will register their functionality without a driver, network cards do not do so until the driver is loaded. But the memory management scan occurs before the network driver is loaded. Because memory management operations occur after the NIC driver is loaded, the memory manager simply overwrites the RAM address of the NIC.

58. **A** The only way to completely isolate the network card is to remove all the expansion boards, including the I/O (serial and parallel) card on some older systems. If you take out the video card, you won't be able to see anything. This is an excellent way to isolate compatibility problems, which are often with other peripherals, not the system itself.

59. **B** The IRQ channels must be properly set. 75% or more of your problems in using a new NIC or a new configuration will likely be traced to an IRQ conflict. For this reason, always use the same manufacturer and, if possible, the model of NIC across your enterprise.

60. **D** The reserved IRQs cannot be used by a NIC or any other expansion device, with the exception of IRQ2, which cascades to IRQ 9. You cannot use both IRQ 2 and IRQ 9. Often times you can freely choose one or the other for your device.

61. **A** The I/O channel is where the device sends data when communicating with the computer. The IRQ, by contrast, alerts the CPU to impending communication.

3.3   Key Words

IRQ

I/O port

Memory management software

Frame type

Protocol

Client software

Server software

IPX/SPX, TCP/IP, NetBEUI

Redirector/requester

3.4   Implement a NetBIOS Naming Scheme for all Computers on a Given Network

NetBIOS is an interface that provides applications with access to network resources. It is *not* a protocol. Every computer on a Windows NT network must have a unique name for it to be accessible through the NetBIOS interface. This unique name is called a computer name or a NetBIOS name.

NetBIOS (Network Basic Input/Output System) is an application interface that provides PC-based applications with uniform access to lower protocol layers. NetBIOS was once most closely associated with the NetBEUI protocol (a poor performer). *NetBEUI*, in fact, is an abbreviation for NetBIOS Extended User Interface. This is confusing when you realize that NetBIOS is actually the interface, and NetBEUI is the protocol. Today, the NetBIOS interface can be carried over IPX and TCP/IP, as well as NetBEUI. NetBIOS over IPX can cause routing problems if not properly configured, but NetBIOS over TCP/IP avoids all these issues.

On a NetBIOS network, every computer must have a unique name. The computer name must be no more than 15 characters long. A NetBIOS name can include alphanumeric characters and any of the following special characters:

> ! @ # $ % ^ & ( ) - _ ' { } . ~

Note that you cannot use a space or an asterisk in a NetBIOS name. Also, NetBIOS names are not case-sensitive.

Within these character limitations, you can choose any name for a PC. The rule of thumb is to choose a name that helps you identify the computer. Names such as PC1, PC2, and PC3 are difficult to visualize and easy to confuse. Likewise, an ad-hoc naming convention, such as SNEEZY, DOC, and BASHFUL does not tell you enough about the PC, especially if you have many computers on your network. The name should include information about the PC's location, department, and primary user.

A list that uses a unique hexadecimal address to identify each PC would satisfy the technical requirements of a NetBIOS naming scheme, but it would be difficult, if not impossible, to administer. It would be better to have a naming system that includes several characters for location or department, several characters for a sub-department (or floor, perhaps), and the remaining characters to identify the primary user, perhaps using an e-mail address.

Consider this naming system:

> ADMIN-013-SALLY
>
> ADMIN-014-BETTY
>
> MRKTG-001-KARL

This naming system uses a department (ADMIN for Administration and MRKTG for Marketing) to identify the location of the computer. Also, the floor of the building was used to pinpoint the location. Finally, the user's e-mail name was used to identify each PC. You can change the name of a Windows 95 or Windows NT computer using the control panel.

A NetBIOS computer name must:

- **Be unique.**
- **Consist of no more than 15 characters.**
- **Consist of a combination of alphanumeric characters and these characters:**
  ! @ # $ % ^ & ( ) - _ ' { } . ~

The Universal Naming Convention is a standard for identifying resources on Microsoft networks. A UNC path consists of the following components:

- A NetBIOS computer name preceded by two backslashes (left-leaning slashes)
- The share name of a shared resource located on the given PC (optional)
- The MS-DOS-style path of a file or a directory located on the given share (optional)

Elements of the UNC path are separated with single backslashes. The following list shows examples of legal UNC names:

\\ADMIN-113-BETTY\CDRIVE

\\MRKTNG-001-KARL\DOCUMENTS

\\PET_DEPT\CATS\SIAMESE.TXT

Various Windows NT commands use UNC paths to designate network resources. For instance, the command

net view \\PET_DEPT

enables you to view the shared resources on the computer with the NetBIOS name PET_DEPT. Like wise, the command

net use G: \\PET_DEPT\CATS

maps the shared directory CATS on the computer PET_DEPT to the drive letter G:.

A computer on a NetBIOS network must have a NetBIOS computer name. The NetBIOS name is configured at installation and, in Windows NT or Windows 95, can be changed later through the Control Panel Network application. Computers use the NetBIOS name (sometimes combined with a share name or a path name) to locate resources on the network.

3.4 Practice Problems

1. A NetBIOS name can have how many characters?

   A. 14

   B. 15

   C. 11

   D. 8 plus a three-character extension

2. Which character cannot be used in a NetBIOS name?

   A. \

   B. !

   C. $

   D. @

3. Using the character limitations, you

   A. Must choose a meaningful name for your computer.

   B. Must choose a name that includes the computer's role.

   C. Must choose a name of 15 characters or less.

   D. Must choose a combination of upper- and lowercase letters.

The following four questions use this situation as a scenario:

Network type:

Windows NT servers, multiple domains

Protocols:

NetBEUI, IPX, TCP/IP

Your workstations:

30 Windows NT workstations

You decide to implement a NetBIOS naming scheme for your network. You are currently part of a standalone network with one server, but you are scheduled to be connected to the multidomain corporate WAN in several

months. Your users have e-mail accounts on the corporate WAN mail hub.

Required objectives:

- The naming scheme must contain unique names.

- The naming scheme must continue to function after the WAN integration.

Desired objectives:

- The naming scheme should help streamline user administration.

- The naming scheme should be informative about the computer's role.

4. You decide to generate a unique hexadecimal number for your workstations. You will keep a list of each number on a list and carefully control which numbers are available. You will submit your list to corporate HQ to guarantee they are not using your unique hexadecimal names. This plan will:

   A. Perform both of the required objectives and both of the desired objectives.

   B. Perform both of the required objectives and one of the desired objectives.

   C. Perform both of the required objectives and none of the desired objectives.

   D. Not perform the required objectives.

5. You decide to use the burned-in MAC address of the Ethernet cards in each system as the NetBIOS name. Because the first several characters of the MAC address indicate the manufacturer, you feel this will help indicate the role of the PC. This plan will:

   A. Perform both of the required objectives and both of the desired objectives.

B. Perform both of the required objectives and one of the desired objectives.

C. Perform both of the required objectives and none of the desired objectives.

D. Not perform the required objectives.

6. You decide to use the user's e-mail address as the computer's name. This plan will:

A. Perform both of the required objectives and both of the desired objectives.

B. Perform both of the required objectives and one of the desired objectives.

C. Perform both of the required objectives and none of the desired objectives.

D. Not perform the required objectives.

7. You create a naming convention that uses a three-character building code, followed by a four-character floor code, followed by the user's e-mail address. This plan will:

A. Perform both of the required objectives and both of the desired objectives.

B. Perform both of the required objectives and one of the desired objectives.

C. Perform both of the required objectives and none of the desired objectives.

D. Not perform the required objectives.

8. The UNC convention

A. Uses the NetBIOS name followed by the drive name.

B. Includes the NetBIOS name for Microsoft computers.

C. Allows use of any alphanumeric character, plus ! @ # $ % ^ & ( ) - _ ' { } . ~, but never slashes because they are reserved.

D. Allows use of no fewer than 15 characters.

9. When using resources with the UNC naming convention, you must

A. Use the MAP ROOT command for NetWare networks.

B. Precede the statement with a username and password.

C. Precede the share name with two slashes and the NetBIOS name.

D. Always use *net use* and use a drive letter.

10. Elements within the UNC name are separated:

A. By servers with NTFS file-level security.

B. By single slashes.

C. By preceding double-slashes.

D. By a hard return on multiple lines.

11. On a Windows 95 workstation,

A. UNC names must be mapped to a drive letter to be used.

B. UNC names are supported via the 32-bit Windows NT kernel.

C. UNC names are built into the Microsoft NetWare Requester.

D. UNC names can be used instead of drive letters.

12. A computer on a NetBIOS network:

A. Must have a NetBIOS name only if it wants to share resources.

B. Must have a unique hexadecimal address.

C. Must have a NetBIOS name to participate in networking.

D. Must have a NetBIOS name of no fewer than 15 characters.

13. Computers use the NetBIOS name:

A. To manage the protocols and network drivers.

B. To view and share resources on the network.

C. To attach to remote printers and files.

D. To populate the ACL (Access Control List).

14. Once the NetBIOS name is created,

A. It cannot be changed because it uniquely identifies that computer on the network

B. It can be used to secure resources.

C. It can be used to select a password.

D. It can be changed easily.

15. Which is the correct NetBIOS statement?

A. net use * \\ago-ncls1\ntw

B. net view g: \\Wednesday\system

C. net use root g: \\server\drive

D. net delete g:

16. The NetBIOS share name

A. Is hidden using the ACL (Access Control List).

B. Is used to access a resource.

C. Cannot be made hidden by using a '$' as the last character.

D. Allows access to users in the local share group only.

17. A computer on a NetBIOS network:

A. Must have a NetBIOS name only if it wants to share resources.

B. Must have a unique hexadecimal address.

C. Must have a NetBIOS name only if it wants to use resources.

D. Must have a NetBIOS name of no more than 15 characters.

18. The statement net use d: \\server\share

A. Is incorrect.

B. May prompt the user for a password.

C. Will not function on Windows 95. Instead, it requires the advanced networking built into Windows NT.

D. Will share the user's d: drive over the network.

19. The statement copy \\cats\docs\burmese.txt

A. Is illegal.

B. Must be mapped to a drive letter to be used.

C. Can be used instead of mapping \\cats\docs to a drive letter.

D. Will not function unless the share name \docs is unique.

20. A UNC name consists of the following components:

A. Server name, share name, MS-DOS style path

B. Server name, NetBIOS name, and drive letter

C. "net use" or "net view" followed by a server name

D. The ACL (Access Control List), the user's SID (Security ID), and the file name

21. Finding resources on a Microsoft NetBIOS network

    A. Uses the User Manager for Domains.

    B. Uses the Windows NT Server Manager.

    C. Is as simple as typing "net view."

    D. Can degrade network performance.

22. NetBIOS names on Windows NT

    A. Are case-sensitive.

    B. Are case-insensitive.

    C. Are maintained in the ACL.

    D. Break the 15-character limitation imposed by Windows for Workgroups.

23. On a NetBIOS network,

    A. Each computer must have a unique name.

    B. Each server must have a unique name, but workstations can be named more leniently.

    C. Servers and workstations create a security-token based on the NetBIOS name and its uniqueness.

    D. The protocol must use NetBEUI.

24. If all NetBIOS names are unique,

    A. The usernames can be shared.

    B. The usernames are case-sensitive.

    C. The users can be connected using "net use \\servername\username."

    D. The usernames must be unique.

3.4   Answers and Explanations: Practice Problems

1. **B**   A NetBIOS name can no more than 15 characters.

2. **A**   The slash (\ ) is reserved for directory names and UNC entries.

3. **C**   You are not required to use a meaningful name or a name that satisfies any other role. The name cannot be more than 15 characters, though.

4. **C**   The hexadecimal naming scheme will make it difficult to administer and will indicate nothing about the computer's role. The carefully controlled list will also be difficult and cumbersome to administer.

5. **C**   The MAC address will only indicate the manufacturer of the NIC. But the numbers would be unique.

6. **B**   This is a great naming scheme, as it is easier to administer and is also unique. In this case, it fails to indicate the computer's role.

7. **A**   This plan will work perfectly, but the e-mail address portion can contain only eight characters or less, because you will have used seven characters on the building and floor codes.

8. **B**   It is true that slashes are reserved for NetBIOS names, but this is not a requirement for the UNC naming convention. However, in a Microsoft network, the NetBIOS name is the computer or server name.

9. **C**   A username is required only if the currently authenticated user does not have access to the network share. The map root command is not necessary for mapping using UNC names. The NetWare MAP command does support UNC naming. It's much easier to use than map root j: server/vol1:dirame\otherdir.

10. **B**   Single slashes separate the elements.

11. **D**   UNC names can be used instead of drive letters for COPY, XCOPY, DIR, and a host of other commands. Batch files can behave erratically when executed from a UNC name, but executables do not suffer from this.

12. **C**   A NetBIOS name is required to be a server *and* a client.

13. **B**   NetBIOS names are also used to access resources on the network, but C is incorrect because files are not attached across the network.

14. **D**   The NetBIOS name can be changed easily in the Control Panel.

15. **A**   B is incorrect: You would not include a drive letter in this manner in a NET VIEW statement. C is incorrect: Only because the drive letter (in \\SERVER\ DRIVE is not used.).

16. **B**   A, C, and D are all false statements.

17. **D**   A NetBIOS name is used for sharing and using resources. The name need not be a hexadecimal address. It must, however, not have more than 15 characters.

18. **B**   If the currently logged in user does not have access to the network resource, the statement will generate a password or username prompt.

19. **C**   COPY can be used with UNC names, and a drive letter is not required. Many applications also support this.

20. **A**   A full UNC file name would include the MS-DOS path in addition to the share name. This MS-DOS path refers to the directories beneath the share.

21. **C**   The NET VIEW command shows all computers within the specified domain or workgroup that are sharing resources.

22. **B**   NetBIOS names are never case-sensitive.

23. **A**   NetBIOS names do not have a lot of requirements, but one is that they must all be unique. If not, users in the conflicting workstations or servers will not be able to access resources.

24. **D**   There can be no duplicate of user names.

3.4   Key Words

UNC

NetBIOS name

Naming scheme

MAC address

NET commands

Resources

Sharing

Accessing

Username

NetBIOS name

3.5 Select the Appropriate Hardware and Software Tools to Monitor Trends in the Network

A. Tools to Use to Document Network Activities

An important part of network management involves monitoring trends on the network. By effectively monitoring network behavior, you can anticipate problems and correct them before they disrupt the network. Monitoring the network also provides you with a *baseline*, a sampling of how the network functions in its equilibrium state. This baseline is beneficial because if you experience a problem later, the changes in certain related parameters could lead you to a possible cause.

Monitoring the network is an ongoing task that requires data from several different areas. The following list details some tools you can use to document network activities:

- A performance-monitoring tool, such as Windows NT's Performance Monitor

- A network-monitoring and protocol-analysis program—such as Windows NT's Network Monitor or the more powerful Network Monitor tool included with Microsoft's BackOffice System Management Server (SMS) package—or a hardware-based protocol analyzer

- A system event log, such as the Windows NT event log, which you can access through Windows NT's Event Viewer application.

B. Keeping Network Records

A detailed history of changes to the network is critical for accurate troubleshooting. When a problem occurs, simply cross-reference the problem's occurrence with the network changes or modifications carried out at the same time.

Your initial configuration records should include descriptions of all hardware, including installation dates, repair histories, configuration details (such as interrupts and addresses), and backup records for each server. In addition, you should maintain a running log that contains the following details:

- A list of all software modifications, version updates, and service packs

- A map of the network showing locations of hardware and cabling details

- Current copies of workstation configuration files, such as CONFIG.SYS and AUTOEXEC.BAT files

- Service agreements and important telephone numbers, such as the numbers of vendors, contractors, and software support lines

- Software licenses to ensure that your network operates within the bounds of the license terms

- A history of past problems and related solutions

C.   Monitoring Performance

Windows NT's Performance Monitor tool lets you monitor important system parameters for the computers on your network. Performance Monitor can keep an eye on a large number of system parameters, providing a graphical or tabular profile of system and network trends. You can use Performance Monitor to track statistical measurements for components such as these:

Network segment

Server

Server work queues

Protocol-related objects, such as NetBEUI, NWLink, and NetBIOS

Service-related objects, such as Browser and Gateway Services for NetWare

D.   Baseline Measurement

You should use Performance Monitor when your network is first upgraded or installed. By identifying acceptable performance standards and relating them to the Performance Monitor, you can establish a *baseline* set of statistics.

A baseline is critical for measuring network performance using the Performance Monitor. Without a baseline, the measurements viewed by Performance Monitor will be basically meaningless. When you experience problems, you can compare the current readings with the readings listed in your baseline. To establish a baseline, follow these steps:

1. Use Performance Monitor to view the statistics you are concerned with.

2. View Performance Monitor over a period of several days to observe where the utilization of each statistic tends to cluster.

3. Associate current spikes in each statistic to correlate these activity spikes with events and performance degradation.

After you establish a baseline, you can refer back to your baseline to monitor against problems you may experience. For example, during your baseline period, you may have observed that a large database query caused a performance spike in server utilization. You would consider this a normal part of your network's performance. If, however, the statistic in question had an abnormal spike duration or spiked much higher than usual, this would indicate a problem. Without your baseline to refer to, such problems would be difficult to distinguish.

E.   Monitoring Network Traffic

Protocol analysis tools monitor network traffic by intercepting and decoding frames. Software-based tools, such as Windows NT Server's Network Monitor, analyze frames coming and going from the computer on which they run.

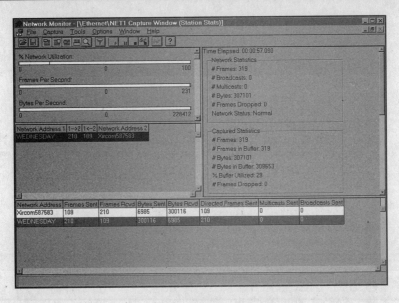

Figure 3.5.1   Windows NT Server's Network Monitor main screen.

An enhanced version of Network Monitor, which is included with the Microsoft BackOffice System Management Server (SMS) package, monitors traffic not just at the local system, but also at other computers on the network.

Other protocol analyzers are more sophisticated. HP Lanalyzer™ and Network Sniffer™ are two examples of dedicated protocol analyzers. For larger networks, you should consider a dedicated network analysis tool.

In addition to keeping network traffic statistics, protocol analyzers can capture bad frames and often isolate which PC is causing the problem. A dedicated protocol analyzer is often a good investment for a large network because it concentrates a considerable amount of monitoring and troubleshooting power into a single, portable unit. Depending on your network, you will want to choose between a dedicated hardware-based or a specific software-based protocol analysis tool.

F. Logging Events

Some operating systems, such as Windows NT, have the ability to keep a running log of system events. That log serves as a record of previous errors, warnings, and other messages from the system. Studying the event log can help you find reccurring errors and discover when a problem first appeared.

Windows NT's Event Viewer application provides you with access to the event log. You can use Event Viewer to monitor the following types of events:

- **System events:** Warnings, error messages, and other notices describing significant system events. Examples of system log entries include browser elections, service failures, and network connection failures.

- **Security events:** Events tracked through Windows NT's auditing features.

- **Application events:** Messages from applications. If you're having a problem with an application, you can check the application log for an application-related error or warning messages.

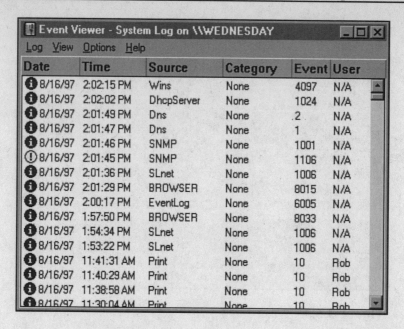

Figure 3.5.2 The Event Viewer main screen.

If you double-click a log entry in Event Viewer, a dialog box called an Event Detail appears on your screen. An Event Detail provides a detailed description of the event.

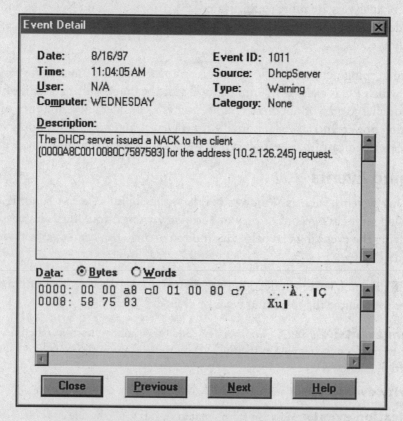

Figure 3.5.3 Event detail describing a system event.

3.5   Exercises

1. Using Network Monitor

Objective: Examine the main window display of Windows NT Server 4.0's Network Monitor application

Estimated time: 15 minutes

1. If Network Monitor has been installed on your system, click the Start menu and choose Programs/ Administrative Tools. Then choose the Network Monitor application from the Administrative Tools group and proceed to step 4.

2. If Network Monitor hasn't been installed on your system, you must install it, along with a component called the Network Monitor Agent. Network Monitor and the Network Monitor Agent can be installed together by using the Control Panel Network application. Click the Start menu and choose Settings/Control Panel. Double-click the Network application and choose the Services tab.

3. In the Network application Services tab, click the Add button. Choose Network Monitor and Agent from the Network Service list and click OK. Windows NT prompts you for the Windows NT installation disk. When the installation is complete, click OK to shut down your system and restart Windows NT. Then start the Network Monitor application, as described in step 1.

4. Examine the four panes of the Network Monitor main screen (refer to Figure 3.5.1). The following list describes the four panes:

    *   The Graph pane is located in the upper-left corner of the display. The Graph section includes five bar graphs describing network activity. Only two of the graphs are visible; use the scroll bar to view the other three graphs.

    *   The Session Statistics pane, which appears below the Graph pane, tracks network activity by session, showing the two computers in the session and the frames sent each way.

    *   The Total Statistics pane, which appears to the right of the Graph pane, lists such important statistics as the number of frames and the number of broadcasts. You can use the scroll bar to reach other entries that are not visible.

    *   The Station Statistics pane, which sits at the bottom of the window, shows statistics for frames listed by network address.

5. Pull down the Capture menu and choose Start. Network Monitor then starts monitoring the network.

6. Ping the Network Monitor PC from another computer on the network. (Go to the command prompt and type **Ping**, followed by the IP address on the Network Monitor computer—for example, ping 111.121.131.141.) Watch the Station Statistics pane at the bottom of the screen to see if any new information appears.

7. Experiment with sending files or other requests to or from the Network Monitor PC. Study the effect of network activity on the values displayed in the four panes of the Network Monitor main window.

8. When you are finished, pull down the Capture menu and click Stop to stop capturing data. Then exit Network Monitor.

2. Creating a Chart in Performance Monitor

Objectives: Become familiar with the process of creating and reading a Performance Monitor chart. Understand the basic components of the Performance Monitor main window and the Add to Chart dialog box. Learn how to turn on disk performance counters using the *diskperf* command.

Estimated time: 25 minutes

1. From the Start menu, select Programs. Choose the Administrative Tools group and click Performance Monitor. The Performance Monitor main window appears on your screen.

2. Pull down the Edit menu and choose Add to Chart. The Add to Chart dialog box appears. You can also open the Add to Chart dialog box by clicking the plus sign in the toolbar of the Performance Monitor main window.

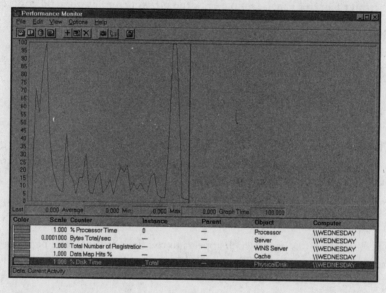

Figure 3.5.4   The Performance Monitor main window.

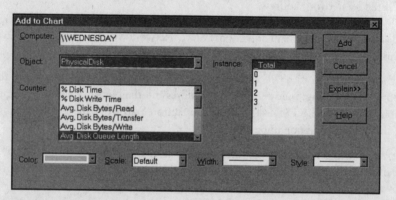

Figure 3.5.5   The Add to Chart dialog box.

3.a. The box labeled Computer at the top of the Add to Chart dialog box tells Performance Monitor which computer you want to monitor. The default is the local system. Click the ellipsis button to the right of the box for a list of computers on the network.

3.b.   The box labeled Object tells Performance Monitor which object you want to monitor. As you learned earlier in this chapter, an object is a hardware or software component of your system. You can think of an object as a *category* of system statistics. Pull down the Object menu. Scroll through the list of objects and look for the Processor, Memory, PhysicalDisk, LogicalDisk, Server, and Network Segment objects described earlier in this chapter. Choose the PhysicalDisk object. If you have more than one physical disk on your system, a list of your physical disks will appear in the Instances box to the right of the Object box. The Instance box lists all instances of the object selected in the Object box. If necessary, choose a physical disk instance.

3.c.   The box labeled Counter displays the counters (the statistical measurements) that are available for the object displayed in the Object box. Scroll through the list of counters for the PhysicalDisk object. If you feel like experimenting, select a different object in the Object box. Notice that the new object is accompanied by a different set of counters. Switch back to the PhysicalDisk object and choose the %Disk Time counter. Click the Explain button on the right side of the Add to Chart dialog box, and a description of the %Disk Time counter appears at the bottom of the dialog box.

3.d.   Click the Done button in the Add to Chart dialog box. The dialog box disappears, and you see the Performance Monitor main window.

4.   In the Performance Monitor main window, a vertical line sweeps across the chart from left to right. You may also see a faint colored line at the bottom of the chart recording a %Disk Time value of 0. If so, you haven't enabled the disk performance counters for your system. (If the disk performance monitors are enabled on your system, you should see a spikey line that looks like the readout from an electrocardiogram. You're done with this step. Go on to step 5.)

   If you need to enable the disk performance counters, click the Start button and go to the command prompt. Enter this command: **diskperf -y**. Then reboot your system and repeat steps 1 through 4. (You don't have to browse through the object and counter menus this time.)

5.   You should now see a spikey line representing the percentage of time that the physical disk is busy reading or writing. Select Add to Chart from the Edit menu. Select the PhysicalDisk object and choose the counter Avg. Disk Queue Length. Click the Add button. Then choose the counter Avg. Disk Bytes/Read. Click the Add button and then click the Done button.

6.   Examine the Performance Monitor main window. All three of the counters you selected should be tracing out spikey lines on the chart. Each line is a different color. At the bottom of the window is a table showing which counter goes with which color. The table also gives the scale of the output, the instance, the object, and the computer.

7.   Below the chart (but above the table of counters) is a row of statistical parameters labeled Last, Average, Min, Max, and Graph Time. These parameters pertain to the counter that is selected in the table at the bottom of the window. Select a different counter, and you see that some of these values change. The Last value is the counter value over the last second. Graph time is the time it takes (in seconds) for the vertical line that draws the chart to sweep across the window.

8.   Start Windows Explorer. Select a file (a graphics file or a word processing document) and choose Copy from Explorer's Edit menu. (This copies the file you selected to the clipboard.) Go to another directory and select Paste from the Edit menu. (This creates a copy of the file in the second directory.) Then minimize Explorer and return to the Performance Monitor main screen. The disk activity caused by your Explorer session is now reflected in the spikes of the counter lines.

9.   Pull down the Options menu and select Chart. The Chart Options dialog box appears on your screen. The Chart Options dialog box provides a number of options governing the chart display. The Update Time section enables you to choose an update interval. The update interval tells

Performance Monitor how frequently it should update the chart with new values. (If you choose the Manual Update option, the chart will update only when you press Ctrl+U or click Update Now in the Options menu.) Experiment with the Chart Options or click the Cancel button to return to the main window.

10. Pull down the File menu and choose Exit to exit Performance Monitor. Note that the Save Chart Settings and Save Chart Settings As options in the File menu enable you to save the collection of objects and counters you're using now so you can monitor the same counters later and avoid setting them up again. The Export Chart option enables you to export the data to a file that you can then open with a spreadsheet or database application. The Save Workspace option saves the settings for your chart, as well as any settings for alerts, logs, or reports specified in this session.

3. Performance Monitor Alerts, Logs, and Reports

Objectives: Become familiar with the alternative views (Alert view, Log view, and Report view) available through the Performance Monitor View menu and log performance data to a log file

Estimated time: 25 minutes

1. Click Programs in the Start menu and choose Performance Monitor from the Administrative Tools group. The Performance Monitor main window appears on-screen (refer to Figure 3.5.4).

2. Pull down the View menu. You'll see the following four options:

   - The Chart option plots the counters you select in a continuous chart.

   - The Alert option automatically alerts a network official if the predetermined counter threshold is surpassed.

   - The Log option saves your system performance data to a log file.

   - The Report option displays system performance data in a report format.

   The setup is similar for each of these view formats. All use some form of the Add to Chart dialog box. All have options that are configured through the first command at the top of the Options menu. (The first command at the top of the Options menu changes its name depending on the active view.)

3.a.   Click the Alert option in the View menu.

3.b.   Click the plus sign in the toolbar or choose Add to Alert from the Edit menu. The Add to Alert dialog box is similar to the Add to Chart dialog box except for two additional items at the bottom of the screen. The Alert If box enables you to enter a threshold for the counter. The Over/Under option buttons specify whether you want to receive an alert if the counter value is over or under the threshold value. The Run Program on Alert box lets you specify a command line that will execute if the counter value reaches the threshold you specify in the Alert If box. You can ask Performance Monitor to send a message to your beeper, to send you an e-mail message, or to notify your paging service.

Don't specify a batch file in the Run Program on Alert box. Performance Monitor uses Unicode format, which can confuse the command-prompt interpreter. (The < and > symbols, which are used in Unicode format, are interpreted as a redirection of input or output.)

3.c.   The default object in the Add to Alert dialog box should be the Processor object. The default counter should be %Processor Time. Enter the value **5%** in the Alert If box and make sure the Alert If option button is set to Over. In the Run Program on Alert box, type **SOL**. Set the Run Program on Alert option button to First Time. This configuration tells Performance Monitor to execute Windows NT's Solitaire program when the %Processor Time exceeds 5%.

> **If the Run Program on Alert option button is not set to First Time, Performance Monitor will execute a new instance of Solitaire every time the %Processor Time exceeds 5%, which happens every time it executes a new instance of Solitaire. You'll probably have to close Performance Monitor using the Close (X) button or reboot to stop the incessant shuffling and dealing.**

3

3.d.   Click the Add button and then click the Done button. The Alert legend at the bottom of the Alert window describes the active alert parameters. The Alert Log shows every instance of an alert.

3.e.   Make some change to your desktop. (Hide or reveal the taskbar, or change the size of the Performance Monitor window, for example—anything that will cause a 5% utilization of the processor.) The Solitaire program should miraculously appear on your screen. In a real alert situation, Performance Monitor would execute an alert application instead of starting a card game.

3.f.   Pull down the Edit menu and select Delete Alert.

4.a.   Pull down the View menu and select Log. Performance Monitor's Log view saves performance data to a log file instead of displaying it on the screen.

4.b.   Pull down the Edit menu and select Add to Log. Notice that only the objects appear in the Add to Log dialog box. The counters and instances boxes don't appear because Performance Monitor automatically logs all counters and all instances of the object to the log file. Select the Memory Object and click Add. If you want, you can select another object, such as the Paging File object, and click Add again. When you are finished adding objects, click Done.

4.c.   Pull down the Options menu and select Log. The Log Options dialog box appears on your screen. The Log Options dialog box enables you to designate a log file that Performance Monitor will use to log the data. In the File Name box, enter the name **exer2**. You also can specify an update interval. The update interval is the interval at which Performance Monitor records performance data to the log. The Manual Update option button specifies that the file won't be updated unless you press Ctrl+U or select Update Now from the Options menu. Click the Start Log button to start saving data to the log. Wait a few minutes, and then return to the Log Options dialog box and click the Stop Log button.

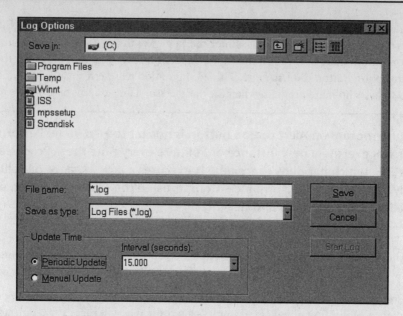

Figure 3.5.6   The Log Options dialog box.

4.d.   Pull down the View menu and switch to Chart view.

4.e.   Pull down the Options menu and select Data From. The Data From dialog box enables you to specify a source for the performance data that appears in the Chart. Note that the default source is Current Activity. (That is why the chart you created in the previous exercise took its data from current system activity.) The alternative to using the Current Activity option is to use data from a log file. Click the Log File option button. Click the ellipsis button to the right of the log file window and select the exer2 file you created in step 4.c. Click OK.

4.f.   Pull down the Edit menu and click Add to Chart. Click the down arrow to the right of the Object menu. Notice that your only object choices are the Memory object and any other objects you selected in step 4.b. Select the Memory object. Browse through the counter list and select Pages/sec. Click the Add button. Select any other memory counters you want to display and click the Add button. Click Done.

4.g.   The log file's record of the counters you selected in 4.f appears in the chart in the Performance Monitor's main window. Notice that, unlike the chart you created in the previous exercise, this chart does not continuously sweep out new data. That is because this chart represents static data from a previous, finite monitoring session.

5.a.   Pull down the View menu and switch to Report view. Pull down the Options menu and select Data From. Switch the Data From setting back to Current Activity. Report view displays the performance data in a report instead of in a graphics format.

5.b.   Select Add to Report from the Edit menu. Select the processor object and choose the %Processor Time, %Interrupt Time, and Interrupts/sec counters. (Hold down the Ctrl key to select all three, and then click Add.) Select the PhysicalDisk object and choose the %Disk Time, Avg. Disk Queue Length, and Current Disk Queue Length counters. Click the Add button. Select the Memory object and choose the Pages/sec, Page Faults/sec, and Available Bytes counters. Click the Add button. Then click Done.

5.c.   Examine the main report window. Performance Monitor displays a report of the performance data you specified in a hierarchical format, with counters listed under the appropriate object.

6.   Select Exit in the File menu to exit Performance Monitor.

3.5   Practice Problems

1. By monitoring the network, you can:

   A. Get a "hands-on" view of problems as they occur.

   B. Anticipate problems before they disrupt network performance.

   C. Keep a permanent record of just how bad performance becomes.

   D. Use a baseline to keep a list of the maximum and minimum performance.

2. A "baseline" set of readings

   A. Is provided by the hardware manufacturer to help tune your network.

   B. Is developed over time and can be used later to compare performance spikes.

   C. Is the foundation based on which network performance can be improved upon.

   D. Can be used by a Microsoft Certified System Engineer to help troubleshoot network performance issues.

3. Tools that you can use to monitor network performance include:

   A. A time-domain reflectometer.

   B. An ohmmeter and cable tester.

   C. Windows NT's *Performance Monitor* and *Network Monitor.*

   D. A NIC set to *promiscuous* mode.

4. Two good tools to create records of network performance are:

   A. Windows NT's Event Viewer and Performance Monitor.

   B. Windows NT's Network Monitor and NetWatcher™.

   C. Windows NT's disk administrator and system monitor.

   D. The MLID and ODI network drivers.

5. You should keep detailed records of your network changes, because

   A. Technical Support won't help you unless you have good records.

   B. A physical disaster could destroy your system, and you must be able to rebuild it.

   C. You can compare your records with performance changes to see if your changes impacted the network.

   D. You may be unable to comprehend your network without them.

6. Your records of the network should include:

   A. Hardware settings, service pack installations, and service agreements.

   B. A detailed map showing cabling layouts and so on.

   C. Current copies of workstation files and other workstation information.

   D. All of the above.

7. Windows NT's Performance Monitor:

   A. Follows the NT security model and, therefore, can be run on only one PC.

   B. Can connect to any Windows NT computer on the network.

   C. Can be used only by the Domain Admins.

   D. Is accessed using the NetBIOS *servername**sharename* convention.

8. Once you develop your system baseline:

   A. Never modify it; you will be unable to make meaningful comparisons unless it stays put.

3

B. Modify and alter your baseline statistics as your network grows.

C. Keep two copies: one that stays with the server and another that stays with the backup tapes.

D. It should be kept safe to prevent intrusion from hackers.

9. You can use *Performance Monitor* to track such items as:

A. Protocol use, drive use, and processor use.

B. A user's performance while using certain applications.

C. How long a computer takes to boot up.

D. Whether the user is suffering from a protocol mismanagement issue.

10. You should take your first baseline reading:

A. When your system is finally stable and functioning normally.

B. As soon as you have installed the operating system.

C. Before installing the NetBIOS networking and unique name.

D. Early in the morning, when there are no users present.

11. To establish your baseline readings:

A. Choose your desired settings and check the minimum levels; this is your baseline.

B. Choose common items such as processor utilization and drive usage and check the minimum levels; this is your baseline.

C. Choose your favorite settings and check where the use tends to cluster; this is your baseline reading.

D. Choose common items such as processor utilization and drive usage and check where they tend to cluster; this is your baseline reading.

12. The time to establish a baseline is:

A. During the morning hours, when users are not there. This will be an accurate benchmark.

B. During peak hours. This is when usage is most critical.

C. During off hours, which you will compare against peak hours.

D. Before you decide which protocol to use.

13. Protocol analysis tools measure performance by:

A. Decoding frames.

B. Filtering packets through NetBEUI, IPX, and TCP/IP.

C. Must use a *gateway*.

D. Checking current network performance against a *baseline*.

14. Windows NT's Network Monitor is:

A. An example of a protocol analyzer.

B. An example of a network analysis tool.

C. The most advanced network utility to date.

D. Required in order to run Systems Management Server.

15. Windows NT's Event Viewer is useful because it records what type of events?

A. Warnings, errors, and events created by the system

B. Messages from applications

C. Events tracked through the auditing features of Windows NT

D. All of the above

16. The Windows NT Event Viewer

    A. Can be opened to provide a great amount of detail for each event.

    B. Is enhanced with the Event Viewer that ships with Systems Management Server.

    C. Views events created in the Performance Monitor.

    D. All of the above.

17. Protocol analyzers

    A. Are advanced software tools used to view the performance of each protocol.

    B. Are hardware or software tools used to view inside network packets.

    C. Analyze protocols for bottlenecks and lost frames.

    D. Can replace the need for detailed paper-based notes.

18. A Performance Monitor chart:

    A. Immediately indicates bottlenecks and performance problems.

    B. Must be analyzed by a seasoned network professional to be understood.

    C. Should be compared with your baseline to get meaningful results.

    D. Should be printed out and hung near the server.

19. Performance Monitor

    A. Is used to view the major portions of the operating system.

    B. Can be configured to use a very high degree of detail to match your particular needs.

    C. Only displays line-charts.

    D. Must be installed separately in Windows 95.

20. Performance Monitor reports

    A. Must be checked diligently if it is to be used.

    B. Should be printed and stored at regular intervals.

    C. Must be viewed using the *Event Viewer.*

    D. Can be used to send an alert if you prefer, to your pager.

3.5   Answers and Explanations: Practice Problems

1. **B**   The overriding reason to keep records is to help you maintain the stability of the network by anticipating and avoiding problems.

2. **B**   Although answer C can be correct in a limited set of circumstances, the baseline is to reflect the ordinary usage of your network.

3. **C**   The other items mentioned will help troubleshoot faults, but not monitor performance.

4. **A**   In addition to Network Monitor, the Event Viewer can be used to track performance-related events, including performance spikes in Network Monitor.

5. **C**   Without detailed records of what you've modified on the network, it will be difficult over time to correlate network changes with performance changes.

6. **D**   All of these items will be most useful in the event of a catastrophe.

7. **B**   The Event Viewer can be connected to any NT computer on the network. This makes it very flexible. The Performance Monitor can also be used this way.

8. **B**   The baseline should be continually changed to reflect the current state of your network.

9. **A**   The Performance Monitor has a very high level of detail.

10. **B** If you wait until your network is finally stable, you may never take a baseline reading. Because it will be modified continually, take the initial reading after the operating system has been installed, and be prepared to update it.

11. **D** You will want to choose critical system items such as processor and disk activity. Look at where the use tends to cluster. Take note of spikes, but spikes are not as important as the average utilization of the items.

12. **B** A baseline is not meant to measure hardware in the absence of users, it is meant to view how your network performs within the organization. So establish your baseline during peak hours. Then compare it to other times and adjust your baseline accordingly.

13. **A** Protocol analysis tools decode frames in order to determine such items as packet source, packet destination, packet size, and data.

14. **B** Network Monitor is not a protocol analyzer; it is a network analysis tool.

15. **D** By default, the Event Viewer does not capture all of these items, but they can be activated in the User Manager for Domains (in the Audit item).

16. **A** Each event can be viewed in detail, down to the hexadecimal level.

17. **B** There are hardware protocol analyzers and software protocol analyzers.

18. **C** Without comparing the chart to your baseline, it is difficult to spot trends or abnormalities.

19. **B** You can use Performance Monitor to view extremely detailed items.

20. **D** The Performance Monitor can be set to trigger an alert if a component reaches a critical level. This alert can be sent to the Event Viewer, to an e-mail account, or to a pager.

3.5 Key Words

Protocol analyzer

Event Viewer

Event

Frame

Baseline

Systems Management Server

Practice Exam: Implementation

1. A network resource can only be:

   A. A file, printer, disk drive, or fax modem.

   B. A gateway, a modem, or a network share or device.

   C. A network-attached scanner.

   D. Any of the above devices and more.

2. Network resources must be shared before they can be

   A. Secured.

   B. Accessed.

   C. Seen.

   D. Placed in the ACL.

3. When using a network share:

   A. The password in the user account is checked against the password in the network resource. If they match, the user is authenticated.

   B. The network resource is checked in the Access Control List (ACL) to see if that user is granted access. If so, the user is granted access.

   C. The username is checked against the user accounts database. If the user exists, the user's password is checked. Then the user is granted access.

   D. There is no need to check the user database because the user is authenticated by the domain controller during login. The server checks the user's password. Then the user is granted access.

4. Global groups

   A. Add a layer of complexity on user management and are, therefore, difficult to administer.

   B. Are available across platforms to Windows NT, Novell NetWare, and Unix.

   C. Must contain users before they can be given access.

   D. Can contain users, local groups, or global groups.

5. Windows NT user accounts are:

   A. Created as part of the installation process and can be created later.

   B. Created with a tool such as *User Manager for Domains* and can be created during the installation process.

   C. Transferable to a Windows 95 workstation.

   D. Used via the Access Control List to manage resources.

6. The primary purpose of a disaster recovery plan is to

   A. Reduce downtime and protect data.

   B. Protect the system from hardware faults and infiltration from hackers.

   C. Avoid monetary losses from lost data.

   D. Keep heads cool during an emergency.

7. A "backup" refers to

   A. A tape backup unit.

   B. A procedural or data backup.

   C. A fully redundant backup network.

   D. A procedure used during an emergency.

8. With a central backup server, the tape unit

   A. Can be more expensive, because they tend to have more capacity than standalone units.

   B. Is always cost-effective because it can do more work per tape unit.

C. Is more useful in larger networks.

D. Is faster than directly connected units.

9. Your network tapes should be

A. Kept in a central safe location.

B. Kept in separate locations. That way if a physical disaster strikes, the data will survive.

C. Secured with passwords to prevent infiltration from hackers.

D. Kept near the server in case they are needed during an emergency.

10. A fault-tolerant design must

A. Not be concerned with price and performance. Fault-tolerance defines only its ability to function.

B. Use a *redundant array* of servers and disks.

C. Use an advanced operating system, such as Microsoft Windows NT or Novell NetWare.

D. Balance the concerns of downtime versus cost and performance. No one solution is best for all users.

11. A fully equipped Network Adapter Card

A. Requires a driver to run.

B. Can be used immediately once it is installed.

C. Will be listed in the manufacturer's HCL.

D. Is used to avoid hardware conflicts with reserved devices.

12. The primary job of the network card is to:

A. Bind the protocols to all layers of the OSI 7-layer model.

B. Bind the clients to the network protocols.

C. Prepare data for transmission over the medium.

D. Avoid collisions on the network .

13. If your NIC supports 10-Base 2 networks:

A. You can connect it to twisted-pair wire using RJ-45.

B. You can connect it using BNC connectors.

C. You must insert it into your token-ring before enabling communications.

D. It will support token-ring but not Ethernet.

14. Plug and Play

A. Works with Windows NT to configure network adapters.

B. Works with Windows 95 to configure network protocols.

C. Works with Windows 95 to configure hardware devices.

D. Works with Windows 95 or Windows NT to configure hardware devices.

15. When configuring your network adapter, typical settings you must configure are:

A. IRQ, I/O port, and RAM address.

B. IRQ, I/O port, and interrupt.

C. Slot number, protocol, and IRQ.

D. I/O port, DMA channel, and adapter ROM.

16. NetBIOS names

A. Can include spaces and are case-sensitive.

B. Include the two slash (\\ ) prefix.

C. Must have 15 or fewer characters.

D. Cannot use the reserved %% variable identifier.

17. One popular NetBIOS naming scheme

    A. Uses randomly generated hexadecimal addressing to retain uniqueness.

    B. Allows users to assign their own names and relies on security for uniqueness.

    C. Combines a location code with a portion of the username.

    D. Avoids the unnecessary slashes (\\ ) of the UNC naming convention.

18. Which of the following is true about this statement: net use d: \\server\share

    A. It is incorrect.

    B. It might prompt the user for a password.

    C. It will not function on Windows 95. Instead, it requires the advanced networking built into Windows NT.

    D. It will share the user's d: drive over the network.

19. Which of the following is true about this statement: copy \\cats\docs\burmese.txt

    A. It is illegal.

    B. It must be mapped to a drive letter to be used.

    C. It can be used instead of mapping \\cats\docs to a drive letter.

    D. It will not function unless the share name \docs is unique.

20. A UNC name consists of the following components:

    A. Server name, share name, MS-DOS style path.

    B. Server name, NetBIOS name, and drive letter.

    C. "net use" or "net view" followed by a server name.

    D. The ACL (Access Control List), the user's SID (Security ID), and the file name.

21. A network baseline:

    A. Becomes the yardstick to measure system performance.

    B. Must be somewhat flexible to grow with the network.

    C. Should be generated during peak times rather than off-times.

    D. All of the above.

22. To establish your baseline readings:

    A. Choose your desired settings and check the minimum levels; this is your baseline.

    B. Choose common items such as processor utilization and drive usage and check the minimum levels; this is your baseline.

    C. Choose your favorite settings and check where the use tends to cluster; this is your baseline reading.

    D. Choose common items such as processor utilization and drive usage and check where they tend to cluster; this is your baseline reading.

23. Windows NT's Event Viewer is useful because it records what type of events?

    A. Warnings, errors, and events created by the system.

    B. Messages from applications.

    C. Events tracked through the auditing features of Windows NT.

    D. All of the above.

3

24. Performance Monitor reports

   A. Must be checked diligently if it is to be used.

   B. Should be printed and stored at regular intervals.

   C. Must be viewed using the *Event Viewer.*

   D. Can be used to send an alert, if you prefer, to your pager.

25. Your initial and ongoing configuration records and baseline reports should *not* include:

   A. A list of the service packs and software installed.

   B. A list of licensing agreements.

   C. The original system administrator password.

   D. A history of past problems and useful solutions.

Answers and Explanations: Practice Exam

1. **D** If a device can be shared over the network, it is a network resource.

2. **B** Some network shares are invisible.

3. **C** This level of redundancy may seem unnecessary, but it is the core of Windows NT security.

4. **D** A global group is a Windows NT group that makes administration easier and can be exported to other Windows NT domains.

5. **A** Two user accounts, ADMINISTRATOR and GUEST are always created during the installation process.

6. **A** The most effective job a system admin can perform during disaster recovery is to get the network back up as quickly as possible.

7. **B** A backup includes more than simply data backups.

8. **A** The costs can vary, but centralized tape servers tend to be more expensive per tape unit. Because of this, they tend to be more effective in small to mid-sized networks.

9. **B** If you keep the tapes in a separate location, you would be able to rebuild the entire network with all new equipment.

10. **D** All system plans should be concerned with the cost of downtime versus the cost of a fault-tolerant system.

11. **A** A network card requires a driver to run. Not all compatible adapters are listed on the Hardware Compatibility List, but it is a good place to start.

12. **C** The network card's job is small but important. It prepares data for transmission over the physical network.

13. **B** 10 Base-2 is defined as using BNC connectors and coaxial cable. RJ-45, by contrast, uses Category 5 twisted-pair.

14. **C** Plug and Play is not supported by the current versions of Windows NT.

15. **A** B is incorrect: The IRQ and interrupt are the same thing. C is incorrect: The slot number is not required. D is incorrect because NICs don't use a DMA channel. A is correct.

16. **C** The NetBIOS name cannot use spaces. Some operating systems, such as Windows 95, allow you to create a name with spaces and may appear to function. But this will cause problems.

17. **C** This is the most useful naming scheme in a large organization, but an e-mail address as the PC name also works very well.

18. **B** If the currently logged in user does not have access to the network resource, the statement will generate a password or username prompt.

19. **C**   COPY can be used with UNC names, and a drive letter is not required. Many applications also support this.

20. **A**   A full UNC file name would include the MS-DOS path in addition to the share name. This MS-DOS path refers to the directories beneath the share.

21. **D**   Each of these elements comprise a baseline.

22. **D**   You will want to choose critical system items such as processor and disk activity. Look at where the use tends to cluster. Take note of spikes, but spikes are not as important as the average utilization of the items.

23. **D**   By default, the Event Viewer does not capture all of these items, but they can be activated in the User Manager for Domains (in the Audit item).

24. **D**   The Performance Monitor can be set to trigger an alert if a component reaches a critical level. This alert can be sent to the Event Viewer, to an e-mail account, or to a pager.

25. **C**   Never write down the Administrator password—ever.

3

CHAPTER 4

Troubleshooting

Troubleshooting is the art of seeking out the cause of a problem and then eliminating the problem by managing or eliminating the cause. With something as complex as a computer network, the list of possible problems and causes is nearly endless. Almost anything can go wrong, and for that reason, you must use all your networking knowledge to troubleshoot network problems.

The troubleshooting questions on the Networking Essentials exam draw from the concepts discussed in all chapters of this book. To solve a specific network problem, for instance, you may need to know that the NetBEUI protocol is non-routable (see Chapter 1) or that only the NTFS file system supports local file-level security (see Chapter 3). Therefore, an essential part of preparing for the troubleshooting section is to study the other sections and be prepared to apply the networking concepts you learned in previous chapters to real-life situations.

Microsoft targets four specific troubleshooting objectives for the Networking Essentials exam. Those objectives center around the following topics:

- Communication problems
- Connectivity problems with cards, cables, and related hardware
- Broadcast storms
- Network performance problems

This chapter focuses on each of these important troubleshooting topics. But keep in mind that almost any problem within the broad subject of networking could fit somewhere in the preceding bulleted list. The distinguishing characteristic of a troubleshooting problem is not its subject but its viewpoint: You are working backwards from a symptom to a cause.

The Troubleshooting Process

Microsoft recommends the following five-step approach to network troubleshooting:

1. Set the problem's priority. Ask yourself a few questions: How serious is this problem? Will the network still function if I attend to other matters first? Can I quantify the loss of work time or productivity the problem is causing?

2. Collect information to identify the symptoms. Ask users to describe the problem. A user's description can lead to further questions, which can lead to a deeper description. Compare the present behavior of the network with the baseline behavior. Search logs and journals for previous occurrences of the problem.

3. Develop a list of possible causes. Is the problem related to connectivity devices? Cabling? Protocols? A faltering workstation? What do past occurrences have in common with the present occurrence?

4. Test to isolate the cause. Develop tests that will prove or disprove each of the possible causes. A test could be as simple as checking a setup parameter or as complicated as studying network traffic with a protocol analyzer.

5. Study the results of the test to identify a solution. Your tests will (ideally) point you to the real problem. After you know the problem, you can determine a solution.

These five steps are sufficient to guide you through a myriad of network problems, and similar approaches appear in the documentation of other network vendors. Part of the challenge of network troubleshooting is to determine how you can apply these five troubleshooting steps to your own situation.

In many cases, network troubleshooting is really a matter of common sense. Few troubleshooting tips will bring you more success than the following:

*   Make sure that all cables and connectors are securely plugged in and that all electrical devices are turned on.

*   Step through the logical and physical pathways of the connection in your mind. Verify that each hardware and software component along the path of the connection is functioning properly. Check cables and adapters; check protocol bindings and system settings; verify that all required services are running.

*   Test and experiment to isolate the problem. Remove and replace suspected components one at a time to isolate the defective component. (Keep extra hard drives, cables, jumpers, and network adapters around in case of emergency.)

Most of the troubleshooting techniques in this chapter are refinements of these simple rules.

4.1 Identify Common Errors Associated with Components Required for Communications

Without communication, there would be no networking, so the components required for communication are essential features for any networking environment. These components were all covered in previous chapters, but they are worthy of second notice here in a troubleshooting context. In particular, this section focuses on the following networking components, which must function properly if communication is to succeed.

- Protocols
- NetBIOS names
- Network services
- Permissions and rights
- Modems

The components discussed in section 4.2 (cables, cards, and cable-related network hardware) are also communication components. In a sense, sections 4.1 and 4.2 belong together. Together they encompass the hardware and software components that pass a message from one computer across the network to another computer.

This section begins with a discussion of some important troubleshooting tools.

A. Troubleshooting Tools

Network administrators use a number of tools to search out network problems. Section 4.2 discusses some of the tools that pertain specifically to network cabling problems. These are a few of the more general-purpose tools:

- **Protocol analyzers.** These hardware or combined hardware and software products are used to monitor network traffic, track network performance, and analyze packets. Protocol analyzers can identify bottlenecks, protocol problems, and malfunctioning network components.

- **Network monitors.** These software-based tools monitor network traffic, displaying packet information and keeping statistics on network usage. Windows NT's Network Monitor is an example of a network monitoring tool. See Chapter 3 (and the discussion later in this section) for more on Network Monitor.

- **Event Log.** Windows NT's Event Log is a log of important system events. If a service or device fails, check the event log for information on the failure and clues about possible causes. See Chapter 3 for a discussion of Windows NT's Event Log and the Event Viewer tool. The Event Log is also an important historical record. You can look for past occurrences of similar failures and compare them with your present situation.

B. Protocol Troubleshooting

Network protocols are at the heart of any networking system, and misused or misconfigured protocols are a common source of network problems. Chapters 1 and 2 discuss network protocols. You should be familiar with when to use which protocol: A common troubleshooting scenario is that a given protocol is implemented in the wrong situation.

After installing and configuring a protocol, you must also *bind* the protocol to the appropriate hardware and services. (See section 1.9 for more on network bindings.) If network bindings are not configured properly, the protocol will not function.

Two computers must be using compatible protocols in order to communicate. If one workstation is using TCP/IP and a second workstation is using only the NetBEUI protocol, the workstations can't establish a connection. Other troubleshooting issues apply to specific protocols:

- **NetBEUI.** NetBEUI is not a routable protocol. Workstations on opposite sides of routers cannot establish communications.

- **DLC.** DLC is used exclusively for network printers and mainframe traffic. Windows NT doesn't use DLC to establish workstation or server sessions.

- **TCP/IP.** Each node on a TCP/IP network must have a unique IP address. Nodes on the same subnet should have the same network ID, which usually means they should have the same subnet mask. Some TCP/IP networks may require additional addressing parameters, such as DNS names, default gateways, and addresses for WINS servers, DNS servers, and DHCP servers.

- **NWLink/IPX.** Each NWLink or IPX node should have a unique network number. Sometimes it is also important to make sure that network nodes are using compatible frame types.

- **SLIP.** The serial line protocol SLIP is not as versatile as its newer counterpart PPP. A typical troubleshooting scenario occurs when the SLIP protocol is applied to a situation for which it was not intended. Specifically, SLIP supports only the TCP/IP protocol and requires a static IP address. See section 1.6 for more on PPP and SLIP.

Sections 1.1, 1.9, and 2.3 discuss network protocols and when to use which protocol.

Windows NT Server's Network Monitor enables you to monitor, filter, and analyze network data frames or packets transmitted and received by the local Windows NT machine. You can use Network Monitor to unravel certain problems with protocols. Each frame of data contains a header that encapsulates information including:

- Protocol type
- Source address
- Destination address
- Data

Network Monitor permits you to investigate intricate details of data frames, including certain types of errors that may be affecting network traffic. If your network is plagued with bad frames or with an overabundance of frames from an unknown source, Network Monitor can help you find the culprit. You can dissect the incoming frames and look for a source address. This strategy is useful if you're trying to find the source of a broadcast storm (discussed later in this chapter).

Network Monitor includes individual modules called *protocol parsers*. Each protocol parser examines a specific protocol. Network Monitor includes more than 60 protocol parsers that cover most of the protocols used in Windows NT network environments.

See section 3.5 for more on Windows NT's Network Monitor tool.

C. NetBIOS Names

Each computer on a Microsoft network must have a unique NetBIOS name (also called a computer name). See section 3.4 for a complete description of NetBIOS names and how to configure them. For a quick summary, NetBIOS names must follow these guidelines:

- They must be unique.

- They can consist of 15 characters or fewer.

- They can contain alphanumeric characters and these characters: ! @ # $ % ^ & ( ) - _ ' { } . ~

A computer cannot participate in the network if its computer name doesn't follow these rules. From the standpoint of troubleshooting, uniqueness is the biggest issue. In most circumstances, a Windows computer won't let you give it a name with too many characters or with illegal characters. If you're trying to connect to a computer and you're using a name that doesn't follow these rules, the name you're using is probably incorrect.

D. Network Services

Network services are processes that enable the network to function. Windows NT includes numerous network services that provide a wide range of capabilities. (Examples include the Browser service, the Replicator service, and the DNS Server service.) The details of these network services are, for the most part, beyond the scope of the Networking Essentials exam, but there are two important services that you should know about:

- **Server service.** The Server service enables a Windows NT system to share resources on the network. In other words, the Server service lets the Windows NT computer offer (serve) its resources to the network. If the Server service on Computer A is stopped or if it isn't bound to the necessary protocols (see section 1.9), other computers will not be able to connect to Computer A.

- **Workstation service (redirector).** The Workstation service enables a Windows NT computer to act as a client. If the Workstation service is stopped or if it isn't bound to the necessary protocols, the computer will not be able to access network resources. The Workstation service is actually what is called a *redirector*. A redirector is a software entity (often a file system driver) that redirects I/O calls to the network. Network client software packages typically include a redirector. If a network client can't connect, make sure the redirector is running properly on the client.

E. Permission and Rights

Security is important on all networks, and Windows NT in particular is a security-conscious operating system. If a user can't make a network connection, it may be because the user doesn't have the necessary rights or permissions to access the resource. See section 3.1 for a discussion of security in Windows NT and Windows 95.

F. Modems

A modem presents all the potential problems you find with any other device. You must make sure that the modem is properly installed, that the driver is properly installed, and that the resource settings are consistent and do not conflict with other devices. Modems also pose some unique problems because they must connect directly to the phone system, because they operate using analog communications, and because they must make a point-to-point connection with a remote machine.

The online help files for both Windows NT and Windows 95 include a topic called Modem Troubleshooter. The Modem Troubleshooter leads you to possible solutions to modem problems by asking questions about the symptoms. As you answer the questions (by clicking the gray box beside your answers), the Modem Troubleshooter zeroes in on more specific questions until (ideally) it leads you to a solution.

Some common modem problems (in addition to the basic device problems such as connectivity and resource settings) include:

- **Dialing problems.** The dialing feature is configured improperly. For instance, the modem isn't dialing 9 to bypass your office switchboard, or it *is* dialing 9 when you're away from your office. The computer also could be dialing an area code or an international code when it shouldn't. Check the dialing properties for the connection.

- **Connection problems.** You can't connect to another modem. Your modem and the other modem might be operating at different speeds. Verify that the maximum speed setting for your modem is the highest speed that both your modem and the other modem can use. Also make sure the Data Bits, Parity, and Stop Bits settings are consistent with those of the remote computer.

- **Protocol problems.** The communicating devices are using incompatible line protocols. Verify that the devices are configured for the same or compatible protocols. If one computer initiates a connection using PPP, the other computer must be capable of using PPP.

G. Troubleshooting RAS

Windows NT Remote Access Service (RAS) is a source of much troubleshooting. Possible problems include faulty user modems and bad lines. As an administrator, you should frequently consult the event log. By investigating the audit and error messages created by RAS, you can often track down problems. The event log might even reveal a bad serial port or driver, indicating a hardware-level problem. Such clues can be vital when intermittent errors occur. You can use the Remote Access Administration tool (in Windows NT Server's Administrative Tools group) to monitor users' logon attempts and to view port usage.

Other problems associated with RAS include:

- Invalid permissions to the resources the user is trying to access

- Invalid user accounts

- Incompatible modems

- Invalid telephone numbers

- Incorrect external modem cables

- Phone system issues (such as dialing 9 for an outside line)

- Phone system has call waiting (dial *70 or get instructions from the local phone company)

- Poor line causing static or noise (In some cases, lowering the baud rate on the modems may create a steady connection.)

- The NT server is down or offline

- User account logon hours violation

- Damaged or faulty modem (Was the user recently operating in an electrical storm?)

- Encryption Authentication level that's set too high or does not match both the server and client

4.1   Exercise: Modem Troubleshooter

This exercise describes how to access Windows NT's or Windows 95's Modem Troubleshooter.

Modem Troubleshooter is part of Windows NT's online help system. The easiest way to access it is to start Help and search for "modems" in the index. Follow these steps:

1. Click the Start button and choose Help.

2. In the Help Topics dialog box, click the Index tab. Enter **modem** in the search box at the top of the screen.

3. Look for the "troubleshooting" subtopic under the "modems" topic in the index. Double-click troubleshooting, and the Modem Troubleshooter appears.

4. Browse through the Modem Troubleshooter's topics. Click the gray box to the left of each symptom for a look at possible causes and/or more diagnostic questions.

5. When you're finished, close the Help window.

4

4.1   Practice Problems

1. If a modem's dial-up phone number is improperly configured (for example, if it's not configured to dial 9 to bypass your office switchboard), the modem has a _____ problem.

   A. Broadcast

   B. Protocol

   C. Connection

   D. Dialing

2. Suppose you start your Windows NT system and receive a message saying the network adapter was not found. Where should you look first for information on what happened?

   A. Performance Monitor

   B. Network Monitor

   C. Windows NT Diagnostics

   D. The event log

3. Your LAN has two Thicknet Ethernet segments, one in the engineering wing and one in the marketing wing. The segments are separated by a router. The distance between the segments is approximately 70 meters. The marketing segment uses the NetBEUI protocol. The engineering segment uses NetBEUI and also TCP/IP. You are unable to make a connection from the engineering segment to the marketing segment. The first thing you should do is:

   A. Make sure all computer names are unique.

   B. Make sure that the router is properly configured and all cables are fastened securely.

   C. Implement TCP/IP on the marketing segment.

   D. Move NetBEUI to a higher priority on the engineering segment.

4. Suppose Computer A can't seem to ping computer B on a TCP/IP network. You know that TCP/IP is installed on both PCs. The next thing you should check is:

   A. The network utilization.

   B. The protocol binding.

   C. To see whether a competing protocol has control of the adapter.

   D. To see whether the Server service is running on Computer A.

5. Which of the following enables a Windows NT computer to act as a client?

   A. Workstation

   B. Server

   C. Browser

   D. NTClient

4.1   Answers and Explanations: Practice Problems

1. **D**   A problem related to dialing information is a Dialing problem. (Forgetting to bypass the office switchboard is a very common dialing problem.)

2. **D**   The event log tracks system events, such as the failure of devices. Windows NT Diagnostics might help you determine the cause of the failure, but you're better off starting with the event log so you know exactly what happened.

3. **C**   NetBEUI is a nonroutable protocol. You'll need to install a different protocol on the marketing segment if you want packets to pass through the router.

4. **B**   You must bind a protocol to a specific adapter in order to use it. The NDIS and ODI standards ensure that you don't have "competing protocols" fighting for control of the adapter. The Server service enables you to share resources, but it isn't required for a simple diagnostic check such as a ping.

5. **A** The Workstation service is Windows NT's redirector. It routes I/O requests to the network and enables the Windows NT machine to act as a client.

4.1 Key Words

Protocol analyzer

Network Monitor

Event log

Protocol binding

Data frame

Packet

Network service

Server service

Workstation service

Redirector

Remote Access Service (RAS)

4.2   Diagnose and Resolve Common Connectivity Problems with Cards, Cables, and Related Hardware

Most network problems occur out on the wires. The components that connect PCs and enable them to communicate are susceptible to many kinds of problems. The following subsections (listed here) discuss these important connectivity and communication components and some of the problems associated with them.

- Cables and connectors
- Network adapter cards
- Hubs and MSAUs
- Connectivity devices (bridges, routers, repeaters, and other network devices)

This section also discusses some cable-related troubleshooting tools.

A.   Troubleshooting Cables and Connectors

Most network problems occur at the OSI Physical layer, and cabling is one of the most common causes. A cable might have a short or a break, or it might be attached to a faulty connector. Tools such as DVMs and TDRs (discussed later in this section) help search out cabling problems.

If a workstation cannot access the network and you think the problem might be the cabling, try disconnecting the network cables and attaching them to a portable PC. If the portable reaches the network, cabling probably isn't your problem.

When troubleshooting any network, begin with the more obvious physical problems. For example, make sure that all connectors are tight and properly connected, that ground wires and terminators are used when required, and that manufacturer's specifications (such as cable grade, cable lengths, and maximum number of nodes) are met and are consistent with the specifications for the transmission medium.

Chapter 2 discusses the various network cabling standards and some of their requirements and limitations. Be aware of the capacity and range limitations for the various transmission media. Typical troubleshooting scenarios include situations in which the cabling distance exceeds the range of the transmission medium or the required throughput exceeds the capacity of the transmission medium. Table 2.1.2 summarizes the requirements and characteristics of the various media standards. One of the best things you can do for yourself as you prepare for the Networking Essentials exam is to memorize the information in Table 2.1.2.

Here are some other guidelines to follow when troubleshooting cable-related network problems:

- With 10baseT, make sure the cable that's used has the correct number of twists to meet the data-grade specifications.
- Look for electrical interference. Electrical interference can result from tying the network cable together with monitor and power cords. Outdoor fluorescent lights, electric motors, and other electrical devices can cause interference.

- Make sure that connectors are pinned properly and crimped tightly.

- If excess shielding on coaxial cable is exposed, make sure it doesn't ground out the connector.

- Make sure that coaxial cables are not coiled tightly together.

- On coaxial Ethernet LANs, look for missing terminators or terminators with improper impedance ratings.

- Watch out for malfunctioning transceivers, concentrators, or T-connectors. Make sure that connectors have not been mixed up (for example, ARCnet connectors cannot be used on an Ethernet network).

- Test the continuity of the cable by using the various physical testing devices discussed in the previous section or by using a software-based cable testing utility.

- Make sure that all the component cables in a segment are connected. A user who moves his client and removes the T-connector incorrectly can break a segment.

- Examine cable connectors for bent or broken pins.

- On token-ring networks, inspect the attachment of patch cables and adapter cables. Remember, patch cables connect MSAUs, and adapter cables connect the network adapter to the MSAU.

One benefit of a token-ring network is its built-in capability to monitor itself. Token-ring networks provide electronic troubleshooting and, when possible, actually make repairs. When the token-ring network can't make its own repairs, a process called *beaconing* narrows down the search for the portion of the ring in which the problem is most likely to exist.

Because cabling problems are so prevalent and, often, so difficult to trace, network administrators use some special tools to seeking out damaged wires. Those tools include the following:

- **Digital Volt Meter (DVM).** This hand-held electronic measuring tool enables you to check the voltage of network cables. You can use a DVM to find a break or a short in a network cable.

- **Time-Domain Reflectometer (TDR).** TDRs send sound waves along a cable to look for imperfections that might be caused by a break or a short in the line.

- **Oscilloscope.** This device measures fluctuations in signal voltage and can help find faulty or damaged cabling.

B. Troubleshooting Network Adapter Cards

Network problems often result from malfunctioning network adapter cards. The process of troubleshooting the network adapter works like any other kind of troubleshooting process: You start with the simple. The following list details some things you can check if you think your network adapter card might be malfunctioning:

- Make sure the cable is connected to the card properly.

- Confirm that you have the correct network adapter card driver and that the driver is installed properly. Be sure the card is properly bound to the appropriate transport protocol.

- Verify that the network card matches your network's topology (for instance, 10baseT versus 100baseT.

- Make sure the network adapter card and the network adapter card driver are compatible with your operating system. If you use Windows NT, consult the Windows NT hardware compatibility list. If you use Windows 95 or another operating system, rely on the adapter card vendor specifications.

- Test for resource conflicts. Make sure another device isn't attempting to use the same resources. (See section 3.3 for more on resolving resource conflicts for network adapter cards.) If you think a resource conflict might be the problem but you can't pinpoint the conflict using Windows NT Diagnostics, Windows 95's Device Manager, or some other diagnostic program, try removing all the cards except the network adapter and then replacing the cards one by one. Check the network with each addition to determine which device is causing the conflict.

- Run the network adapter card's diagnostic software.

- If necessary, remove the card and clean the connector fingers (don't use an eraser because it leaves grit on the card).

- Examine the jumper and DIP switch settings on the card. Make sure the resource settings are consistent with the settings configured through the operating system.

- Make sure the card fits properly in the slot.

- Replace the card with one that you know works. If the connection works with a different card, you know the card is the problem.

Token-ring network adapters with failure rates that exceed a preset tolerance level might actually remove themselves from the network. Some token-ring networks experience problems if a 16 Mbps card is inserted into a 4 Mbps ring. (Other 16 Mbps cards can adjust to a 4 Mbps network.)

Broadcast storms (discussed later in this chapter) are often caused by faulty network adapters.

Review your event log on a regular basis. The event log may reveal a network adapter that experiences intermittent problems.

C.   Troubleshooting Hubs and MSAUs

If you experience problems with a hub-based LAN, such as a 10baseT network, you often can isolate the problem by disconnecting the attached workstations one at a time. If removing one of the workstations eliminates the problem, the trouble may be caused by that workstation or its associated cable length. If removing each of the workstations doesn't solve the problem, the fault may lie with the hub. Check the easy components first, such as ports, switches, and connectors. Then use a different hub (if you have it) and see if the problem persists. If your hub doesn't work properly, call the manufacturer.

If you're troubleshooting a token-ring network, make sure the cables are connected properly to the MSAUs, with ring-out ports connecting to the ring-in ports throughout the ring. If you suspect the MSAU, isolate it by changing the ring-in and ring-out cables to bypass the MSAU. If that makes the ring functional again, consider replacing the MSAU. In addition, if your network has MSAUs from more than one manufacturer, you might find that they are not wholly compatible. Impedance and other electrical characteristics can show slight differences between manufacturers, causing intermittent network problems. Some MSAUs (other than the 8228) are active and require a power supply. These MSAUs fail if they have a blown fuse or a bad power source. Your problem also might result from a misconfigured MSAU port. MSAU ports might need to be reinitialized with the setup tool. Removing drop cables and reinitializing each MSAU port is a quick fix that is useful on relatively small token-ring networks.

Isolating problems with patch cables, adapter cables, and MSAUs is easier to do if you have a current log of your network's physical design. After you pinpoint the problem, you can isolate potential problem areas from the rest of the network and then use a cable tester to find the actual problem.

D. Connectivity Devices (Bridges, Routers, Repeaters, and Other Network Devices)

If you are experiencing problems with a bridge, router, or repeater, your troubleshooting effort should begin where it begins for other network hardware: Make sure that the unit is plugged in and turned on and that all cables and connectors are fastened securely. Your problem might also be that you are deploying the unit in an inappropriate situation. Each of these connectivity devices is designed for a specific role, and if you deploy the device in the wrong situation, you may not get the results you expect. Section 2.4 outlines the roles of bridges, routers, repeaters, switches, brouters, and gateways.

The following list offers some important troubleshooting considerations:

- If you are extending your network using repeaters, remember the 5-4-3 rule (see section 1.8.B). Use a maximum of five repeated segments, with no more than four repeaters, and only three of the five segments should be populated.

- A repeater can extend the length of a LAN segment, but the maximum distance is still limited by the propagation delay (see section 2.4.A).

- Bridges and repeaters do not filter broadcast traffic and thus do not prevent or contain broadcast storms (see section 2.4.B).

- Bridges and repeaters cannot connect dissimilar LAN types (such as an Ethernet segment and a token-ring segment). See sections 2.4.A and 2.4.B.

- A router can route only routable protocols. (Routable protocols include TCP/IP, NWLink, IPX/SPX, and AppleTalk; Nonroutable protocols include NetBEUI and DLC.) See section 2.4.D.

- A router can connect dissimilar LAN types (such as Ethernet and token-ring), but it cannot connect dissimilar protocol systems (such as a TCP/IP network and an IPX network). Use a gateway to connect dissimilar protocol systems (see section 2.4.F).

4.2 Exercise: Using the Event Log to Diagnose Trace Problems

Exercise 4.2 shows you how you can trace problems quickly using the event log and Windows NT's Event Viewer application. The problem with an exercise in network problems is that you must induce a problem in order to perform the exercise. In this case, you'll simulate a network problem by disabling your network adapter. Here's how:

1. On a Windows NT system, start Control Panel and double-click the Devices application icon.

2. Look for your network adapter card driver in the list of devices. Select your network adapter card and click the Startup button.

3. Write down your current startup type setting so you'll remember what it is. Then, under Startup Type, click Disabled and select OK.

4. Close the Devices application and shut down your system.

5. Reboot Windows NT and log on.

6. Click the Start button and choose Programs, Administrative Tools, Event Viewer.

7. In the Event Viewer main window, make sure the System log is active. If it isn't, pull down the Log menu and select System.

8. Look for red error icons in the left column of Event Viewer. On most systems, the absence of a network adapter causes some services (such as the Remote Procedure Call (RPC) service and protocol-related services) to fail. Double-click a line with a red error icon for an *event detail*—a description of the event. In a real-life failure situation, the event detail gives you clues about the cause of the failure.

9. (Very important!) When you finish inspecting the event log, start the Control Panel Devices application, find your network adapter card in the devices list, click the Startup button, and restore the startup type to its original setting (most likely Automatic). Then reboot. (You can start your adapter directly from the Devices application, but starting your adapter might not automatically resurrect all the failed services.)

4.2   Practice Problems

1. Which of the following can you use to look for breaks in network cables by measuring cable voltage?

    A. Protocol analyzer

    B. DVM

    C. TDR

    D. MSDL

2. Which of the following sends sonar-like pulses down the cable to look for imperfections?

    A. DVM

    B. Oscilloscope

    C. TDR

    D. None of the above

3. Of the following possible problems, which two relate to token-ring network adapters?

    A. Broadcast messages from the card are not timed properly.

    B. The card is not bound to a network service.

    C. The card removed itself from the network.

    D. A 16Mbps card exists on a 4Mbps ring.

4. Most network problems occur at which layer of the OSI model?

    A. Physical

    B. Data Link

    C. Network

    D. Session

5. Which of the following suggestions offers a means of isolating a network problem on a hub-based 10baseT network?

    A. You can disconnect the attached workstations one at a time to isolate a bad cable, a bad network card, or a bad workstation.

    B. You can isolate a bad hub by bypassing it.

    C. By changing port assignments of all the workstations, you can isolate a potential network problem.

    D. By disconnecting all of the attached workstations simultaneously, you can isolate a bad cable, a bad network card, or a bad workstation.

4.2   Answers and Explanations: Practice Problems

1. **B**   A DVM (Digital Voltage Meter) measures cable voltage.

2. **C**   TDRs (Time-Domain Reflectometers) send sonar-like pulses.

3. **C, D**   A token-ring card can remove itself from the network. A disparity between the speed of the card and the speed of the other cards in the ring can cause problems. A network adapter is not bound directly to a service; it is bound to a protocol.

4. **A**   Most network problems occur at the Physical layer.

5. **A**   Of the choices given, the easiest way to isolate a network problem on a hub-based network is to disconnect workstations from the hub one at a time.

4.2   Key Words

Electrical interference

Beaconing

Digital Volt Meter (DVM)

Time-Domain Reflectometer (TDR)

Oscilloscope

Resource conflict

Jumper

DIP switch

Broadcast storm

Connectivity device

Multistation Access Unit(MSAU)

4

4.3   Resolve Broadcast Storms

A *broadcast storm* is a sudden flood of broadcast messages that clogs the transmission medium, approaching 100 percent of the bandwidth. Broadcast storms cause performance to decline and, in the worst case, computers cannot even access the network. The cause of a broadcast storm is often a malfunctioning network adapter, but a broadcast storm also can occur when a device on the network attempts to contact another device that either doesn't exist or for some reason doesn't respond to the broadcast.

If the broadcast messages are viable packets (or even error-filled but partially legible packets), a network-monitoring or protocol-analysis tool often can determine the source of the storm. If the broadcast storm results from a malfunctioning adapter throwing illegible packets onto the line, and a network monitor or protocol analyzer can't find the source, try to isolate the offending PC by removing computers from the network one at a time until the line returns to normal. (For more information, see "Troubleshooting Network Adapter Cards," earlier in this chapter.)

The Windows NT Network Monitor tool, discussed earlier in this chapter and in Chapter 3, can help you find the source of a broadcast storm.

4.3   Practice Problems

1. A broadcast storm is

    A. A network broadcast that begins properly but doesn't terminate.

    B. An infinite loop caused by a faulty redirector.

    C. A sudden deluge of network traffic.

    D. A hard drive consecutively outputting all its bits to the network.

2. Which two of the following problems are the most common causes of network broadcast storms?

    A. A malfunctioning network adapter card.

    B. A short in a section of the transmission medium.

    C. Incorrect transport protocol assignments.

    D. A device on the network that is unable to contact another device because the other device either does not exist or, for some reason, does not respond.

3. Which is the best tool to locate the source of a broadcast storm?

    A. TDR

    B. DVM

    C. Performance Monitor

    D. Network Monitor

4. If the broadcast storm contains illegible packets, a good way to find the source is to

    A. Use an analysis tool to decode the packets.

    B. Isolate the offending PC by removing computers from the network one at a time.

    C. Disable the current default protocol and then test the network using a different protocol with the same adapter.

    D. All of the above.

4.3   Answers and Explanations: Practice Problems

1. **C**   A broadcast storm is a large, sudden increase in network traffic.

2. **A, D**   The most common causes of broadcast storms are a malfunctioning adapter and a device looking for a missing network node.

3. **D**   TDRs and VDMs find cabling problems. Performance Monitor can help you discover that there is a broadcast storm, but it cannot directly discover the source. Network Monitor is the best candidate for finding the source of an incoming packet.

4. **B**   An analysis tool can't decode the packets if they're illegible. If the broadcast storm is caused by a malfunctioning adapter, it won't help to use a different protocol with the same adapter. The fastest way to find the offending computer is to remove the computers from the network one at a time.

4.3   Key Words

Broadcast storm

Protocol analyzer

Network monitor

Network adapter

4

4.4   Identify and Resolve Network Performance Problems

If your network runs slower than it used to run (or slower than it ought to run), the problem might be that the present network traffic exceeds the level at which the network can operate efficiently. Some possible causes for increased traffic are new hardware (such as a new workstation) or new software (such as a network computer game or some other network application). A generator or another mechanical device operating near the network could cause a degradation of network performance. In addition, a malfunctioning network device could act as a bottleneck. To determine which is true, ask yourself what has changed since the last time the network operated efficiently, and begin there with your troubleshooting efforts.

The increased traffic could be the result of increased usage. If usage exceeds the capacity of the network, you might want to consider expanding or redesigning your network. You also might want to divide the network into smaller segments using a router or a bridge. A protocol analyzer can help you measure and monitor the traffic at various points on your network. If your Ethernet network is using more than 20–25 percent bandwidth utilization, this would be a good time to either break the network into segments or use a router. This also applies to a token-ring network that has more than 50 percent bandwidth utilization.

Underdesigned networking components can sometimes cause performance problems for an entire network. A busy server, for instance, should use a high-end bus mastering 32-bit or 64-bit network adapter card. A 16-bit network adapter can cause performance degradation.

If you suspect that a particular component is slowing down your network, you can use Windows NT's Performance Monitor to look for the bottleneck. Performance Monitor is an essential tool for troubleshooting network performance problems. Performance Monitor collects performance-related statistics and enables you to graph, log, or tabulate those statistics. See section 3.5 for a discussion of Windows NT's Performance Monitor tool.

If possible, spend some time with Performance Monitor so you can become familiar with the kinds of statistics it measures. If you see an exam question on network performance, look for clues in the question that point toward a particular measurement. Even if you aren't an expert on Performance Monitor, you can usually find the appropriate counter if you think through the problem logically and you have a good understanding of the PC's components (processor, hard drive, protocols, network adapters, and so forth).

Performance Monitor has a vast selection of counters relating to both hardware and software components: processors, adapters, protocols, disks, services. This means you can monitor several suspected bottleneck candidates simultaneously to determine problems and possible solutions. You may discover, for instance, that a protocol is rarely used, indicating that you could increase your network's bandwidth by disabling or removing that protocol.

Section 3.5 describes some other strategies for record keeping and discusses the importance of maintaining a baseline of performance data. A baseline helps you troubleshoot network performance by providing you with a reference point from which you can measure later fluctuations in performance.

A. Handling Other Network Problems

The following list details some other common problems that could affect your network:

- **Operating system conflicts.** Operating system upgrades sometimes cause older programs to become incompatible with the operating system itself. This problem is compounded in network environments because, during the transition to a new network operating system, some servers run the new version for a period of time while others are still running the previous version. Microsoft recommends that you perform a test upgrade on an isolated part of the network to ensure that all hardware and software systems function properly when the upgrade is made.

- **Server crashes.** A server disk crash can be disastrous if you aren't adequately prepared for it. You should devise a system of regular backups and, depending on the nature of your data, explore other safeguards such as a RAID fault-tolerant system.

- **Power fluctuations.** A small fluctuation in the power supply can make the network misbehave. If the power goes off completely—even for a moment—the whole network could shut down, causing users to lose their work in progress. A disorderly shutdown also can cause problems with file servers. The best solution is to prepare for a power outage before it happens. Connect each server to an Uninterruptible Power Supply (UPS), and encourage your users to perform occasional saves as they work.

If you implement all the measures discussed so far and you still experience problems, your next step may be to consult the experts. Or, even before you start your own troubleshooting, you may want to consult the available information to learn more about the problem. The next section discusses some online and offline sources of help.

B. Getting Support

You are rarely alone when you are troubleshooting network problems. An important aspect of troubleshooting is knowing where to turn for critical information about your network environment. Many online and offline sources can provide troubleshooting information. Some of these sources (in addition to the online help provided with your operating system), include the following:

- **Vendor documentation and help lines.** Hardware and software vendors often provide troubleshooting tips with the documentation. Vendors also often provide technical assistance by phone.

- **Bulletin board services.** A number of electronic bulletin boards supply networking information. You can download information on Microsoft network products from the Microsoft Download Library (MSDL), which you can reach by dialing 206-936-6735. Other vendors also have active bulletin board systems, such as Novell's NetWire BBS. See vendor documentation for more information on how to reach a particular vendor's official BBS.

- **The Internet.** The major network vendors all sponsor active forums and newsgroups on the Internet, CompuServe, and other online services. See your vendor's documentation.

- **CD-ROMs.** Several vendors now market CD-ROMs with network and PC hardware information. These are some examples:

    Windows NT Server's Books Online (located on the Windows NT Installation CD-ROM) provides an additional source of documentation that isn't available with online help.

Microsoft's TechNet contains product information, technical information, articles, and announcements. TechNet is available on a subscription basis through Microsoft (call 800-344-2121).

Novell's NSEPro CD-ROM is a NetWare-oriented encyclopedia of network information.

The Micro House Technical Library (MHTL) is another impressive database of technical information. The MHTL addresses such items as BIOS settings for IDE drives and jumper settings for popular peripheral boards. The MHTL comes with a rich collection of informative illustrations.

4.4   Practice Problems

1. Which three of the following could degrade network performance?

   A. A generator or mechanical device near the network

   B. A computer game

   C. A sudden disorderly shutdown of a workstation

   D. New hardware

2. Which one of the following devices is a solution for power fluctuation problems?

   A. Uninterruptible Power Supply (UPS)

   B. NT Clustering

   C. RAID

   D. Grounded circuit

3. To avoid potential operating system conflicts, what course of action does Microsoft recommend when upgrading?

   A. Do not upgrade any servers or nodes on any network, unless absolutely necessary.

   B. Upgrade the entire network simultaneously.

   C. Perform a test upgrade on an isolated part of the network to ensure that all hardware and software systems function properly when the upgrade is made.

   D. Use only Microsoft products to ensure complete compatibility.

4. Suppose there appears to be some interference on network cables installed over an acoustic tile ceiling. What is a possible (probable) cause for the interference?

   A. Fluorescent lights

   B. Adverse weather

   C. Electrical motors and devices

   D. Network cables tied together with monitor wires

5. You should consider subdividing your Ethernet network if the bandwidth utilization exceeds

   A. 25%.

   B. 50%.

   C. 90%.

   D. 95%.

4.4   Answers and Explanations: Practice Problems

1. **A, B, D**   A shutdown of a workstation typically won't affect network performance. A mechanical device could cause electrical interference. A computer game or a faulty new device could disrupt or slow down the network.

2. **A**   A UPS protects the network from power fluctuations.

3. **C**   Microsoft recommends that you test a part of the network first to ensure that all systems are compatible.

4. **A**   If you are experiencing interference in network cables installed over an acoustic tile ceiling, fluorescent lights are a logical first guess for the cause.

5. **A**   Ethernet networks use a contention-based access control method, and performance can start to degrade a seemingly low network utilization of 25%.

4.4   Key Words

Bandwidth utilization

Performance Monitor

Baseline

Operating system conflict

Power fluctuation

TechNet

Practice Exam: Troubleshooting

1. Which of the following services enables a Windows NT computer to share its resources?

    A. Workstation

    B. Server

    C. Browser

    D. NTClient

2. Suppose you are not able to establish a SLIP connection to an IPX/SPX network. The most likely cause is:

    A. You are using an incompatible frame type.

    B. Your network number is not unique.

    C. Your modem speed is different from the speed of the modem to which you're connecting.

    D. SLIP won't work with IPX/SPX.

3. Your network is a small workgroup of Windows 95 machines. You want to switch from share-level to user-level security. You go to the Access Control tab in the Control Panel Network application, select the option button for user-level access control, and enter the name of your workgroup. You receive an error message. A likely cause for this is:

    A. Windows 95 machines do not have an account database that supports user-level access.

    B. The other machines in the workgroup are all set for share-level access.

    C. You must cancel all network shares before you switch to user-level access.

    D. All of the above.

4. The PPP protocol requires:

    A. TCP/IP.

    B. A static IP address.

    C. A point-to-point connection.

    D. All of the above.

5. You access a directory on an NTFS partition through a network share. You then discover that you can't access a file on the NTFS partition. Which of the following might be the cause?

    A. The share permissions do not provide access to the file.

    B. Your user rights specifically exclude access to that file.

    C. The file-level permissions for the file exclude you from accessing the file.

    D. All of the above.

6. Which troubleshooting tool can you use to verify that a network card does not have a resource conflict?

    A. Windows NT Diagnostics

    B. Windows 95 Device Manager

    C. Network adapter card's diagnostic software

    D. A third-party diagnostic utility

    E. All of the above

7. From the following list, which two devices can be used to monitor network traffic, track network performance, and analyze packet frames?

    A. Oscilloscopes

    B. Network monitors

    C. Protocol analyzers

    D. Time-Domain Reflectometers

8. On a Windows NT system, which tool would you use to change a conflicting IRQ setting for a network adapter card?

    A. Windows NT Diagnostics

    B. Control Panel Devices Application

    C. Control Panel Network Application

    D. Device Manager

9. Your 10Base5 network is not behaving reliably. Which three of the following things do you need to verify?

   A. The maximum length for the entire network is 2500 meters.

   B. The maximum network segment length is 500 meters.

   C. The minimum drop cable length is 2.5 meters.

   D. The maximum drop cable length is 50 meters.

10. Your laptop communicates with the internal network using scatter infrared, and you are experiencing reliability problems. Your office contains a large quantity of high-voltage electrical equipment. You typically roam around the office within a range of approximately 150 feet from the access point, and your path takes you around corners where you are not always in a direct line of sight to the access point. Which of the following is a likely source of the problems?

   A. You are not always in direct line of sight to the access point.

   B. You exceed the reliable distance to the access point.

   C. The electrical equipment is causing interference that disrupts the signal.

   D. All of the above.

11. You should consider subdividing your token-ring network if the bandwidth utilization exceeds

   A. 25%.

   B. 50%.

   C. 90%.

   D. 95%.

12. Using Performance Monitor, you have discovered that the frequency with which your Windows NT Server system accesses the paging file (Pages/sec) is unusually high. This could indicate that you should:

   A. Increase the size of the paging file.

   B. Spread the paging file over multiple disks.

   C. Upgrade memory.

   D. Upgrade your processor.

13. The number of interrupts per second processed by your PC recently increased drastically. A possible cause is:

   A. The processor is overloaded.

   B. A network adapter is malfunctioning.

   C. The operating system is searching for a missing hardware component.

   D. An application is incompatible with the operating system.

14. Which tool would you use to determine whether a network slowdown is caused by a slow hard disk?

   A. Disk Administrator

   B. Task Manager

   C. Server Manager

   D. None of the above

15. Of the following possible solutions, which two are most likely to improve the performance of a Windows NT Server system acting as a file server?

   A. Replace the hard disk to add capacity.

   B. Replace the hard disk for better I/O performance.

   C. Replace the 16-bit network adapter with a 32-bit adapter.

   D. Implement disk mirroring.

4

Answers and Explanations: Practice Exam

1. **B** The Server service enables a computer to share resources.

2. **D** SLIP works only with TCP/IP; you can't use it with IPX/SPX.

3. **A** A Windows 95 machine cannot access user information on a Windows NT or NetWare machine in order to support user-level security. Because the workgroup contains only Windows 95 machines, user-level security is not an option.

4. **A** PPP (Point-to-Point Protocol) is designed for point-to-point connections. Unlike its forerunner, SLIP, it does not require TCP/IP or a static IP address.

5. **C** The file permissions for the file may exclude you from accessing the file. Share permissions apply to a directory, and you have already accessed the directory, so you know share permissions are not a problem. A user right applies to a type of activity, not to a specific resource such as a file.

6. **E** All of the choices could help you verify the resource settings for a network adapter card.

7. **B, C** Protocol analyzers and network monitors perform sophisticated network analysis functions. Oscilloscopes and TDRs diagnose only network cabling problems.

8. **C** The Network application lets you change the IRQ settings. Windows NT Diagnostics lets you view the setting, but not change it. Device Manager is a Windows 95 tool. The Devices application lets you start and stop devices, but not reconfigure them.

9. **A, B, D** There is no minimum length for drop cables. The other choices are limits included in the 10Base5 specification (see section 2.2.C.2).

10. **B** Infrared broadcasts are reliable up to 100 feet. Scatter infrared does not require a line-of-sight connection, and infrared is not affected by electrical interference.

11. **B** Token-rings can support more utilization than Ethernet networks, but they still operate more efficiently at >50% bandwidth utilization.

12. **C** If you increase the RAM memory, you'll reduce the need for paging.

13. **B** A device such as a network adapter card uses interrupts to contact the processor. A malfunctioning adapter may be flooding the system with interrupt requests.

14. **D** None of the options listed will give you any direct statistics on the performance of the hard disk. Your best choice is Performance Monitor.

15. **B, C** A faster hard disk will spend less time reading and writing to files. The network adapter is often the bottleneck for a busy server. Disk mirroring doesn't improve, and could actually slow down, I/O performance. Adding capacity could have a secondary effect on performance in some situations, but B and C still are the best answers.

Practice Exam 1

The exam consists of 58 questions that cover four major topics. You have 75 minutes to complete this test. Remember that time is a factor. You should be around question 19 after 33 minutes and question 37 after 60 minutes.

Before the actual exam begins, the exam program will give you the option of taking a sample orientation exam to familiarize yourself with the way the exam operates. You should take that orientation exam. If you are unsure about how to use the testing equipment or software, or if you have any questions about the rules for the exam, ask the exam administrator before the exam begins.

1. An infrared network can transmit at what speed?
   A. 10 Mbps
   B. 100 Mbps
   C. 1 Mbps
   D. 1.544 Mbps
   E. 2 Mbps
   F. 4 Mbps
   G. 100 Kbps
   H. None of the above

2. Thicknet is used as a backbone in some installations to connect a number of Thinnet-based networks. Why would it be an advantage to use Thicknet cabling as a backbone solution?
   A. Thicknet can transfer data much faster than Thinnet cable can.
   B. Thicknet can carry data over greater distances than Thinnet cable can.
   C. You cannot mix Thicknet and Thinnet cable.
   D. Thicknet is less expensive and easier to install than Thinnet.
   E. Thicknet is the most common type of cable used in most networks.
   F. You cannot use Thicknet as a backbone cable; it is used only for cable TV transmissions.

3. Which of the following are used for Infrared Networks (choose all that apply):
   A. Reflective
   B. Line-of-sight
   C. Scatter transmissions
   D. Spread-spectrum

E. Broadband optical

F. Narrow-band

G. RF

H. AF

4. Which method is used in TCP/IP protocol to isolate the host ID from the network ID in a 32-bit address?

A. Network Address

B. Node Address

C. Class A

D. Class B

E. Class C

F. Default gateway

G. Subnet mask

H. None of the above

5. Which utility under the Windows NT operating system is used to create accounts on the PDC?

A. User Profile Editor

B. User Manager for Domains

C. Server Manager

D. Client Administrator

E. Registry Editor

6. You have a Thinnet cable in your network. How far can the cable transmit correct data frames before it degrades (attenuates) the data signal?

A. 500 Meters

B. 250 Meters

C. 100 Meters

D. 75 Meters

E. 50 Meters

F. 10 Meters

G. 185 Meters

7. In a primary rate ISDN system, what is the D channel used for?

A. 16 Kbps

B. 32 Kbps

C. 64 Kbps

D. Voice, Data, and Images

E. Signaling and link management data

F. Handshaking only

8. What is the definition of *attenuation*?

A. The signal crossover in wires

B. The signal overflow from an adjacent wire

C. The loss of a signal strength in a wire as the data signal travels further

D. The signal increase in a data packet in a long distance cable run

9. In Windows NT, a redirector is used for which of these two things?

A. To assign a logical drive letter to a share resource on the network.

B. To divide the hard disk into multiple sectors.

C. To intercept requests in the computer.

D. To determine if the specific task should be on the local computer's bus, or it should be sent to the remote computer on the network.

E. To determine the degree of sharing of resources on the network.

F. To redirect SMB blocks into NetWare NCP blocks.

G. There is no such thing as a redirector.

10. Your service provider just installed ISDN service in your home. What are the 64Kbps channels known as?

    A. Z Channel

    B. Y Channel

    C. D Channel

    D. C Channel

    E. A Channel

    F. B Channel

11. What is the most common type of digital line used in most networks today?

    A. 56 Kbps

    B. T1

    C. T3

    D. E1

    E. Asynchronous modems

12. The RJ-45 connector used in networking has how many connections?

    A. Eleven

    B. Seven

    C. Four

    D. Six

    E. Eight

    F. Sixteen

13. Which of the following statements is true of Time Domain-Reflectometers (TDR)?

    A. TDR is an advanced cable tester used for WANs.

    B. TDR sends light to locate breaks or shorts in a cable run.

    C. TDR sends SONAR to locate breaks or shorts in a cable run.

    D. TDR sends a laser signal to locate breaks or shorts in a cable run.

14. Which level of RAID divides data into 64K blocks and spreads it equally in a fixed organized order under a fault-tolerance setup with parity?

    A. RAID 0

    B. RAID 1

    C. RAID 2

    D. RAID 3

    E. RAID 4

    F. RAID 5

    G. RAID 10

15. Which of the following techniques enables you to reduce network traffic by backing up several Unix servers across the network?

    A. Back up only once a year.

    B. Schedule backups after business hours.

    C. Back up only the operating system.

    D. Back up only files and directories.

    E. Place the backup computer on an isolated network.

    F. Back up during business hours only.

16. In which layer of the OSI model does packet assembly begin?

    A. Network

    B. Presentation

    C. Session

    D. Physical

    E. Data Link

    F. Application

    G. Transport

    H. ATM

    I. FDDI

17. Which type of cable does a 10BT network used?

   A. Thicknet

   B. Thinnnet

   C. RJ-11

   D. Fiber

   E. Unshielded Twisted-Pair (UTP)

   F. RJ-56

18. Your company purchased 100BaseTX cable. Which category of UTP cable is required?

   A. CAT 1

   B. CAT 2

   C. CAT 3

   D. CAT 4

   E. CAT 5

   F. CAT 10

   G. CAT 100

19. Which of the following categories supports transmission for 10BaseT?

   A. 1

   B. 2

   C. 3

   D. 4

   E. 5

   F. 10

   G. 50

20. Which of the techniques listed below does broadband transmission use?

   A. Digital signaling

   B. Analog signaling

   C. Bidirectional signal flow

   D. Unidirectional signal flow

   E. Repeaters to amplify signals

   F. Repeaters to regenerate signals

   G. Hon/Hoff signaling

21. You installed DHCP service in your Windows NT network. Which of the following statements is true of DHCP?

   A. It serves as an Internet server service.

   B. It serves as a gateway service.

   C. It serves as a NIC card address service.

   D. It serves as a TCP/IP service to automatically issue TCP/IP addresses.

22. Which of the following is contained inside a packet header frame?

   A. Data

   B. CRC

   C. TTL

   D. SA (source address)

   E. DA (destination address)

   F. Alert signal

   G. None of the above

23. Which of the following cables would you think is the least expensive?

   A. Fiber

   B. 10Base5 – Thicknet

   C. 10Base2 – Thinnet

   D. 10BaseT – UTP

   E. IBM TYPE 2

24. Which of the following describes the 10Base5 cable type?

   A. CAT 5 UTP

   B. CAT 3 UTP

   C. Thin coaxial (Thinnet)

   D. Thick coaxial (Thicknet)

   E. None of the above

25. Which of the following wireless transmission techniques is the slowest method of transmitting a data packet from location A to location B?

    A. Infrared

    B. Laser

    C. Narrow-band radio

    D. Spread-spectrum radio

    E. 10BaseT

26. You're a consultant. You are asked what is the maximum distance for 10BaseT (UTP) cabling for a proposal. Which of the following is the correct answer?

    A. 100 meters (328 feet)

    B. 500 meters (1,640 feet)

    C. 25 meters (82 feet)

    D. 185 meters (607 feet)

    E. 50 meters (164 feet)

    F. 1 meter (3 feet) without a repeater

27. You installed a Windows 95 client in your network, and you're running a Novell Network with version 3.12. What is needed to gain access to the application GAMES on the Novell NetWare server?

    A. NDS

    B. NCP

    C. NWLink with GSNW

    D. NWLink with CSNW

    E. IPX/SPX with Microsoft Client for NetWare

28. What is the function of CSMA/CD?

    A. It's part of token-ring algorithm.

    B. It breaks data into smaller formats.

    C. It's an Ethernet tool for finding wiring faults.

    D. It regulates traffic on the segment.

    E. It is a cable repeater system.

    F. It's a 1000BaseT protocol only.

29. *Impedance* is defined as:

    A. The opposite of resistance.

    B. Signal overflow errors.

    C. Resistance to DC.

    D. Resistance to AC.

    E. The CAT 5 standard.

30. To avoid data loss, which is the best method you could use and still access data?

    A. UPS system

    B. RAID 5

    C. RAID 0

    D. Tape backup

31. What type of hardware connector assembly is used by 10Base2 for connection to a standard Network Adapter Card?

    A. A BNC barrel connector assembly.

    B. A BNC T connector assembly.

    C. An RJ-11 connector assembly.

    D. An RJ-45 connector assembly.

    E. An AUI connector assembly.

32. Which media access method is used commonly by IEEE 802.3 standards?

    A. CDMS/CA

    B. Ethernet Passing

    C. Token Passing

    D. Demand priority

    E. CSMA/CD

33. Which of the following is a non-routable transport protocol?

    A. NetBEUI

    B. DLC

    C. IPX

    D. IP

    E. AppleTalk

34. 10Base5 cable has another name. Which of the following is the correct term?

    A. CAT 2

    B. CAT 4

    C. Thinnet

    D. Outernet

    E. Thicknet

    F. None of the above

35. Raw data bits that convert into data frames are handled by which layer of the OSI model?

    A. Transport

    B. Session

    C. Physical

    D. Presentation

    E. Data Link

36. Which of the following is true of a star topology design?

    A. An opening in the cable segment can take down the entire network infrastructure.

    B. It is more difficult to configure than a ring design.

    C. It provides centralized monitoring and management control.

    D. It requires less cable than a bus design.

37. Translating the data format is the responsibility of which layer of the OSI model?

    A. Application

    B. Physical

    C. Data Link

    D. Communication

    E. Presentation

38. Which type of connector assembly is responsible for twisted-pair?

    A. AUI

    B. BNC

    C. BBC

    D. RJ-55

    E. RJ-45

39. Which of the following protocols is an NDIS x.x-compliant version of the Internetwork Packet Exchange protocol?

    A. IP

    B. SMB

    C. NCP

    D. NWLink

    E. NetBEUI

40. Which sublayer of the Data Link layer directly communicates with the Network Adapter Card assembly?

    A. LLC

    B. LAC

    C. MAC

    D. DAC

    E. None of the above

41. Which system parameter determines whether a file request is intended for the local computer or for a remote computer on the network?

    A. The frame type
    B. The networking protocol
    C. The redirector
    D. The transceiver
    E. The TDI

42. Which of the following statements is true of NetBEUI?

    A. NetBEUI is routable.
    B. NetBEUI is slow in a LAN design.
    C. NetBEUI is a NetWare protocol only.
    D. NetBEUI is a small, very fast, and efficient transport layer protocol used primarily with Microsoft networks.

43. Which of the following devices can use all seven layers of the OSI model?

    A. Bridges
    B. Routers
    C. Repeaters
    D. Mux
    E. Modems
    F. Gateways

44. Which of the following networks typically use a design with star bus topology?

    A. 10BaseT
    B. 10Base5
    C. 100Base5
    D. 100BaseX
    E. 100BaseVG-AnyLAN
    F. None of the above

45. Which of the following are dial-up data communications protocols?

    A. FTP
    B. TCP
    C. SLIP
    D. PPP
    E. ATM

46. Which of the following devices can perform protocol conversions in an infrastructure setup?

    A. Gateways
    B. Routers
    C. Bridges
    D. Brouters
    E. Repeaters
    F. None of the above

47. Which of the following cable types can be used for 100 Mbps networks?

    A. RG-58 A/U
    B. RG-58 U
    C. CAT 3
    D. CAT 5
    E. CAT 1

48. Which of the following types of cable can transmit 1,000 meters without a repeater working at the Physical layer of the OSI model?

    A. CAT 3
    B. CAT 5
    C. CAT 1
    D. 10Base 5
    E. Fiber optic

49. Which of the following tasks can a bridge accomplish?

    A. Connecting a 10BaseT segment with a 10Base5 segment.
    B. Translating network protocols.

C. Segmenting a network traffic load.

D. Connecting a token-ring segment with an Ethernet segment.

50. If your goal is to increase the strength of a broadband signal (10Base2) over a long cable length, which device would solve this problem in your design?

A. Repeaters

B. Oscilloscopes

C. Amplifiers

D. Multiplexers

E. Switches

51. Which of the following is an implementation of packet switching technology?

A. ISDN

B. Modem

C. ATM

D. Switched 56

E. T1

52. You have just finish a design that connects Unix and Windows NT operating systems. Which protocol is used in your design to enable communication between the two systems?

A. NetBEUI

B. DLC

C. NWLink

D. TCP/IP

E. FDDI

53. You want to change the parallel data stream used on the computer's PCI bus into a serial data stream. Which

device in your system is responsible for this conversion?

A. Hub

B. Terminator

C. Bridge

D. Multiplexer

E. Transceiver

54. Which of the following protocols uses a distance-vector algorithm to determine routes?

A. RIP

B. NFS

C. SNA

D. DLC

E. XNS

F. AAP

55. You want to implement sector sparing on your network. Which of the following devices can perform sector sparing?

A. IDE

B. ESDI

C. AT

D. AT Advanced

E. SCSI

F. PCI

G. ISA

56. Which of the following is a TCP/IP protocol for monitoring networks?

A. SMP

B. NCP

C. SMTP

D. SNMP

E. FTAM

57. You are setting up a network in your new office for the first time, and there is no preinstalled wiring. Which type of cabling should you consider first?

    A. Thicknet

    B. Thinnet

    C. STP

    D. UTP

    E. Flatnet

58. You want to allow users to access network resources freely, but you also want to protect a few resources with special passwords. Which of the following security models should you implement?

    A. Domain-level security

    B. Share-level security

    C. User-level security

    D. Server-level security

    E. None of the above

Answers and Explanations

1. **A**   10 Mbps is the current specification for infrared network.

2. **B**   It can support the same data over longer distances that Thinnet can, which is 10Base2 cabling.

3. **A, B, E, F**   Reflective, line-of-sight, broadband optical, and narrow-band are used in the transmission of infrared data.

4. **A**   Network Address is used to separate the host ID (16-bits) from the network ID (16-bits) of the total 32-bit address.

5. **B**   User Manager for Domains is the utility used to create accounts and groups.

6. **G**   The specification is 185 meters for 10Base2 (Thinnet cable).

7. **E**   It is used only for signaling (handshaking) and Link Data Management at 16 Kbps speed.

8. **C**   As the length increases beyond IEEE specifications, attenuation takes place and degrades the signal.

9. **A, E**   It assigns a logical drive letter to a share resource on the network. (A *logical drive letter* is a drive letter outside the local drive assignments, such as the floppy drive, local hard disk drive, and CD-ROM in the computer.) It also determines the degree of sharing of resources on the network.

10. **F**   B Channel is described as 64 Kbps. When two channels are used, the total combination is 128 Kbps, which is two B Channels.

11. **B**   T1 is the most common type at 1.544 Mbps.

12. **E**   RJ-45 cable has eight connections, four pairs of wire assembly.

13. **C**   TDR sends a SONAR signal to locate breaks or shorts in a cable run. It is an excellent tool for the network professional.

14. **F**   RAID 5 divides the data into 64K blocks of equal increments across disks. These disks must be three physical drives and greater in order for RAID 5 to function.

15. **E**   By placing the server on an isolated network, you can reduce the amount of traffic on the network. This is also called *segmentation network traffic*.

16. **F**   The Application layer is number seven in the OSI model, and that is where the packet assembly begins and transcends to the lowest layer (the Physical layer—number one).

17. **E**   UTP is a four pair cable that 10BaseT topology uses.

18. **E**   CAT 5 cabling will use 10BaseT, 100BaseTX, and 100BaseT.

19. **C, D, E**   CAT 3 cable, CAT 4 cable, CAT 5 cable.

20. **A, B, E, F**   Digital signaling, analog signaling, repeaters to amplify signals, and repeaters to regenerate signals.

21. **D**   DHCP assigns TCP/IP addresses automatically when the client computer comes on-line and issues a DHCP LEASE IP ADDRESS from the DHCP server.

22. **D, E, F**   The source address, destination address, and alert signal are required fields in a packet header frame.

23. **D**   Unshielded Twisted-Pair is the cheapest per foot in comparison to coaxial (Thicknet and Thinnet), fiber cable, and IBM TYPE 2 (which is used for token-ring signaling).

24. **D** Thick coaxial or Thicknet is used only for 10Base5 cabling. The disadvantages of using 10Base5 are its handling for installations, its difficulty to install, and the cost per foot. It serves as a backbone for Thinnet networks interconnecting to Thicknet.

25. **D** Spread-spectrum radio has a maximum output between 2 Mbps and 10 Mbps, whereas infrared can scale over 10 Mbps, and laser can scale at the speed of light.

26. **A** 100 meters or 328 feet is the exact IEEE specification for CAT 5 cable with 10BaseT cable.

27. **E** You must load IPX/SPX protocol with a Windows 95 client. You must also load Microsoft Client for NetWare, which is a service under Windows 95. GSNW is Gateway Services for NetWare and is part of the Windows NT server service. CSNW (Client Services for NetWare) is used in the Windows NT workstation product.

28. **D** CSMA/CD (which stands for Carrier Sense Multiple Access with Collision Detection) regulates traffic on the segment.

29. **D** Impedance is the opposite of conduction. In signals flowing in a network cable, impedance is the resistance factor to AC (alternating current). AC is the type of voltage that is sent in network cabling topologies.

30. **B** RAID 5 will provide complete access to your data on-line, even when a disk failure occurs.

31. **B** For 10Base2, which is termed Thinnet, a BNC T connector is used to join the network interface card in the local computer to the cable assembly, which is in the form of a coaxial cable.

32. **E** CSMA/CD is a standard called Carrier Sense Multiple Access with Collision Detection and is a media access method used in Ethernet networks. With CSMA/CD, a computer "listens" to the physical medium to determine whether another computer is transmitting the data frame.

33. **A** NetBEUI is a popular transport protocol that is used in a small non-routable network and is very fast.

34. **E** 10Base5 cabling is Thicknet by trade name. This coaxial cable is very rigid in material and serves as an excellent backbone for signals up to 500 meters in length.

35. **E** At the Data Link layer, the conversion of data frames from raw bits takes place. This layer is also responsible for transferring frames from one computer to another. After the Data Link layer sends a frame, it waits for ACK, which is an acknowledgment from the receiving computer.

36. **A** In a star design, cable segments to a centralized component device called a *hub* that connects the computers. Signals transmitted by a computer on the star pass through the hub to all computers on the network.

37. **E** The Presentation layer is responsible for translating data from the Application layer into an intermediary format. The Presentation layer is also responsible for security issues and the compression of data.

38. **E** The RJ-45 connector assembly is an eight-wire modular connector used by twisted-pair cables.

39. **D** NWLINK is an NDIS-compliant version of the IPX protocol that is used with Microsoft products.

40. **C**   The MAC (Media Access Control) layer communicates directly with the network adapter card and is responsible for delivering error-free data between two computers on the network.

41. **C**   The redirector is a small section of the code in the NOS that intercepts requests in the computer and determines if the requests should be local to be redirected out to the network computer.

42. **D**   NetBEUI is a small, efficient, and fast Transport layer protocol. It is very dynamic in the way it can be optimized for very high performance when used in mostly departmental LANs that are not routable.

43. **F**   Gateways are used to connect networks using different protocols so that information can be passed from one system to another. For example, Microsoft SNA Server for Windows NT is a gateway product that connects one form of protocol to another for connectivity to a mainframe system.

44. **A, D**   100BaseX Ethernet uses the CSMA/CD in a star wired bus design, similar to 10BaseT where all cables are attached to a hub. Also, 10BaseT and 100BaseX are configured in a star pattern, but internally they use a bus signaling system like other Ethernet configurations.

45. **C, D**   The two protocols have been adopted by the Internet community to transmit Internet Protocol (IP) datagram over serial point-to-point lines.

46. **A**   A gateway can perform protocol conversions that act as a translator between two systems that do not use the same communication protocols, data formatting structures, languages, or architecture.

47. **D**   CAT 5 supports speeds up to and including 100 Mbps in an unshielded twisted-pair design. CAT 3 and RG-58U will support signal speeds up to 10Mbps in both unshielded twisted-pair and coaxial cable designs.

48. **E**   Fiber optics can transmit speeds in excess of 100 Mbps in a distance of 1,000 to 2,000 meters without any special fiber repeaters.

49. **A, C, D**   All three are correct. Bridges can perform the same functions as repeaters, but they can also reduce traffic by segmenting the network. Bridges can join dissimilar physical media such as twisted-pair and coaxial networks.

50. **A**   A repeater is an amplifier that increases the power factor of the electrical signal so that it can travel beyond the specification of the cable length depending on the type of cable. A repeater strengthens baseband signals in LANs.

51. **C**   ATM, which stands for Asynchronous Transfer Mode, is a packet-switch technology that provides high-speed data transmission rates for sending fixed-size cells over broadband LANs or WANs.

52. **D**   TCP/IP is a standard routable protocol and is the most complete and accepted protocol available that is used to connect dissimilar systems such as Unix and Windows NT.

53. **E**   A transceiver is a device that connects a computer to the network. A transceiver is basically a device that receives data and transmits the signal.

54. **A**   Routing Information Protocol uses a distance-vector algorithm to determine routes. With RIP, routers

transfer information among other routers to update their internal routing tables, and they use that information to determine the best routes.

55. **E** SCSI devices do perform *sector sparing*, which is a fault-tolerance system that automatically adds sector-recovery capabilities to the file system during operating. All other devices (other than SCSI) do not perform sector sparing at all.

56. **D** SNMP (Simple Network Management Protocol) is a TCP/IP protocol for monitoring networks. In SNMP, agents monitor the network traffic and gather statistical data, which they put into a management information base (MIB).

57. **C** CAT 5 cable design would be appropriate because it can support transmission speeds of 100 Mbps, and because all new installations have CAT 5 cable as a de facto standard in cable designs. CAT 5 can support video, multimedia, and imaging at higher data-transfer speeds than other categories of cable.

58. **B** Implementation of share-level security involves assigning a password to each shared resource. Access to a shared resource is granted when a user enters the appropriate password.

Practice Exam 2

The exam consists of 58 questions that cover four major topics. You have 75 minutes to complete this test. Remember that time is a factor. You should be around question 19 after 33 minutes and question 37 after 60 minutes.

Before the actual exam begins, the exam program will give you the option of taking a sample orientation exam to familiarize yourself with the way the exam operates. You should take that orientation exam. If you are unsure about how to use the testing equipment or software, or if you have any questions about the rules for the exam, ask the exam administrator before the exam begins.

The first three questions use the following scenario.

Situation

You have to design a simple network given the following parameters:

- You have five users located in offices on the same floor less than 100 meters apart.
- These users do not have dedicated network cabling.
- These users do have additional open pairs with their telephone wiring (CAT 3).

- They want to share each other's files and printers.
- They do not want to have their applications file served.
- All users use Windows 95 in a standalone environment.
- The owner does not have a large budget for this project.

1. Which network cabling scheme would you choose to implement?
   A. Coaxial
   B. Twisted-pair
   C. Wireless
   D. Infrared

2. Which operating system would you choose to use?
   A. Windows NT
   B. Novell
   C. Windows 95 Peer to Peer
   D. Lantastic Peer to Peer

3. Based on your answer to question number 2, which type of networking equipment would support your cable solution?
   A. A repeater
   B. A hub

C. A transmitter

D. A router

4. From the types of cable listed below, which can be used for a LAN with a maximum distance of 370 feet between network devices?

   A. Thicknet coaxial

   B. Thinnet coaxial

   C. Twisted-pair

   D. Fiber optic

5. Which wireless LAN transmission method typically has the slowest response time?

   A. Laser

   B. Narrow-band radio

   C. Spread-spectrum radio

   D. Infrared

6. Which categories of Unshielded Twisted-Pair cable are certified to carry data transmissions faster than 10Mbps?

   A. 1

   B. 4

   C. 2

   D. 5

   E. 3

The next two questions use the following scenario.

Situation

You have a small office with three users who are located six feet apart and are separated by half-wall cubicles.

You do not have an existing network, and there are no additional free pairs in the phone cable.

You want to share files and printers, but you do not want to serve applications.

All of your users are using Windows 95.

You have a very, very limited budget.

7. Based on the information above, which network cabling scheme makes sense?

   A. Coaxial

   B. Twisted-pair

   C. Fiber

   D. Microwave

8. Which network operating system would work best?

   A. Windows 95 (Peer to Peer)

   B. Windows NT

   C. Novell

   D. Appleshare

9. Select three attributes of a server-based network:

   A. Individual users are responsible for the security of their resources.

   B. It has a dedicated server.

   C. Files are stored on a central file server.

   D. Applications are centrally managed on a central file server.

   E. System managers are responsible for the security and protection of resources.

10. What are two functions of a network operating system's redirector?

    A. To determine the level of sharing between network resources.

    B. To segment the hard disk into different areas.

C. To intercept requests and forward them to the computer.

D. To assign a letter to a shared resource.

E. To determine if a task should be left on a local computer or sent to another server on the network.

11. In which layer of the OSI model does the packet creation begin?

A. Physical

B. Network

C. Transport

D. Session

E. Application

F. Presentation

12. Choose three parts of a packet header:

A. Source address

B. Destination address

C. Alert signal

D. Actual address

13. In a bus topology, how many computing devices can communicate at one time?

A. 10

B. 2

C. All computing devices

D. 1

E. Only the computing device with the assigned token

The next two questions use the following scenario.

Situation

You have an office with 20 people who have an open CAT 5 cable next to their phone connections.

This open CAT 5 cable runs into a central wiring closet.

Your users currently use Windows 95.

You want to serve applications to save on concurrent application usage.

You want to have centrally managed IP addresses for your users.

The person identified as the Network Administrator is very proficient in Windows 95.

You are willing to spend a reasonable amount of money to implement this solution.

You are concerned about how reliable your power source is.

14. Which type of network cabling scheme would work best?

A. Fiber

B. Coaxial

C. Twisted-pair

D. Microwave

15. Your supervisor has requested that you centrally manage the IP addresses in your network. Which protocol could you use to perform this task?

A. ARP

B. HTTP

C. SLIP

D. PPP

E. DHCP

Question 16 uses the following scenario.

Situation

You're planning an addition to your current network, and you want to connect two networks that are on different floors of a multifloor building. Your main objective with this design is to reduce the risk of someone tapping into your network.

16. Which media would work best in this scenario?

   A. Coaxial cable

   B. UTP cable

   C. Wireless

   D. Fiber optic cable

The next four questions use the following scenario.

Situation

You are assigned the task of designing a network for a lab at a local school. Listed below are your operating conditions:

- You will network 10 workstations together (all IBMs).

- The workstations are currently standalone, so they cannot be networked.

- The workstations are all in a row on four tables.

- You do not have enough money to have a dedicated file server.

- You want to run applications locally but share printers and files.

- You will be connected to an Internet provider and given the IP addresses 134.93.4.10 through 134.93.4.25.

- This design should be built to expand in the future to include other network cabling schemes where appropriate.

- You will be hired to install this system, but the librarian (who is Windows 95 literate) will manage it after installation.

17. Suppose you were contracted to install this network. Of the following questions and statements, which three represent major concerns you will face?

   A. What type of experience does the librarian have?

   B. How old is the school?

C. A security plan needs to be addressed.

D. Identify the existing hardware to ensure a minimum platform for your solution.

18. What type of network cabling would be the simplest to install and the most cost-effective?

   A. Fiber

   B. Coax

   C. Twisted-pair

   D. Wireless

19. Based on the requirement for future expansion, what type of network card would be appropriate?

   A. Combo card with coax and twisted-pair

   B. Combo card with fiber and twisted-pair

   C. Twisted-pair only

20. Which operating system would be a good choice here?

   A. Lantastic

   B. Windows NT

   C. Windows 95

   D. Novell Lite

21. How far can a signal be reliable when transmitted over a Thinnet cable?

   A. 100 meters

   B. 50 meters

   C. 250 meters

   D. 185 meters

22. What is the theoretical capacity of STP cable?

   A. 200Mbps

   B. 400Mbps

C. 500Mbps

D. 100Mbps

23. Which of the three statements below are true characteristics of Category 3 cables?

    A. These cables are suitable for 100Mbps data rates.

    B. These cables are suitable for 4Mbps data rates.

    C. This cable is considered to be the lowest data-grade cable.

    D. This cable uses four twisted pairs with three twists per foot.

24. What is the most common type of connector used with twisted-pair cabling?

    A. RJ-11

    B. RJ-24

    C. RJ-45

    D. RJ-8

25. Select three valid reasons for implementing wireless networking:

    A. For people who move around a lot within their work environments.

    B. For temporary installations within your network.

    C. For spaces where cabling would be impossible or inconvenient to implement.

    D. For people who want to use their cell phones to contact their resources at work.

26. What is the typical maximum transmission distance for infrared signals?

    A. 50 feet

    B. 10 feet

C. 100 feet

D. 150 feet

27. What is the outdoor operating range of a frequency-hopping scheme under a spread-spectrum radio transmission?

    A. 100 feet

    B. 500 feet

    C. 1 mile

    D. 2 miles

28. What is the transmission rate of a frequency-hopping transmission scheme?

    A. 10Mbps

    B. 100Mbps

    C. 250Kbs

    D. 4Mbs

Question 29 uses the following scenario.

Situation

Suppose you are implementing a network with the following requirements:

Servers: 6 that run Microsoft Windows NT; 3 that run Novell 3.12

Client computers: 800 that run Windows 95

Hubs: 40

Routers: 6

29. Which protocols should you configure on each router in order for traffic to pass freely across your network?

    A. NetBEUI, TCP/IP

    B. AppleTalk, TCP/IP

    C. IPX, TCP/IP

    D. TCP/IP, AppleTalk

30. Your existing 10Base2 Ethernet cable is 185 meters long. You are planning to extend your network by adding another 100 meters of cable. Therefore, the total length of the cable will be 285 meters. If the network uses NetBEUI, which of the following devices should you use?

    A. Gateway
    B. Hub
    C. Repeater
    D. Router

31. Of the statements below, which three describe 10Base5?

    A. 10Mbs data rate
    B. Signal range of 500 meters per cable segment
    C. Uses thin coaxial cable
    D. Referred to as Thicknet

32. From the list below, select the four Windows NT special groups created during the installation of Windows NT.

    A. Active user
    B. Everyone
    C. Network
    D. Interactive
    E. Creator-owner

33. At which layer of the OSI model does a repeater operate?

    A. Physical
    B. Network
    C. Session
    D. Transport
    E. Presentation

34. Select three types of backups identified by Microsoft.

    A. Full backup
    B. Semi-contingent backup
    C. Incremental backup
    D. Differential backup

35. From the list below, select three network standards that employ token-passing access control.

    A. FDDI
    B. IEEE Standard 802.3
    C. IEEE Standard 802.4
    D. Token-ring

36. Of the following statements, which four describe benefits of using a dedicated file server?

    A. Files are in a specific place where they can be reliably archived.
    B. Central file servers can be managed more efficiently, with user and security data located in a single database.
    C. Dedicated file servers have a single point of failure.
    D. Dedicated file servers allow data backups to be implemented more easily.
    E. The cost of specialized file server technology is shared by a large number of users.

37. What is *disk mirroring*?

    A. The function of simultaneously writing data to separate disks using one channel on one disk controller.
    B. The function of simultaneously writing data to separate disks on different servers.

C. The function of simultaneously writing data to disks using separate channels.

38. What is the minimum number of disks needed to configure a stripe set with parity on a Windows NT server?

    A. Seven

    B. Two

    C. Three

    D. Four

39. From the list below, select three duties of a network adapter.

    A. To format and prepare data

    B. To control the flow of data in and out of the computer

    C. To send the data

    D. To identify network cabling issues within the network

40. A characteristic of Ethernet networks is that data flows from the network adapter card to the transmission medium in which of the following forms?

    A. Serial

    B. Parallel

    C. Both serial and parallel

    D. Neither parallel or serial

41. Select four basic data-bus architectures in use today.

    A. ICI

    B. EISA

    C. PCI

    D. Micro Channel

    E. ISA

42. From the options below, identify three typical resource settings.

    A. IRQ

    B. SQA

    C. Base I/O port addresses

    D. Base memory address

43. Suppose you're designing a network and you need to install network adapters in 10 ISA computers. Which rule must you follow when installing the NICs?

    A. All network adapters in all computers on the same network must be set to different IRQs.

    B. All adapters in a computer, including the network adapter, must be set to the same IRQ.

    C. All network adapters in all computers on the same network must be set to the same IRQ.

    D. All adapters in a computer, including the network adapter, must be set to different IRQs.

44. What tool helps a network administrator view operations in real-time and record time for processors, hard disks, memory, network utilization, and the network as a whole on a Windows NT server?

    A. Network management tools for software vendors

    B. Problem device

    C. Performance Monitor

    D. Systems Management Server

45. Which tool would you use to check the physical condition of the cable including excess collisions and congestion errors?

    A. DV

    B. Protocol analyzer

C. Advanced cable tester

D. TDR

46. What is the set of message-handling standards developed by the CCITT?

A. X.400

B. MHS

C. SMTP

D. X.500

47. What service would you need to install on a Macintosh to bring it into a Windows NT environment?

A. Gateway

B. GSNW

C. Services for Macintosh

D. Redirector

48. What tool does Microsoft have that provides a broader scope on network systems management with centralized administration of all computers in a WAN?

A. Performance Monitor

B. TraceRoute

C. Ping

D. SMS

49. What happens in the Network layer if the network adapter on the router cannot transmit a data chunk as large as the source computer sends?

A. It causes network activity failure.

B. It retransmits the data chunk.

C. It breaks the data into smaller units.

D. It organizes the data frame.

50. A terminal sends a request for information to a mainframe. The mainframe retrieves the information and displays it on the terminal. What type of computing is this ?

A. Client-server

B. Peer to peer

C. Centralized

D. Decentralized

The next three questions use the following scenario.

Situation

You are in charge of installing cables for an Ethernet network in your office. Your building has limited workspace, and the cable will have to share an existing conduit with the phone system cable. The maximum length of a cable segment is 320 feet.

51. Which type of cable should you install in this situation?

A. Fiber optic

B. Thicknet coax

C. CAT 3 UTP

D. CAT 1 UTP

52. Based on the situation above, how many pairs are needed to connect to a 10BaseT network?

A. 1 pair

B. 2 pairs

C. 3 pairs

D. 4 pairs

53. If you choose to use Ethernet and use 10BaseT, what type of cable connector should you use?

A. RJ-11

B. RJ-45

C. RJ-6

D. RJ-12

54. Your company has a corporate-wide Windows NT network using TCP/IP protocol. You have been receiving a lot of complaints that client computers are getting IP address conflicts. What is Microsoft's preferred solution to this problem?

   A. Increase the TCP window size.

   B. Implement a DHCP server.

   C. Change the MAC address for each network.

   D. Manually configure IP addresses on each computer.

55. Which two layers of the OSI model define how multiple computers can simultaneously use the network without interfering with one another?

   A. Media Access Control and Logical Link Control

   B. Session and Transport

   C. Physical and Data Link

   D. Transport and Network

56. What blocks out a portion of the IP address so TCP/IP can distinguish the network ID from the host ID?

   A. Node number

   B. Subnet mask

   C. Default gateway

   D. Network address

57. Of the Internet tools listed below, which two assist in validating hosts that are active on the Internet?

   A. PING

   B. FTP

   C. TraceRoute

   D. Multi-homing

58. Which e-mail standard is used on the Internet and is part of the TCP/IP protocol?

   A. MHS

   B. SNMP

   C. X.400

   D. SMTP

Answers and Explanations

1. **B** Because there are open Category 3 pairs from the phone system, the fastest and most cost-effective approach would be to implement a twisted-pair network solution. Another important piece of information here is that the users are fewer than 100 meters apart, which means a twisted-pair solution would work fine.

2. **C** Because each of the users currently uses Windows 95 and their only requirement is to share one another's files and printers, Windows 95 Peer to Peer is the clear choice. Choosing Windows 95 is the most cost-effective solution. Another advantage here is that the learning curve for the end user is smaller because they currently are using the Windows 95 interface.

3. **B** In a twisted-pair network, hubs are a requirement for connectivity.

4. **A, B, D** All of these cables have been tested and approved to operate at or above the 370 foot requirement. Twisted-pair cabling is guaranteed to work reliably at 362 feet. With newer technology in twisted pair cabling (CAT 5), vendors are hyping longer distances for twisted-pair; however, the IEEE recommendation for twisted-pair is still 362 feet.

5. **C** Spread-spectrum radio transmission speeds are typically 1.54Mb or slower.

6. **B, D** To date, Category 4 and 5 cables are the only cables rated that are certified to operate faster than 10Mbps.

7. **A** Because the users are close together and their cubicles are half-walled, it makes sense to choose a coaxial solution. Other major factors in this decision are that there are no available twisted-pair cables in the phone cable, and that this network needs to be installed at minimum cost.

8. **A** Because each of the users currently uses Windows 95 and their only requirement for networking is to share one another's files and printers, the logical solution here is to implement Windows 95 Peer to Peer networking.

9. **B, C, E** Server-based networks consist of dedicated servers, centrally located files on one or many servers, and centrally managed applications. Server-based networks also put more responsibility on systems managers for the security and protection of system resources and files.

10. **C, E** A network operating system's redirector intercepts requests and forwards them to the computer. The redirector also determines if a task should be left on a local computer or sent to another server on the network.

11. **E** The Application layer is the first layer where the raw data is housed. In layers under the Application layer, the major focus is shaking hands both electronically and physically.

12. **A, B, C** A packet header consists of a source address, a destination address, and an alert signal.

13. **D** In a bus topology, only the computing device with the assigned token can communicate at one time.

14. **C** Because there is an available twisted-pair cable in each office and it is home run to a central wiring closet, the most logical choice here is twisted-pair cabling.

15. **E** Windows NT's DHCP enables you to distribute and manage your IP addresses centrally.

16. **D** Fiber would be the best choice here because tapping into fiber is virtually impossible. Fiber connectivity requires a high level of expertise; the other media types are easier to connect to.

17. **A, C, D** When planning a network such as the one described here, you must first diagnose your existing hardware to make sure you understand the current operating environment. This information establishes a base from which to plan. You also need to be concerned with the level of knowledge the librarian has to ensure that he will be able to manage your solution at his level of expertise without having to rely on you. The issue of security should always be discussed.

18. **B** In this situation, coax seems to be appropriate because the workstations are all lined up in a row in the same room. This would be the simplest and most cost-effective approach.

19. **A** Because the CPUs are together in a line, coax would be the current cable of choice. To plan for future expansion, a combo card with coax and twisted-pair would be the best choice because a combo of fiber and twisted-pair card is not available.

20. **C** Because the librarian is familiar with Windows 95 and because Peer to Peer networking will solve all of the networking issues, the best choice for this situation is Windows 95.

21. **D** A signal transmitted over Thinnet can reliably run 185 meters.

22. **C** The theoretical capacity of STP cable is 500Mbps.

23. **A, C, D** Category 3 cabling is the lowest data-grade cable. This type of cable is generally suited for data rates up to 10Mbps, although some innovative schemes enable the cable to support data rates up to 100Mbps. Category 3 cabling uses four twisted pairs with three twists per foot and is now considered to be the standard cable for most telephone systems.

24. **C** RJ-45 connectors are the most common type of connector used with UTP cables.

25. **A, B, C** Wireless networks are great solutions for people who move around a lot within their environments and for temporary installations within networks. Wireless networks are also great solutions where cabling would be impossible or inconvenient to implement.

26. **C** The maximum transmission distance for infrared signals is 100 feet.

27. **D** The outdoor operating range of a frequency-hopping scheme under a spread-spectrum radio transmission is two miles.

28. **C** Frequency-hopping typically transmits at up to 250Kbps.

29. **C** In order to get access to NetWare servers, IPX must be able to be routed across routers. Windows NT can be accessed by TCP/IP, IPX, and NetBEUI. Therefore, the only answer that works in this situation is C because of the IPX for NetWare resources.

30. **C** Because the maximum signal distance of a 10base2 segment is 185 meters, you would want to add a repeater in this scenario to regenerate the signal.

31. **A, B, D** 10Base5 has a data rate of 10Mbs with a signal range of 500 meters per cable segment. This type of cable is also referred to as Thicknet.

32. **B, C, D, E** Windows NT creates four special groups, each of which has special uses and access privileges. These groups are Everyone, Creator-owner, Interactive, and Network.

33. **A** Repeaters operate at the Physical layer of the OSI model.

34. **A, C, D** Microsoft identifies the following backup types: full, incremental, and differential.

35. **A, C, D** Three network standards that employ token-passing access control are FDDI, IEEE Standard 802.4, and token-ring.

36. **A, B, D, E** Benefits of using dedicated file servers include:

    Files are stored in a specific place where they can be reliably archived.

    Central file servers can be managed more efficiently with user and security data located in a single database.

    Dedicated file servers enable data backup to be implemented more easily.

    The cost of specialized file server technology can be shared by a larger number of users.

37. **A** Disk mirroring is the function of simultaneously writing data to separate disks using one channel on one disk controller.

38. **C** Three disks is the minimum number needed to configure a stripe set with parity on a Windows NT server.

39. **A, B, C** Network adapters format and prepare data, control the flow of data in and out of the computer, and send data to other resources.

40. **A** Data travels on the network in serial form, one bit at a time.

41. **B, C, D, E** In today's networking environments, EISA, PCI, Micro Channel, and ISA data-bus architectures are used most often.

42. **A, C, D** Typical resource settings are IRQs, base I/O port addresses, and base memory addresses.

43. **D** The rule for IRQs is that no two components can use an IRQ at the same time. Therefore, option D is the only viable answer.

44. **C** Windows NT uses Performance Monitor to track these resources.

45. **C** An advanced cable tester will provide more information, including collisions and congestion errors, than a TDR.

46. **A** The CCITT standards committee is responsible for developing and maintaining the X.400 set of message-handling standards.

47. **C** After loading Services for Macintosh on a Windows NT server, you have to define Macshare files so that Macs can access the files.

48. **D** Microsoft uses its SMS product to monitor Windows NT networks.

49. **C** When a router is sent a data stream that is larger than it can handle in one session, it breaks the data into smaller units and transmits them in smaller units.

50. **C** In a centralized network model, terminals send requests for data to a mainframe. The mainframe then retrieves the data and displays it on the requesting terminal.

51. **C** The length of the maximum cable run meets the requirement of CAT 3, and 95 percent of all existing phone systems use CAT 3 cabling. Therefore, CAT 3 UTP is the best choice for this situation.

52. **B** Because the logical choice for cabling here is twisted-pair, you will need 2 pairs (4 wires) to comply with 10BaseT connectivity.

53. **B** RJ-45s are required connectors for 10BaseT specifications.

54. **B** By implementing a DHCP server, you will be guaranteed that no duplicate addresses will ever be served.

55. **C** In the OSI model, the Physical and Data Link layers are responsible for allowing multiple computers to simultaneously access the network without interfering with one another.

56. **B** A subnet mask is used to block out a portion of the IP address so TCP/IP can distinguish the network ID from the host ID.

57. **A, C** These two tools enable a user or network administrator to validate host machines that are active.

58. **D** SMTP is the e-mail standard used on the Internet. SMTP is also part of the TCP/IP protocol.

The Microsoft Certification Process

Microsoft has a variety of certifications available for its products. You can find out more about the certifications at http://www.microsoft.com/train_cert/.

The Microsoft Education and Certification Roadmap is a publication from Microsoft that provides a thorough outline of the certification process. The Roadmap Assessment Exam includes the best available examples of the kinds of questions you'll find on the certification exam. The Roadmap also includes the Planning Wizard, an online tool that helps you quickly map out a plan for achieving your certification goals.

Most Roadmap Assessment Exams are based on specific product versions, and new elective exams are available on an ongoing basis. The Microsoft Education and Certification Roadmap is a quarterly publication. You can obtain updates of the Roadmap at any of the following locations:

Microsoft Education: Call (800)636-7544

Internet: ftp://ftp.microsoft.com/Services/MSEdCert

World Wide Web: http://www.microsoft.com/train_cert/default.htm

CompuServe Forum: GO MSEDCERT

Becoming a Microsoft Certified Product Specialist (MCPS)

The Microsoft Certified Product Specialist is the entry level of Microsoft's certifications, and it requires passing a minimal number of exams. Microsoft Certified Product Specialists are required to pass one operating system exam, proving their expertise with a current Microsoft Windows desktop or server operating system, and one or more elective exams from the MCSE or MCSD tracks. Table A.1 shows the choices for the operating system exam.

Table A.1   Operating System Exam Choices

Exam Number	Exam Title
70-073	Implementing and Supporting Microsoft Windows NT Workstation 4.0
OR	
70-042	Implementing and Supporting Microsoft Windows NT Workstation 3.51
70-067	Implementing and Supporting Microsoft Windows NT Server 4.0
OR	
70-043	Implementing and Supporting Microsoft Windows NT Server 3.51
70-030	Microsoft Windows 3.1
70-048	Microsoft Windows for Workgroups 3.11-Desktop
70-063	Implementing and Supporting Microsoft Windows 95
70-160	Microsoft Windows Architecture I
70-161	Microsoft Windows Architecture II

In addition, all elective exams for the premium certifications (Microsoft Certified Systems Engineer and Microsoft Certified Solution Developer) are available and provide further qualification of skills with Microsoft BackOffice products, development tools, or desktop applications.

Becoming a Microsoft Certified Systems Engineer (MCSE)

The Microsoft Certified Systems Engineer is probably the most rapidly growing certification in the world. It proves that you are knowledgeable in advanced operating systems such as Windows 95 and Windows NT, that you excel in networking-related skills, and that you have a broad enough background to understand some of the elective products.

MCSE candidates need to pass four operating system exams and two elective exams. The MCSE certification path is divided into two tracks: the Windows NT 3.51 track and the Windows NT 4.0 track.

Table A.2 shows the core requirements (four operating system exams) and the elective courses (two exams) for the Windows NT 3.51 track.

Table A.2   Windows NT 3.51 MCSE Track

Take These Two Required Exams (Core Requirements)	Plus, Pick One Exam From the Following Operating System Exams (Core Requirement)	Plus, Take the Following Networking Exam (Core Requirement)	Plus, Pick Two Exams from the Following Elective Exams (Elective Requirements)
Implementing and Supporting Microsoft Windows NT Server 3.51 #70-43	Implementing and Supporting Microsoft Windows 95 #70-63	Networking Essentials #70-58	Implementing and Supporting Microsoft SNA Server 3.0 #70-13
AND	*OR*		*OR*
Implementing and Supporting Microsoft Windows NT Workstation 3.51 #70-42	Microsoft Windows for Workgroups 3.11-Desktop #70-48		Implementing and Supporting Microsoft Systems Management Server 1.2 #70-18
	OR		*OR*
	Microsoft Windows 3.1 #70-30		Microsoft SQL Server 4.2 Database Implementation #70-21
			OR
			Implementing a Database Design on Microsoft SQL Server 6.5 #70-27
			OR
			Microsoft SQL Server 4.2 Database Administration for Microsoft Windows NT #70-22
			OR
			System Administration for Microsoft SQL Server 6.5 #70-26
			OR

continues

Table A.2   Continued

Take These Two Required Exams (Core Requirements)	Plus, Pick One Exam From the Following Operating System Exams (Core Requirement)	Plus, Take the Following Networking Exam (Core Requirement)	Plus, Pick Two Exams from the Following Elective Exams (Elective Requirements)
			Microsoft Mail for PC Networks 3.2-Enterprise #70-37
			OR
			Internetworking Microsoft TCP/IP on Microsoft Windows NT (3.5-3.51) #70-53
			OR
			Internetworking Microsoft TCP/IP on Microsoft Windows NT 4.0 #70-59
			OR
			Implementing and Supporting Microsoft Exchange Server 4.0 #70-75
			OR
			Implementing and Supporting Microsoft Internet Information Server #70-77
			OR
			Implementing and Supporting Microsoft Proxy Server 1.0 #70-78

Table A.3 shows the core requirements (four operating system exams) and elective courses (two exams) for the Windows NT 4.0 track. Tables A.2 and A.3 have many of the same exams listed, but there are distinct differences between the two. Make sure you read each track's requirements carefully.

Table A.3   Windows NT 4.0 MCSE Track

Take These Two Required Exams (Core Requirements)	Plus, Pick One Exam from the Following Operating System Exams (Core Requirement)	Take the Following Networking Exam (Core Requirement)	Plus, Pick Two Exams from the Following Elective Exams (Elective Requirements)
Implementing Microsoft Windows NT Server 4.0 #70-67	Implementing Microsoft Windows 95 #70-63	Networking Essentials #70-58	Implementing and Supporting Microsoft SNA Server 3.0 #70-13
AND	*OR*		*OR*
Implementing and Supporting Microsoft Windows NT Server 4.0 in the Enterprise #70-68	Microsoft Windows for Workgroups 3.11-Desktop #70-48		Implementing and Supporting Systems Management Server 1.2 #70-18
	OR		*OR*
	Microsoft Windows 3.1 #70-30		Microsoft SQL Server 4.2 Database Implementation #70-21
	OR		*OR*
	Implementing and Supporting Microsoft Windows NT Workstation 4.0 #70-73		Microsoft SQL Server 4.2 Database Administration for Microsoft Windows NT #70-22
			OR
			System Administration for Microsoft SQL Server 6 #70-26
			OR
			Implementing a Database Design on Microsoft SQL Server 6 #70-27

continues

Table A.3   Continued

Take These Two Required Exams (Core Requirements)	Plus, Pick One Exam from the Following Operating System Exams (Core Requirement)	Take the Following Networking Exam (Core Requirement)	Plus, Pick Two Exams from the Following Elective Exams (Elective Requirements)
			OR
			Microsoft Mail for PC Networks 3.2-Enterprise #70-37
			OR
			Internetworking Microsoft TCP/IP on Microsoft Windows NT (3.5-3.51) #70-53
			OR
			Internetworking Microsoft TCP/IP on Microsoft Windows NT 4.0 #70-59
			OR
			Implementing and Supporting Microsoft Exchange Server 4.0 #70-75
			OR
			Implementing and Supporting Microsoft Internet Information Server #70-77
			OR
			Implementing and Supporting Microsoft Proxy Server 1.0 #70-78

Becoming a Microsoft Certified Solution Developer (MCSD)

The Microsoft Certified Solution Developer (MCSD) program is targeted at people who use development tools and platforms to create business solutions. If you are a software developer or programmer working with Microsoft products, this is the certification for you.

Table A.4   Microsoft Certified Solutions Developer

Take These Two Required Exams (Core Requirements)	Plus, Pick Two Exams from the Following Elective Exams (Elective Requirements)
Exam 70-160:Microsoft Windows Architecture I	Exam 70-021: Microsoft SQL Server 4.2 Database Implementation
AND	*OR*
Exam 70-161:Microsoft Windows Architecture II	Exam 70-027: Implementing a Database Design on Microsoft SQL Server 6.5
	OR
	Exam 70-024: Developing Applications with C++ Using the Microsoft Foundation Class Library
	OR
	Exam 70-065: Programming with Microsoft Visual Basic 4.0
	OR
	Exam 70-165: Developing Applications with Microsoft Visual Basic 5.0
	OR
	Exam 70-051: Microsoft Access 2.0 for Windows-Application Development
	OR
	Exam 70-069: Microsoft Access for Windows 95 and the Microsoft Access Developer's Toolkit
	OR
	Exam 70-052: Developing Applications with Microsoft Excel 5.0 Using Visual Basic for Applications

continues

Table A.4   Microsoft Certified Solutions Developer

Take These Two Required Exams (Core Requirements)	Plus, Pick Two Exams from the Following Elective Exams (Elective Requirements)
	OR
	Exam 70-054: Programming in Microsoft Visual FoxPro 3.0 for Windows
	OR
	Exam 70-025: Implementing OLE in Microsoft Foundation Class Applications

Becoming a Microsoft Certified Trainer (MCT)

MCTs are product evangelists who teach Microsoft Official Curriculum (MOC) courses to computer professionals through one or more of Microsoft's authorized education channels. MCTs have special access to current Microsoft product information and invitations to Microsoft conferences and technical training events. This certification is designed for people who want to teach official Microsoft classes. The process of becoming a certified trainer is relatively simple and consists of both a general approval for the MCT program as well as an approval for each course you want to teach.

MCT Application Approval

There are three steps in the MCT application approval process:

1. Read the MCT guide and the MCT application at http://www.microsoft.com/train_cert/mct/.

2. Send a completed MCT application to Microsoft, including proof of your instructional presentation skills.

3. Send proof of your MCP status to Microsoft.

After you have completed these steps, you have satisfied the general part of the MCT application process. You only have to do this the first time.

MCT Course Certification Approval

The second part of becoming an MCT is that an MCT must be separately certified for each individual class he teaches. There are four required steps to become certified to teach a Microsoft Official Curriculum course.

1. Pass any required prerequisite MCP exams to measure your knowledge.

2. Study the Official Microsoft Trainer Kit for the course for which you seek certification.

3. Attend the MOC course for which you seek certification.

4. Pass any additional exam requirements.

After you've completed both the MCT application and the MCT course certification, you'll be authorized to begin teaching that MOC class at an official Microsoft Authorized Technical Education Center (ATEC).

Registering and Taking an Exam

A

When you are ready to schedule your exam, contact the Sylvan Prometric test registration center that is most convenient for you from the following table:

Country	Telephone Number
Australia	1-800-808-657
Austria	0660-8582
Belgium	0800-1-7414
Canada	800-755-3926
China	10800-3538
France	1-4289-8749
Germany	0130-83-9708
Guam	001-61-800-277583
Hong Kong	800-6375
Indonesia	001-800-61571
Ireland	1-800-626-104
Italy	1-6787-8441
Japan	0120-347737
Korea	007-8611-3095
Malaysia	800-2122
Netherlands	06-022-7584
New Zealand	0800-044-1603
Philippines	1-800-1-611-0126
Puerto Rico	800-755-3926
Singapore	800-616-1120
Switzerland	155-6966
Taiwan	008-061-1142
Thailand	001-800-611-2283
UK	0800-592-873
United States	800-755-3926
Vietnam	+61-2-9414-3666

If this is your first time registering for a Sylvan Prometric exam, Sylvan assigns you an identification number. You are asked to use your Social Security or Social Insurance number as your identification number, which works well for most people because it's relatively easy for them to remember. You also have the option of having them assign you a Sylvan ID number if you prefer not to disclose your private information.

If this is not your first exam, be prepared to give Sylvan your identification number. It's very important that you use the same identification number for all your tests—if you don't, the tests won't be credited to your certification appropriately.

You have to provide Sylvan Prometric with the following additional information:

Mailing address and phone number

E-mail address

Organization or company name

Method of payment (credit card number or check)

Sylvan requires that you pay in advance. Microsoft certification exam prices are related to the currency exchange rates between countries. Exams are U.S. $100, but certification exam prices are subject to change. In some countries, additional taxes may apply. Please verify the price with your local Sylvan Registration Center when registering.

You can generally schedule exams up to six weeks in advance or as late as the day before.

You can cancel or reschedule your exam if you contact Sylvan Prometric at least two working days before the exam or by Friday if your test is scheduled on Monday. If you cancel, exams must be taken within one year of payment.

Same-day registration is available in some locations if space is available. You must register at least 30 minutes before test time.

The day of the test, plan to arrive a few minutes early so you can sign in and begin on time. You are provided with something to write notes on during the test, but you are not allowed to take these notes with you after the test.

You are not allowed to take in books, notes, a pager, or anything else that could contain answers to any of the questions.

Hints and Tips for Doing Your Best

The exam incorporates a variety of questions from a question bank intended to determine if you have mastered the subject. Here are some tips to keep in mind as you prepare for your exam:

- Make sure you understand the material thoroughly.
- Go through all the practice problems. Reread sections that you are having trouble with.

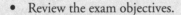

- Make sure you are comfortable with the style of the scenario questions. These probably are the most challenging part of the exam.

- Review the exam objectives.

The Microsoft certification exams are all between 75 and 90 minutes long. The more familiar you are with the test material and the actual test's style, the easier it will be for you to concentrate on the questions during the exam.

You can divide your time between the questions however you like. There are 58 questions on this exam. If there are any questions you don't know the answers to, mark them and come back later if you have time. You have 75 minutes for the actual exam, but you are scheduled for 90 minutes so you can spend up to 15 minutes on a practice pre-test (on unrelated subjects) to get familiar with how the test engine works. Make sure you think about whether you want to try the practice test before you sit down to take your exam—some people find the additional familiarity helps them, but others find it increases their stress level.

Question Presentation

In the actual Microsoft Networking Essentials exam (#70-58), radio (circle) buttons are used to signify only one correct choice, and check boxes (squares) are used to imply multiple correct answers. Whenever there is more than one correct answer, the number you should select is given in the wording of the question.

Scoring

For the Networking Essentials exam, a score of 714 or higher is considered passing. Each objective category is further broken down into categories; a percentage correct is given for each of the 12 categories.

Things to Watch For

Make sure you read each question and all its possible answers thoroughly. This is especially important for the scenario questions. Many people lose points because they select the first answer that looks correct when there is often a better answer lurking right on their screens.

After you've made sure you understand the question, eliminate answers that you know to be wrong. If you still have two or three choices, consider which of them is the *best* answer and select it.

Marking Answers for Return

If you aren't quite sure of an answer, you can mark the question by selecting a box in the upper left. You can then return to the question at the end when you are given the option to review your answers. Pay particular attention to related questions later in the test, in case you can learn enough from them to figure out the answer to the question you were unsure of before.

If you pay close attention, you will probably find that some of the other questions help to clarify questions you were uncertain of originally.

Attaching Notes to Test Questions

When you finish a Microsoft exam, you are allowed to enter comments about individual questions as well as about the entire test. This feature enables you to give the team that reviews Microsoft exams some feedback. If you find a question that is poorly worded or seems ambiguous, this is the place to let them know about it. Microsoft wants to have good tests, and this is your best opportunity to let them know how they're doing.

Glossary

10Base2 Also called *Thinnet*. Ethernet implemented in a bus topology using coaxial cable.

10Base5 Also callezd *Thicknet*. Ethernet implemented with thick coaxial cable.

10BaseF Ethernet implemented over fiber optic cable.

10BaseT Ethernet implemented with Unshielded Twisted-Pair (UTP) cabling.

10Broad36 Ethernet implemented over a broadband system.

5-4-3 rule 5 is the maximum number of repeated segments, 4 is the maximum number of repeaters, and 3 is the maximum number of segments of the five that can be populated.

Access Control Entry (ACE) An ACE is an entry in an Access Control List for any type of object under Windows NT. The ACE contains access information about a user or group for each object. Each object under Windows NT contains an ACL.

Access Control List (ACL) The ACL is a collection of ACEs containing access information for each object under Windows NT. Examples of objects are files, subdirectories, and printers.

access mask Each ACE has an access mask. The access mask defines all possible permissions for a particular user to that object. Permissions include read, write, and change.

access permission security Another phrase for *user-level access*. Rights to network resources are assigned on a user-by-user basis.

access point A stationary transceiver connected to the cable-based LAN that enables the cordless PC to communicate with the network.

ACE See *Access Control Entry*.

ACL See *Access Control List*.

active monitor Used in 802.5 token-ring networks to monitor the health of the network and correct problems.

Address Resolution Protocol (ARP)   Determines the MAC layer address associated with a logical network address.

amplitude   The difference between the highest and lowest points of a signal, often measured by voltage.

analog   Type of signal that changes continuously and can take on many different values.

antivirus software   Software that locates and eliminates computer viruses.

AppleTalk   Protocol family used by Apple computers.

Application layer   Layer 7 or the topmost layer of the OSI model. This layer exposes all the network services to the applications. When an application accesses the network, all actions are carried out through this layer.

application server   An application server runs all or part of an application on behalf of the client and then transmits the result to the client for further processing.

ARP   See *Address Resolution Protocol.*

Asynchronous Transfer Mode (ATM)   A cell-based networking technology that scales to tremendous speeds.

ATM   See *Asynchronous Transfer Mode.*

Attachment Unit Interface (AUI)   The connector used with Thicknet.

attenuation   A measure of how much a signal weakens as it travels through a medium.

AUI   See *Attachment Unit Interface.*

bandwidth   The measure of the capacity of a medium to transmit data.

bandwidth utilization   The percent of total network capacity that is actually used by the network.

baseband   The entire capacity of the medium is used for one communication channel.

baseline   A collection of performance statistics depicting the average (typical) behavior of the network. Later fluctuations in network performance can be measured against the baseline.

beacon   A message sent in a token-ring network to indicate a problem and start the auto-reconfiguration process. Beaconing is a process used by token-ring networks to narrow down the portion of the ring in which a problem is most likely to exist.

bit-oriented protocol   A protocol that identifies the beginning and end of a packet with bit patterns referred to as flags.

bridge   Passes only frames targeted for a computer on the other side of the bridge (and all broadcast frames).

broadband Two or more communication channels can share the bandwidth of the communications medium.

broadcast storm A sudden deluge of network traffic often caused by a faulty network adapter.

brouter A device that can simultaneously perform both routing and bridging.

bus A topology in which all devices connect to a common shared cable.

carrier detection Transmission method in which computers continue to listen to the network as they transmit in order to detect whether another signal interferes with their signal.

Carrier Sense Multiple Access with Collision Avoidance (CSMA/CA) Each computer signals a warning that says it is *about* to transmit data. The other computers then wait for the transmission.

Carrier Sense Multiple Access with Collision Detection (CSMA/CD) Carrier detection and carrier sensing used together form the protocol used in all types of Ethernet.

carrier sensing Transmission method in which computers listen to see if the network is busy before they attempt to transmit.

Category 5 Data-grade cable, which consists of four twisted pairs and can support data rates of 100 Mbps.

clients The computers that use the shared resources in a server-based network.

coaxial cable Two conductors in the cable share a common axis.

connection-oriented mode Assuming that communication errors will occur between computers, these protocols are designed to make sure data is delivered in sequential order and error-free to its destination. TCP/IP is an example of connection-oriented protocol.

connectionless-oriented mode These systems assume that data will reach its destination with no errors; thus there is no protocol overhead associated with these systems. Without this overhead, these systems are typically very fast. User datagram protocol is an example of connectionless-oriented protocol.

connectivity device A device used to extend or subdivide a network or to connect a network to a larger network.

contention Computers are contending for use of the transmission medium.

CRC See *Cyclical Redundancy Check.*

crosstalk Interference caused by adjacent wires.

CSLIP A compressed version of SLIP.

CSMA/CA See *Carrier Sense Multiple Access with Collision Avoidance.*

CSMA/CD See *Carrier Sense Multiple Access with Collision Detection.*

B

Cyclical Redundancy Check (CRC)   A procedure used on disk drives to verify that data written to a sector is read correctly later and to check for errors in data transmission. This is known as a redundancy check because each data transmission includes extra (redundant) error-checking values in addition to data. The sending device generates a number based on the data to be transmitted and sends its result along with the data to the receiving device. The receiving device repeats the calculation after transmission. If both devices obtain the same result, it is assumed that the transmission is error-free.

data   The content of a network packet.

data frame   A unit of network data; the term "frame" is typically used with Ethernet and token-ring (see also *packet*).

Data Link Control (DLC)   Protocol most commonly used to access mainframes and Hewlett-Packard JetDirect network printers.

Data Link layer   The Data Link layer of the OSI model adds information to each packet coming from the Network layer. Thus, the Data Link layer has knowledge of the packet structure and fields.

data transmission rate   The speed at which information is sent over network media.

datagram   An independent data packet being transported by a stateless protocol.

digital   A signal that can take only one of two discrete states.

Digital Audio Tape (DAT)   A reliable and fast tape media.

Digital Volt Meter (DVM)   A hand-held electronic measuring tool that checks the voltage of network cables.

DIP switch   A small switch on a circuit board (typically in a group) that enables you to physically configure a resource setting for the board.

direct sequence modulation   Breaks original messages into parts, which are transmitted on separate frequencies.

discretionary access control   The owner of an object is allowed to assign permissions to the object.

disk duplexing   Disk duplication using a separate controller for each disk.

disk mirroring   Duplication of data across multiple disks, which means that any failed disk can simply be replaced.

DLC   See *Data Link Control*.

DNS   See *Domain Name System*.

B

domain model   In a domain model, one Security Account Manager (SAM) database is maintained for all members of the domain in a network.

Domain Name System (DNS)   Provides a name as a service to client applications.

ElectroMagnetic Interference (EMI)   Outside noise that distorts the signal in a medium.

EMI   See *ElectroMagnetic Interference*.

Ethernet   The most popular OSI layer-two networking technology.

event log   A log of system events. Windows NT's event log includes a system log, a security log, and an application log. You can view the event log using Windows NT's Event Viewer tool.

fault-tolerant   The ability of a system to withstand a failure and continue to function.

FDM   See *Frequency-Division Multiplexing*.

fiber optic   Cable that consists of a highly refined glass or plastic core designed to transmit light signals.

file server   A computers whose main task is to provide file sharing to computers on a network.

File Transfer Protocol (FTP)   Enables users to transfer files between diverse host types.

flag   A distinct sequence of ones and zeroes used to delineate packets.

frame   The minimum unit of data at OSI layer two.

frame relay   A type of WAN packet service that is especially well-suited for data traffic.

Frequency-Division Multiplexing (FDM)   Dividing bandwidth into frequency bands on broadband media.

frequency hopping   Switching among several available frequencies, yet staying on each frequency for a specified interval of time.

FTP   See *File Transfer Protocol*.

gateway   A device or program that enables communication between systems that use dissimilar protocols.

Hardware Specific Module (HSM)   In the ODI model, the HSM directly communicates with the hardware.

header   Signifies the start of the packet and contains important parameters.

HSM   See *Hardware Specific Module*.

hub   A central connection point where all workstations are physically connected. A multiport repeater.

IEEE standard   A standard endorsed by the IEEE.

impedance   A measure of a medium's resistance to an alternating current.

infrared   A low-frequency light used in some wireless LANs.

Integrated Services Digital Network (ISDN)   A set of standards for delivering digital telephone service.

Internet Protocol (IP)   A connectionless protocol that provides datagram service.

Internetwork   A set of connected networks.

Internetwork Packet eXchange protocol (IPX)   A network layer protocol that is primarily used in NetWare networks.

Internetwork Packet eXchange protocol/Sequenced Packet eXchange (IPX/SPX)   A protocol suite used by NetWare and Microsoft's NWLink stack.

IP   See *Internet Protocol.*

IP address   A logical network and host ID that consists of a 32-bit number. It's typically represented in a four octet dotted-decimal form.

IPX   See *Internetwork Packet eXchange protocol.*

IPX/SPX   See *Internetwork Packet eXchange protocol/Sequenced Packet eXchange.*

ISDN   See *Integrated Services Digital Network.*

jumper   A small connector on a circuit board that enables you to physically configure a resource setting for the board.

LAN   See *Local Area Network.*

laser   A light source that produces an especially pure light that is monochromatic and coherent.

laser transmission   Sending a data signal using a laser, typically on fiber optic cable.

late collision   When a collision is missed on an 802.3 network due to propagation delay.

LED   See *Light-Emitting Diode.*

Light-Emitting Diode (LED)   A low-powered light source used with multimode fiber optic cable.

Link Support Layer (LSL)   In the ODI model, the LSL is the packet router.

Local Area Network (LAN)   A group of computers interconnected within a building or campus setting.

logical node names   Human-readable names for computer devices that can be mapped to a protocol-specific address.

logical topology   The logical pathway a signal follows as it passes among the network nodes.

LSL   See *Link Support Layer.*

MAC address See *Medium Access Control address.*

MAU See *Multistation Access Unit.*

Media Support Module (MSM) In the ODI model, the MSM manages the hardware configuration tables and performs initialization functions independent of the media.

Medium Access Control address (MAC address) The NIC address on an 802.5 network. Each workstation has a unique MAC address.

microwave transmission Sending a signal using microwave frequencies. Typically requires line-of-sight connectivity.

MLID See *Multiple Link Interface Drivers.*

mobile computing Uses portable PCs or PDA devices and connects to the network via some form of telephone.

MSAU See *Multistation Access Unit.*

MSM See *Media Support Module.*

Multiple Link Interface Driver (MLID) The MLID has two basic functions: to build up and strip media headers off packets and to send and receive packets at the Physical layer.

multiplexing Enables a medium to support multiple data channels.

Multistation Access Unit (MAU or MSAU) A concentrator used in token-ring networks.

MUX A device that has the capability of acting as a multiplexer and a demultiplexer.

N connector Used in Thicknet, a connector that screws on.

narrow band radio transmission Transmissions that occur at a single radio frequency.

NDIS See *Network Device Interface Specification.*

NetBEUI A non-routable protocol used to carry NetBIOS information on a local LAN only.

NetBIOS The Network Basic Input/Output System, which extends all the way to the Session layer and is used to handle naming and file services.

network A group of interconnected computers that share information and resources.

network adapter A device that provides physical access to a network. The term network adapter is typically used for an internal card that connects a PC to an Ethernet or token-ring network.

Network Device Interface Specification (NDIS) Microsoft and 3Com jointly developed Network Device Interface Specification in 1989. This standard defined an interface between the MAC sublayer and higher layers of the OSI model.

Network File System (NFS) A family of file-sharing protocols for TCP/IP.

B

Network layer   The Network layer of the OSI model determines the route a packet must take to reach its destination.

Network Monitor   A software-based tool that monitors network traffic, displaying packet information and keeping statistics on network usage. Windows NT's Network Monitor is an example of a network monitoring tool.

network service   A process (running on a PC) that facilitates networking. Windows NT includes numerous network services.

network topology   The physical layout of a network.

New Technology File System (NTFS)   This is the transaction-based file system native to Windows NT.

NFS   See *Network File System*.

NTFS   See *New Technology File System*.

NWLink   Microsoft's version of the IPX/SPX protocol.

ODI   See *Open Data-Link Interface*.

Open Data-Link Interface (ODI)   Open Data-Link Interface was jointly developed by Novell and Apple Computer Corporation and released in 1989. The goals of ODI are similar to the goals of NDIS: to provide a seamless integration between the Data-Link layer and the Transport layer of the protocol stack.

Open Shortest Path First (OSPF)   A link-state routing protocol.

operating system conflict   A situation in which an application is not fully compatible with the operating system.

oscilloscope   The device that measures fluctuations in signal voltage.

OSI model   A seven-layer model used primarily as a reference model.

OSPF   See *Open Shortest Path First*.

packet   A unit of network data transmitted from a sending PC to a receiving PC; sometimes called a *Protocol Data Unit* (*PDU*).

passive topology   The interconnection of passive systems using no power or electronics.

patch cable   Relatively short, flexible cable used to connect two network devices.

peer-to-peer network   The simplest network configuration that allows users to access each other's resources.

Performance Monitor   A tool included with Windows NT that monitors system and network statistics.

Physical layer   The lowest layer of the OSI model.

physical topology   The actual physical layout of the network.

Plenum-grade cable   Cabling specially designed to be used without conduit in areas where fire codes prohibit PVC cabling.

Point-to-Point Protocol (PPP)   A very popular dial-up protocol that allows dynamic negotiation of IP addresses and multiple protocols over a single serial connection.

power fluctuation   A fluctuation in the power supply that can cause the network to misbehave.

PPP   See *Point-to-Point Protocol.*

Presentation layer   The Presentation layer defines the format used by applications to exchange data. This layer is also called the *translator*. This layer is responsible for protocol conversion, data encryption, and data compression, and it is where the redirector service operates.

print server   A print server maintains a single printer or group of printers across the network. It manages access to a shared printer, making it accessible to users at other network machines.

propagation delay   A delay resulting from the amount of time it takes an electrical signal to travel through cable and associated electronics before arriving at its destination.

PROTMAN   See *Protocol Manager.*

protocol analyzer   A hardware or combined hardware and software product that monitors network traffic, tracks network performance, and analyzes packets.

protocol binding   A potential logical pathway from a network/transport protocol (such as TCP/IP) to a specific adapter. In Windows NT, you must also bind the protocol to certain higher-level network services, such as the server and workstation services.

Protocol Manager (PROTMAN)   The protocol manager routes packets from the MAC layer to the correct protocol stack in the NDIS model.

PVC cable   Cable that is covered with polyvinyl chloride.

RAID   See *Redundant Arrays of Inexpensive Disks.*

RAID 0   A non-fault tolerant method of speeding disk access.

RAID 1   Disk duplexing and disk mirroring.

RAID 5   Disk striping with parity. The ability for an array of multiple disks to have one disk fail and continue to function.

RAS   See *Remote Access Service.*

redirector   A software module (typically implemented as a file system driver) that redirects I/O requests to the network and thus allows a networked computer to act as a client.

Redundant Arrays of Inexpensive Disks (RAID)   A method of paralleling many disks to make them appear as one large disk with the option of fault tolerance.

Remote Access Service (RAS)   A feature of Windows NT that allows remote users to dial in to and access the network. It is a versatile dial-up server service.

repeater   Repeaters regenerate weak incoming signals. Because no packet information is necessary to perform this task, repeaters reside at the Physical layer. A repeater simply retransmits any frame it receives, including frames with errors.

resource conflict   A situation in which two or more devices simultaneously attempt to use the same system resource (such as interrupts, base I/O port address, or base memory address).

RG-58   A type of coax commonly used interchangeably with Thinnet.

RI   See *Ring In.*

ring   A descriptive term used for the logical path used in a token-ring network.

Ring In (RI)   Type of port on a token-ring MSAU.

Ring Out (RO)   Type of port on a token-ring MSAU.

RIP   See *Routing Information Protocol.*

RJ-45   Common term for the 8-pin modular connector or jack used in most networks today.

RO   See *Ring Out.*

router   Internetwork connectivity device that connects different networks or subnetworks. Especially useful for containing broadcasts.

Routing Information Protocol (RIP)   Distance-vector routing protocol.

Sequenced Packet eXchange (SPX)   Extends IPX to provide connection-oriented service with reliable delivery.

Serial Line Internet Protocol (SLIP)   An older dial-up protocol that is being replaced by PPP.

server-based network   A network that contains computers designated for management and sharing of resources.

Server Message Block (SMB)   An Application layer protocol primarily used for file and print sharing.

Server service   A Windows NT service that enables a Windows NT machine to act as a server (provide resources to the network).

Session layer   The Session layer creates a virtual connection between two applications on separate computers. This virtual connection is called a *session*. The Session layer maintains synchronization between applications by placing checkpoints in the data stream. It is this layer that performs name recognition and security that allows the applications to communicate.

share-level security   Security level in which each shared resource on the network has an associated password. To access the resource, the user must simply enter the correct password. No user authentication is required in share-level security models.

shield   The outer conductor that serves as a ground and protects the inner conductor.

Shielded Twisted-Pair (STP)   Cable that consists of one or more twisted pairs of cables enclosed in a foil wrap and woven copper shielding.

Simple Mail Transfer Protocol (SMTP)   A protocol used to transport electronic mail through internetworks.

Simple Network Management Protocol (SNMP)   Network management protocol used with TCP/IP networks.

SLIP   See *Serial Line Internet Protocol*.

SMB   See *Server Message Block*.

SMTP   See *Simple Mail Transfer Protocol*.

SNMP   See *Simple Network Management Protocol*.

spooler   Accepts print jobs and spools the jobs to disk until the printer is ready to accept data.

spread-spectrum radio transmission   Type of radio transmission that changes frequencies regularly.

SPX   See *Sequenced Packet eXchange*.

standalone system   A computer that isn't connected to a network.

star   Descriptive term for the physical layout of certain network types, such as 10Base-T.

STP   See *Shielded Twisted-Pair*.

T connector   Used in Thinnet-based LANs, this connects the network interface card to the cable.

T1   Digital line that provides point-to-point connections and transmits 1.544 Mbps in a total of 24 DS-0 channels. Also called a *DS-1*.

T3   Digital line that can transmit data at up to 45 Mbps. Made up of 28 MUXed T1 circuits.

TCP   The Internet's reliable Transport layer protocol.

TCP/IP   Typically used to refer to the entire family of Internet protocols.

TDM   See *Time-Division Multiplexing*.

TDR   See *Time-Domain Reflectometer*.

TechNet   A CD-ROM-based repository of technical information available from Microsoft.

Telnet   A protocol that enables PCs and workstations to function as dumb terminals in sessions with host systems on internetworks.

terminator   A special connector that includes a resistor.

terrestrial microwave   Land-based microwave.

Thicknet   Also known as *10Base5,* the Thicknet topology employs RG6 cable, which is much thicker and harder to work with than RG58. It is the oldest standard for coax-based Ethernet.

Thinnet   Also known as *10Base2,* Thinnet is the most common bus topology. This topology employs RG58 cable, which has a 50 ohm impedance. It is the newest standard for coax-based Ethernet.

Time-Division Multiplexing (TDM)   Supports digital signals.

Time-Domain Reflectometer (TDR)   A device that sends sound waves along a cable and looks for imperfections that might be caused by a break or a short in the line.

token   A special network frame passed around some networks to control which station has permission to transmit.

Token-ring   A type of network that uses token-passing.

topology   Defines the arrangement of nodes, cables, and connectivity devices that make up the network.

trailer   Marks the end of the packet and contains error-checking information.

transceiver   Used with Thicknet as part of the network-host connection.

transmission media   The network medium used to send data signals.

transmission medium   The physical pathway in which computers are connected.

Transport layer   The Transport layer ensures that packets are delivered in sequence and error free. The Transport layer breaks large messages from the Session layer into manageable packets to be sent out to the network.

Transport protocol   Protocol that operates at the Transport layer of the OSI model and is responsible for reliable packet delivery.

UDP   See *User Datagram Protocol.*

Uninterruptible Power Supply (UPS)   Usually a large battery that plugs into the wall and supplies about 15 minutes of power.

Unshielded Twisted-Pair (UTP)   Cable that doesn't incorporate a shield into its structure.

UPS   See *Uninterruptible Power Supply.*

User Datagram Protocol (UDP)   Unreliable, connectionless Transport protocol.

user-level security   Security level in which rights are assigned on a user-by-user basis and authentication is employed.

UTP   See *Unshielded Twisted-Pair*.

vampire tap   A clamp-on transceiver that forces sharp teeth into the Thicknet cable.

WAN   See *Wide Area Network*.

Wide Area Network (WAN)   A group of computers connected over long distances. These are typically created using telephone lines, but they can also be created with fiber links, microwave radio, leased lines, and satellite links.

wireless   A type of network that doesn't rely on physical network cabling.

wireless bridging   A bridge that uses something such as satellite or radio frequency instead of standard network cabling to connect two segments of a network.

workgroup model   The model in which each server within the network maintains its own SAM database for its shared resources.

Workstation service   Windows NT's redirector (see *redirector*).

X.25   A packet-switching network standard best suited for low-speed use. (This is fading from use.)

Index

O

Q-R